Loving Your Partner
Without Losing Your Self

This brilliant and fertile book is key to creating a new partnership society. The potent and practical methods offered by Martha Beveridge can deepen and empower virtually every kind of relationship. The stories she tells, the exercises she offers are state of the art. Rarely has so keen and sensitive an analysis been applied to boundary issues. As a guide to transformational relationship in a time when all social forms are in transition and we must meet each other in new ways if we are to survive and grow, this book is simply the best there is.

— **JEAN HOUSTON, PH.D.,** author of *A Mythic Life, Jump Time,* and
A Passion for the Possible

Loving Your Partner Without Losing Your Self is a gift of great value to all those couples who can't seem to get it right. Martha's writing is interesting, insightful, and helpful in the most practical way. Anyone in a relationship will benefit from what she has to say. As a marriage and family therapist, I will use the ideas, exercises, and personal stories in this book to help me do better by those who seek my help.

— **MARJORIE R. BARLOW, PH.D.,** author of *The Possible Woman*

Through the use of her Safe Dialogue Process and heart focused centering, Martha moves couples from their turmoil to a place of mutual respect and eventually to the love that created their relationship in the first place. It is in this safe space that couples can address the boundary issues that plague us all.... This book will help all who read it."

— **RON ROTH**

~ Dedication ~

In loving memory of
Barbara Ann Allen, Ph.D., MSW, MPH,
healer, mentor, and sister of the heart,

and

in loving honor of my children and grandchildren,
Lucie and Joe Voves and Joseph, Jordan, and Lindsay Voves,
Leigh and David Reece and Canon, Holland, and Eden Reece.

ORDERING

Trade bookstores in the U.S. and Canada please contact:

Publishers Group West
1700 Fourth Street, Berkeley CA 94710
Phone: (800) 788-3123   Fax: (800) 351-5073

Hunter House books are available at bulk discounts for textbook course adoptions;
to qualifying community, health-care, and government organizations; and for special
promotions and fund-raising. For details please contact:

Special Sales Department
Hunter House Inc., PO Box 2914, Alameda CA 94501-0914
Phone: (510) 865-5282   Fax: (510) 865-4295
E-mail: ordering@hunterhouse.com

Individuals can order our books from most bookstores, by calling
(800) 266-5592, or from our website at **www.hunterhouse.com**

Loving Your
Partner
Without
Losing
Your Self

MARTHA BALDWIN BEVERIDGE, MSSW

Hunter House PUBLISHERS

Hunter House Inc., Publishers
PO Box 2914
Alameda CA 94501-0914

LIBRARY OF CONGRESS CATALOGING-IN-PUBLICATION DATA

Beveridge, Martha Baldwin, 1941-
Loving your partner without losing yourself / Martha Baldwin Beveridge. —1st ed.
p. cm.
Includes bibliographical references and index.
ISBN-13: 978-0-89793-355-1 (cloth) — ISBN-13: 978-0-89793-354-4 (paper)
ISBN-10: 0-89793-355-9 (cloth) — ISBN-10: 0-89793-354-0 (paper)
1. Man-woman relationships. 2. Interpersonal relations—Psychological aspects.
3. Intimacy (Psychology). I. Title.
HQ801 .B497 2001
306.7—dc21   2001039454

PROJECT CREDITS

Cover Design: Brian Dittmar Graphic Design
Book Production: Hunter House & Jinni Fontana
Developmental and Copy Editor: Kelley Blewster
Proofreader: Lee Rappold
Indexer: Deanna Butler
Acquisitions Editor: Jeanne Brondino
Associate Editor: Alexandra Mummery
Editorial and Production Assistant: Emily Tryer
Sales and Marketing Assistant: Earlita K. Chenault
Publicity Manager: Sara Long
Customer Service Manager: Christina Sverdrup
Warehousing and Shipping: Lakdhon Lama
Administrator: Theresa Nelson
Computer Support: Peter Eichelberger
Publisher: Kiran S. Rana

Manufactured in the United States of America

8 7 6 5 4 3   First Edition   10 11 12 13

Contents

Foreword ix

Acknowledgments xii

Introduction 1

CHAPTER 1: Boundaries Are Basic **8**

    Firm and Flexible 10

    Childhood Boundary Wounds 11

    Reclaiming Our Missing Parts 12

    Your Boundaries and Your Spirit 14

CHAPTER 2: Safe Dialogue **16**

    Honoring Boundaries When You and Your Partner Talk 17

    A Near-Divorce Experience 21

    Preparing for Safe Dialogue on Your Own 23

    Practicing Safe Dialogue at Home 25

    Exercises 26

    The Five Stages of Safe Dialogue 29

CHAPTER 3: Bonding and Boundary Blurring **38**

    "Blest Be the Tie That Binds" 39

    Romantic Boundaries 40

    Bonding and Release 43

    Love You...Love You Not 44

    Bonding Doesn't Stop with Romance 44

    When Romantic Boundaries Begin to Fade 46

CONTENTS (CONT'D.)

The Enmeshment-Making Process 48

Exercises 53

CHAPTER 4: Breaking Out of Enmeshment 55

Emotional Digestion 56

Beginning the Enmeshment-Breaking Process 57

The Anger/Appreciations Exchange 57

The Smoke-Screen Issues: Time, Money, and Sex 63

Lost Selves 71

Exercises 77

CHAPTER 5: Boundary Violations 79

When Our Boundaries Are Violated 79

Three Types of Boundary Violations 80

Four Levels of Boundary Violations 82

Intrusive/Rejective Boundary Violations 83

Neglecting/Abandoning Boundary Violations 91

Freezing/Denying Boundary Violations 99

Boundary Violations Are Defensive Styles of Relating 106

Exercises 107

CHAPTER 6: Reenactment Trances 111

Re-Playing Family Dramas 112

Reenactment Trance Patterns 117

Seeing Partners as Parents 124

Waking Up from Entrancement 128

Exercises 132

CHAPTER 7: Creating Healthy Boundaries 135

Updating the Inner Parent 138

Identifying Danger Signals 139

Stopping the Blame Game 142

CONTENTS (CONT'D.)

Practicing Tough Self-Love 145

Exercises 150

CHAPTER 8: Stopping Boundary Violations **153**

The Internal Saboteur 154

The Saboteur Masks Our Fears 156

Reclaiming the Shadow 157

Identifying Your Saboteur's Favorite Masks 158

Taming Your Saboteur 162

Uncovering Core Fears 173

Framing Life in Love Rather Than Fear 174

Stopping Boundary Violations Is About Consciousness,
    Not Control 176

Exercises 178

CHAPTER 9: The Boundary-Healing Process **182**

Step One: WAIT 184

Step Two: BE SILENT 185

Step Three: WRITE 186

Step Four: SHARE 187

Step Five: GO DEEPER (Now or Later) 188

Step Six: FORGIVE 191

Step Seven: HEAL 192

Step Eight: COMMIT 193

Exercises 198

CHAPTER 10: Embracing the Whole of You **200**

Let Me Introduce You 201

Appreciating Your Shadow Side 202

Going Backstage 203

Your Higher Self 211

CONTENTS (CONT'D.)

Embracing Your Shadow Side Clears Your Vision 214
Embracing Your Shadow Side Creates Inner Peace 215

CHAPTER II: Letting Go **217**
Fear Interrupts Healthy Connecting and Releasing 217
Letting Go Demands Courage and Faith 218
Letting Go of What Might Be 222
Letting Go and the Gift of Forgiveness 224
Letting Life Flow 225
Letting Go and Letting God 226

Glossary of Terms 229

Notes 231

Index 233

Foreword

We meet; we fall in love; we marry. Then, we become frustrated, confused, and disillusioned. We experience feelings of helplessness, often resulting in depression. When our depression turns into despair, we restore our sense of power by activating our anger. Changing our tactics from courtship to coercion, we try to restore the original bliss with actions that produce more pain. This results in alienation and disconnection. The ecstasy of romantic love changes into conflict and a struggle for power that can last for years.

This scenario, its causes and cures, have occupied my attention for more than twenty years, and it has been the subject of research by the discipline of marital therapy for nearly a century. In the early years, researchers leaned toward the explanation that the causes were inside each person in the relationship. Internal conflict, with its roots in childhood, was seen as the source of interpersonal conflict. The obvious cure was to help each person, in individual sessions, resolve his or her internal war. Then they would be able to have a good relationship. With unconvincing results from this approach, the diagnosis shifted to communication problems between partners. This analysis required that partners attend sessions together in order to learn communication skills that would help them solve their problems. But the success rate of only 30 percent was still alarming, so therapists added behavior modification to communication skills, producing better, but still unsatisfactory, statistics.

This is the theoretical and clinical environment that Helen, my partner in life and work, and I inherited when we began our explorations of the dynamics of committed partnership in the late 1970s. In the course of our discussions, we developed the thesis that marital choice is influenced by unmet needs in childhood. Over time, we integrated communication theory, behavior modification, emotional restructuring, developmental stage theory, and positive reinforcement into a synthesis and extension we named Imago Relationship Therapy.

Using this approach to study and help couples, we discovered that partners in stress are, paradoxically, using coercive methods to restore connection ruptured in childhood. As a result of inappropriate parenting, they lost connection with parts of themselves, their intimate context, and with the universe. This helped us understand that the temporary euphoria of romantic love is fueled by a transient experience of original wholeness and that the power struggle is an attempt to recover that experience with methods that further rupture the experience of connection. As I crafted the theory, I developed a therapeutic process called the Couples Dialogue that helps couples connect at deep levels, thus achieving the goals of the power struggle and eventually restoring the feelings of romantic love. Using this theory and process has produced statistics that are not only satisfactory, but also amazing.

Martha Beveridge, in *Loving Your Partner Without Losing Your Self*, has built upon this theoretical and clinical edifice with a brilliant extension of the theory and therapy by focusing on the central importance of boundaries. From her perspective, the childhood rupture is a result of an invasion of the child's physical, emotional, and spiritual boundaries by abuse and/or neglect. When boundaries are invaded, children cannot develop a cohesive and centered self, and their boundaries become rigid or diffuse. To deal with the situation of not knowing where they begin and end or where others begin and end, they develop an internal saboteur. This negative inner voice interferes with emotional development and prepares the way for enmeshment in their adult intimate relationships. In the process of attempting to become distinct from their partner, they repeat the boundary invasions on their partner that were visited upon them by their parents.

Given this working hypothesis, Martha develops a clear description of how boundaries look and work and how to deal with the internal saboteur. She then presents a process called "Safe Dialogue" that couples can use to extricate themselves from enmeshment and create a relationship that honors their reality as distinct selves and connects that at deep levels of respect and love.

Nothing is more important than honoring boundaries—national, social, and personal. Not to do so will inevitably result in conflict. In this exceptional book, Martha Beveridge helps us understand the meaning of personal boundaries in intimate partnerships. She also helps us understand how to recognize and prevent boundary violations. More importantly, she demonstrates how healthy boundaries are essential for intimacy between partners.

This book will be useful to all couples who read it. It is substantive in theory, comprehensive in practice, and humanized by the inclusion of many couples' stories and clinical processes. Many couples will find descriptions of themselves here, and every couple will be helped by a disciplined use of the charts and exercises. We hope, in reading this text, you will use it as a guide to learning how to "love your partner without losing your self." I encourage all couples to read it. It is a must read.

—— HARVILLE HENDRIX, PH.D., and HELEN LAKELLY HUNT, PH.D.
New Jersey, 2001

Acknowledgments

I am grateful for all the help and support I have received while writing this book. Priscilla Stuckey, my developmental editor, worked with me every step of the way. Her expertise and insight inspired me and kept me energized and on track. Our weekly telephone consultations created a warm friendship as well. Kelley Blewster, who provided the final editing and polishing, made valuable and much-appreciated contributions in bringing the manuscript to its published form. Thank you to everyone I've worked with at Hunter House and especially to Jeanne Brondino and Alex Mummery.

I also thank my agent, Susan Schulman, for her work on behalf of this book and Betty Wright of Rainbow Books for her astute guidance. I appreciate Susan Crawford's assistance as well.

I thank all my therapy clients who are my daily teachers. They honor me with their trust and delight me with their courage in growing through their life challenges. I am especially indebted to the members of my Monday and Tuesday night groups.

Pat Pelton and Cindy Thomason give me invaluable support tending to the practical details at my office and consistently encouraging me as I write. Terrisa Bruce is my wonderfully creative web master, radio announcer, and co-host. Ladenia Jackson takes care of me at home and is my long-time trusted friend.

I am deeply grateful to Harville Hendrix and Helen LaKelly Hunt, co-creators of Imago Relationship Therapy. They have encouraged and inspired me through their example and their extraordinary vision. My colleagues in the Association for Imago Relationship Therapy are exceptional therapists who help heal and nurture relationships throughout the United States and in nineteen countries around the world. I appreciate them all and am especially thankful for Joyce Buckner, my first Imago teacher. Her friendship and loving support are invaluable. She has stood with me through the difficult places along with Margie and Dave Mc-Keon and Hedy and Yumi Schleifer. Pat Love is a delight as is my wise and wonderful friend, Marge Barlow. I'm also gifted by my friendships with Maya Kollman and Barbara Bingham, Tom Simpson, Allan Schiffer, Sunny and Mark Shulkin, Bob and Wendy Patterson, Larry Weckbaugh, Saundra Dickinson, Bonnie Brinkman, Gay Jurgens, Dawn Lipthrott, Bill and Gerrie Brennan, Bruce Crapuchettes, and Francine Beauvoir.

I have experienced profound healing and spiritual awakening through workshops and seminars with Brugh Joy, Carolyn Conger, Jean Houston, Hal and Sidra Stone, and Ron Roth. I am also richly blessed through my healing work with Janene Sneider.

I am grateful for the joyous times I've shared with Norwood Beveridge, his sons, Norwood and Richard, and his daughter, Susi. I especially treasured our summer days on North Haven and the inspiration I found there. I also honor Miriam, James, and Catie Beveridge.

My friends gift me with their love and steadfast presence in my life. I honor each of them through this work and especially thank Vicki and Kent Williams, Linda and George Massad, Mary Kay and John Bullard, Evalie and Preston Edwards, Brenda Walters, Jennifer Kavanaugh, Jan O'Neill, Patti Brandon, Liz Holt, Peggy Adkism, Phyllis and Reg Libby, Carolyn and Ron McGarrough, Anne and Jim Williams, Edith Alston, Carol and Chris Witze, Julie Stevens Manson, Julia Ann Allen, Linda and Bob Reece, Susan Collins Fowler, Bill Brown, Sunnie Williams, and Paula Homsey. Lynne Looney is my cousin and soul sister. I thank her for her steadfast love and encouragement.

Finally, I am most deeply grateful for my daughters, Lucie Voves and Leigh Reece, and their husbands, Joe Voves and David Reece. They honor me with their love and generosity and light my life with happy memories, hope for the future, and joy in the present.

IMPORTANT NOTE

The material in this book is intended to provide a review of resources and information related to healing and enhancing intimate relationships by developing healthy boundaries. Every effort has been made to provide accurate and dependable information. However, professionals in the field may have differing opinions, and change is always taking place. Any of the treatments described herein should be undertaken only under the guidance of a licensed health-care or mental-health-care practitioner. The author, editors, and publishers cannot be held responsible for any error, omission, professional disagreement, outdated material, or adverse outcomes that derive from use of any of the treatments or information resources in this book, either in a program of self-care or under the care of a licensed practitioner.

Introduction

This is the book I needed thirty-five years ago when I began my search for my self. It's no accident that I've written it, because I know I teach best what I also am learning. My great life lessons have been about loving my partner without losing myself. Though it took me many years to discover what I now know about healthy boundaries, it doesn't have to take you anywhere near that long to learn to love your partner without losing yourself. What I share with you in the pages you're about to read could have saved me years of pain and turmoil— had I found this book when I was in my twenties, thirties, or forties.

The question I address here is one I have pondered for a long time: "How can two people love each other and sustain a lasting, trusting, and committed relationship while also being true to themselves as individuals—changed as each of them is by their connection with the other?"

I have devoted much of my professional life to helping my clients master their dilemmas with intimate relationships. Since I was a little girl I have wanted to find the magic that makes grown-ups happy with each other. I was an only child in a family that looked great from the outside but was filled with pain and confusion behind our closed doors. I longed for parents who truly liked each other and enjoyed me. Though my parents' marriage lasted until they died, the good they shared was coupled with deep unhappiness and disappointment in my mother, and anxiety, depression, and paranoia in my father.

They didn't see divorce as an option. This was Alabama in the 1940s and '50s—before the civil rights movement, before the women's movement, before any consciousness about the meaning of child abuse. Mother had "made her bed" with Daddy and knew she was financially dependent on him. Daddy carried the pressure of all the responsibility he felt. He worried about money and his health much of the time. I was their joint possession—their pride and joy as well as the scapegoat for their pain.

Now I see that what our family lacked was healthy boundaries. There was nothing to define my mother, my father, and me as separate people with distinct needs, feelings, rights, and privileges that ought to be honored and respected. Given the culture, given the times, given their psychological problems, we were lost as individuals in the emotional stew created by the distorted belief system that dictated our lives.

Again and again I heard them proclaim that children should be seen and not heard. I saw that boys were clearly more important and enjoyed more privileges than girls. Not upsetting Daddy was vital. What the neighbors might think was of prime importance. Gossip bound women to each other. How things looked counted more than how they actually were. Some people were more valuable than others. A great deal depended upon sex, race, ancestors, social position, and money. The past was more highly valued than the present or the future.

Each of these social dictums reflected distorted, unhealthy boundaries. They were based upon the assumptions that people are not to be respected equally and that some therefore should sacrifice their own wishes and desires to serve others.

My parents were immersed in these cultural edicts. I don't think it occurred to them that I was a sensitive being whose needs and feelings differed from their own. Because of this, I doubt that they realized how their behavior harmed me. I remember hearing them say that because I was a child I would not remember or be affected by the ways they abused me—physically, emotionally, and sexually.

Despite the ways they hurt me they were dedicated to giving me a sound education, so I left home to go to boarding school in the eleventh grade and after graduation attended Wellesley College in Massachusetts. I was astounded to discover how good I felt and how successful I could be on my own. I kept my secret emotional demons at bay—hidden behind my accomplishments and chronic illnesses.

I looked wonderfully well adjusted until my first divorce when I was thirty-one. At that point the façade I had so carefully constructed all those years came crashing down. Within two years my mother was senile. Within four years both my parents were invalids—confined to a nursing home and completely dependent upon my supervising their care.

Those devastating experiences brought me to my knees emotionally and spiritually. Therapy with a number of excellent teachers woke me up to how my relationships with my mother and father affected my adult life.

One of my first therapists introduced me to the concept of boundaries. I realized I didn't have any, nor did I have any real sense of myself—that is, an identity to place within them. I was like water without a glass—losing myself in merging with those I loved. Or, when I tried to assert myself and define who I was in relationship to others, I was like a glass without water—empty, fragile, and not very interesting.

Repairing my badly broken boundaries was not a simple matter. God, time, patience, lots of loving support from others, good teachers, writing, dreaming, and sticking with my task saw me through my thirties and forties and into my fifties. As I healed I unleashed my creativity. I wrote two books, became a radio therapist, taught on television, and watched my now adult daughters launch their separate lives. And I developed the ideas and techniques you will find in this book—ways of helping couples heal troubled relationships and enhance valued partnerships they want to nurture and preserve.

I came to realize that adequate boundaries are the backbone of healthy relationships. They provide the skeletal structure that allows love to survive and thrive. Genuine intimacy is possible only when healthy boundaries are in place and are respected by both partners in a committed relationship.

Loving others freely while also loving and respecting oneself is the hallmark of healthy boundaries. Love does not equal self-sacrifice. Love does not give people power over each other, as I had been taught by my parents as well as at school and church. Instead, love honors people as unique individuals who count equally without hierarchies based on sex, age, financial and social status, lifestyle choice, race, or religious preference. Though self-sacrifice is often necessary, sacrifices must be freely chosen and freely made—not demanded and coerced.

I also discovered through my work with clients over the past thirty years that my family and the Southern community where we lived were not unique. The issues I've encountered in my life are variations on a theme that plays throughout our culture. The women's movement and the civil rights movement have brought major changes. Yet much continues to revolve around hierarchical distinctions. It isn't a simple matter to change behaviors based upon generations of cultural programming.

Given the new standards that are evolving, mates struggle to discover how to relate to each other within marriage and other forms of committed relationships. Divorce is rampant. With the social changes that have occurred, traditional roles assigned to men and women have shifted dramatically. There are no working models for the ideal we seek.

How can intimate partners live together as equals, respect each other as peers, and be honest with each other about what they feel, need, and desire? Men are exhorted to be sensitive to their emotions. But it isn't easy to throw off the armor they have developed through many generations of being taught to conceal their feelings behind facades of toughness and power. Women strive to be powerful while remaining sensitive to their feelings and the feelings of the people they love. Yet for generations we have been programmed to sacrifice ourselves to the needs of our mates and children.

Loving Your Partner Without Losing Your Self is my contribution to helping intimate partners adjust to the new paradigm that positions them as peers. Both men and women benefit from developing healthy boundaries. Equal partners with healthy boundaries can love each other freely without sacrificing their own desires and identity.

The book's early chapters tell you what boundaries are and why they are so necessary in the context of intimate relationships. Here, I introduce Safe Dialogue—a heart-centered sharing process. The structure of Safe Dialogue helps establish and sustain respectful boundaries. With these boundaries in place, you and your mate will be able to have satisfying talks about even the most difficult, highly charged subjects that concern you.

The second part of the book focuses on how personal and circumstantial boundaries become blurred as partners bond with each other during the early romantic phase of developing a committed partnership. It describes the enmeshment-making process and shows how blocked anger manifests as guilt and feeds symbiotic relating. It also shows you how to take beginning steps out of enmeshment.

The third section helps you and your partner recognize when and how you fall into boundary-violating patterns of relating. One chapter explains reenactment trances: automatic, trancelike repetitions between mates of boundary violations they experienced in childhood.

The fourth section addresses creating and sustaining healthy boundaries. It assists you in learning to recognize your Internal Saboteur—the fearful self within you that orchestrates boundary-violating patterns of relating. This part of the book offers specific suggestions for healing broken boundaries, stopping boundary-violating behaviors, and interrupting reenactment trances.

The final section of the book is about embracing the whole of who you are so you can also accept the whole of your partner. The last chapter is about letting go of efforts to control what you cannot control while also owning your creative power to frame relationship experiences in the light of love rather than in fear and destructive negativity.

There is a glossary on page 229 to assist you with words and concepts used in this book that may not be familiar to you.

You may want to read through the entire book before doing the exercises suggested at the end of each chapter and practicing the healing processes that are presented within the text. Or you can take your time, practice the processes with your partner, and work with the exercises as you read and integrate the material chapter by chapter. Pay special attention to any exercises or processes that you resist. Your reluctance may tell you that these are exactly the experiences that will be most healing for you.

Ideally, you and your partner might read the book together and use the Safe Dialogue process to talk with each other about what you discover. If your partner is unwilling to join you in such a joint venture, you can still practice what you learn whenever you encounter challenging situations between you. Even without your partner's involvement in these activities, your own new behaviors will create changes in your relationship. And your growth may inspire your mate to join you in discovering more new options for healthy relating.

At the end of Chapter 11 you will find affirmations you can use every day to help you establish a loving framework of beliefs about your relationship. Select one or two affirmations to work with each week, and copy those affirmations onto post-it notes or index cards. You can put them in places where you will be reminded of them frequently—on your mirror, on the refrigerator door, in your car, or beside your bed.

All that I share in the chapters that follow flows from my life experiences, my professional training (especially in Imago Relationship Therapy and Transpersonal Healing), and many years of working as a therapist with individuals, couples, families, and groups. Writing this book is the culmination of thousands of hours of journaling, meditation, reading, healing, and exploring life and relationships with my family, my friends, my mentors, and my clients.

It is also the result of my exploring the spiritual dimension of life. I was raised in the Episcopal church and continue to worship there. I have studied the teachings of many different spiritual masters, both Christian and otherwise. I pray and meditate every day. I ask for God's guidance in silent prayer many times each day as I work with my clients, live my life, write, and play. I ask others to pray for me when I face difficult challenges. Each day I experience the healing power of what I feel as the Holy Spirit in my life. I find God in the beauty of nature, in the eyes and hearts of the people I love, and at the core of me. I believe through experiencing God's presence with and in me that there is much more to me than the physical body I see.

Throughout this book you will find evidence of my faith as it informs my life and my relationships with others. I respect the fact that your spiritual tradition and practices may be quite different from mine. My desire is not to present my point of view as the only way or the way you should adopt. Rather I want to share with you as honestly as I can how important I believe it is to address the spiritual dimension of consciousness as you seek to enhance your relationship with yourself and with your partner. Yet I also recognize that spiritual belief—in whatever form it takes—is an evolving process rather than a single event, an unfolding journey rather than a one-time destination. I hope you will read what I share with an open heart and be willing to make whatever translations are necessary if the terms I choose do not match your system of belief.

What I present here is not a new theory of relationships but a practical approach to making them work. I offer "how to" methods for recognizing, reframing, defusing, and then effectively dealing with the everyday concerns as well as the major issues encountered in all partnerships. These techniques have been proven to work—for my clients and in my own life.

As you read I invite you to hold in your heart my best and most loving intentions for the joy of your intimate relationship, the nurturing of your children, and the healing of the troubled yet rapidly transforming planet we call home. May you and your mate thrive in a partnership that honors both of you, nurtures your growth, and blesses you with peace and joy.

CHAPTER ONE

Boundaries Are Basic

Your boundaries embrace all the facets of the unique person you are. You might imagine them as the circumference of a circle that radiates out from the center of you and extends well beyond your physical body. As imaginary borders, they define you as separate and distinct from others. Yet they do not isolate you from other people. Rather they allow you to connect with others and to establish satisfying, constructive relationships.

Physical boundaries are obvious; your body is separate from others' bodies. But emotional, mental, and spiritual boundaries are more difficult to notice and respect and can be easily confused because they aren't tangible and visible.

You can picture your emotional, mental, and spiritual boundaries as concentric circles that encompass a field of energy surrounding you. Your emotional boundaries are closest to your body and directly affect your physical state. Your mental boundaries lie beyond your emotional ones. What you think determines how you feel. Your spiritual boundaries are at the farthest reaches of your being. They link you with the realms that lie beyond physical form—and connect you with all other beings. Your spirit, mind, and emotions constantly interact and permeate the whole of your being.

Honoring all these boundaries is a core issue in relationships. Doing so helps us feel safe enough to relate to each other in loving ways. Without adequate boundaries we become enmeshed with our mates and lose touch with important parts of ourselves.

When we argue with our partner by interrupting, blaming, criticizing, or shutting them out, we violate the invisible boundaries that define each of us as distinct people who deserve love and respect. Instead of revealing who we are, we point our finger at our partner; we plead for the other person to change so we won't have to address our own part in the difficulties between us.

When we discount our own boundaries or our mate violates them, we behave as if we are not separate beings with distinct needs, feelings, perceptions, and desires. At the moment boundaries are violated, fear strikes its dissonant chord within us. We feel threatened—as if our very survival is at stake. Our guard goes up. Automatically we do whatever we know to do to try to keep ourselves safe. In our state of red alert, we are afraid to be really honest. We're afraid to look at our part in our problems. We're afraid to trust and be real. We're also afraid we might lose our intimate relationship—that we will be rejected and abandoned by the other. That's a lot of fear to handle. All too easily it escapes our control and fuels hurtful fights. We attack and violate each other's boundaries in escalating rounds of defensive behavior—each of us trying desperately to protect ourselves from both real and imagined threats. Instead of being respectful peers, we act like angry, bossy parents or resentful, rebellious kids.

With mature, well-established personal boundaries, we are equals and we enjoy our connection with each other. Neither of us presumes to try to mold, shape, or control the other. Rather, we honor our differences, seek to understand rather than change each other, and are clear about what belongs to one person and not to the other.

Just as each cell within your body has its unique function and is enclosed by a wall that marks its limits and distinguishes it from other cells, your boundaries limit and distinguish you from all others. And just as each cell in your body is both separate and a vital part of the whole of your physical being, you are both separate and connected with all other beings as integral parts of a much greater whole. In a healthy body, each cell sustains its boundaries and respects the boundaries of its neighboring cells. Cells that lose their boundaries become malformed and destructive. They are deselected by an immune system that says no to whatever threatens our overall health and well-being. If the immune system fails to function adequately, diseased cells go on a rampage, invading other cells and creating life-threatening diseases like cancer. In a similar way, destructive relationships are marked by disregard for the boundaries of others. Healthy intimate relationships are marked by respect for our own boundaries and the boundaries of our partners.

Firm and Flexible

Healthy, flexible boundaries clothe us appropriately—for all kinds of emotional weather. Ideally they fit comfortably and are neither too tight nor too loose. They feel good to wear and are suitable for the climate and season. In warm, friendly conditions they can be lightweight and relatively revealing. In a cold, hostile emotional climate they need to be much heavier, warmer, and designed to protect from overexposure.

People with inadequate boundaries are likely to "wear" the equivalent of a bathing suit during an emotional snowstorm. They are too naively open and blindly trusting. Others with too much protection turn up in a ski suit on a mild day. They sweat too much, because they fear too much!

Like dressing appropriately, the trick with boundaries is to wear what fits for the climate we are in—while at the same time having extra layers available to put on or take off should we need to adjust to unexpected changes in the emotional weather. At times we need to dress warmly and stand firm about issues that are essential to our well-being. On other occasions we profit from wearing lighter garments, remaining open and willing to try on new possibilities.

Flexibility is vital so we can respond appropriately to whatever emerges in our relationships. Without adequate flexibility, we are so rigid that we can snap and break when the winds of change bear down on us. With too much flexibility we are too easily swept away by outside forces.

Healthy boundaries are both firm and flexible—they bend with the blowing wind and stand sturdy through the storms of life. They are grounded in consciousness, love, and choice. They allow us to nurture and protect ourselves as individuals while also honoring our partnerships with others. Establishing healthy personal boundaries and a clear sense of who we are as individuals empowers us to contribute the best of our unique talents to the well-being of the whole of creation—a wondrous universe that, like the physical body, is much greater than the sum of all its separate "cells."

Childhood Boundary Wounds

Had you and your partner followed an optimal pathway of growth through childhood and adolescence, you each would have come into your adult relationship with healthy boundaries embracing the whole of you. But parents are only human and can only pass along to their children what they themselves experienced in childhood or learned as adults. They tend to criticize and reject in their children what they believe is unacceptable in themselves and in the world in general. At the same time they encourage in their children the attributes they themselves value. When parents try to prune away important parts that they don't appreciate in their children, they violate their children's boundaries. Consequently, most of us experience many boundary transgressions during our growing-up years. We enter our adult partnerships with less than ideal boundaries and with important parts of ourselves missing.

As children we needed to know we were loved, respected, and accepted. It was important to feel safe with our parents and secure in the knowledge that they would care for us properly and adequately protect us from danger. We needed clear limits and reasonable consequences when we lost control of ourselves and misbehaved. We wanted to feel visible to our parents and to know they were interested in helping us be the unique person we are. We wanted our parents to listen to us and accept our feelings while not allowing us to manipulate and control them with unreasonable demands and annoying behavior.

Our parents violated our boundaries if they attacked us with words or aggressive, hurtful behavior rather than calmly setting limits and consistently invoking judicious consequences when we got out of line. We also were wounded if our parents neglected us, ignored our needs and feelings, failed to protect us from harm, or even harmed us themselves, through physical, emotional, or sexual abuse.

Such boundary violations disturb normal emotional development. Each incident is like a pebble dropped into still water. It creates spreading ripples of aftershock that affect the ways we relate to others. These sometimes tiny, sometimes big pebbles of pain come to rest in the deep waters of our unconscious inner space. They lie buried there and weigh us down with depression, anxiety, and conflicted relationships until we make the conscious effort required to heal our hurts and repair our damaged sense of self.

Reclaiming Our Missing Parts

We lose touch with the parts of ourselves that were unacceptable to our parents. These lost inner selves are cast into the shadows deep within us so we can hide them from others and bury the pain and shame we feel about them. Many of our most valuable personal resources languish in the dark basement of our unconscious space, waiting for us to discover them and invite them back into the light of our lives.

The lost selves we hide inside us act like magnets. They draw us to other people who have permission to be and express what we do not. When we meet someone who is well developed—or even overly developed—in ways that were forbidden to us, we feel an irresistible urge to get to know them. The chemistry between us compels us to connect. We find their idiosyncrasies charming. But once we establish a close relationship, those same quirks may seem to be the most annoying and difficult parts of our partners.

We don't like in them what we learned was unacceptable in ourselves. We want them to change so they will be more like us. Meanwhile, the same thing is going on with them: they see in us what is lost in them. It doesn't take long for ugly power struggles to mar the bliss we felt when first we met. Each of us becomes intent on extinguishing in the other what was extinguished in us. In our battling we violate each other's boundaries, hurting each other as we were hurt. Ultimately we may destroy the relationship or settle into a disappointing stalemate. Alternatively, we may find and follow the path of a conscious relationship: we may wake up and discover how we and our partner are each other's perfect teachers, calling on each other to reclaim the parts of ourselves we lost when we were children and teens.

~ *Magic and Mirrors* ~

It's like magic—the way you are drawn to your partner when first you meet. You feel delighted and delightful, curious and interested, alive and filled with hope. Before you know it you are hooked. You've found the mate of your dreams, and you are ready to dive into life together. Everything is coming up roses!

The partner you attract stirs up deep memories in you—memories that are outside your conscious awareness. You sense in him something compelling and familiar—something you know you want to claim though you are not sure exactly what it is. You just know you feel the magic when you are together. And you are right. There is magic—and there are also mirrors. The surprising secret you may not yet recognize is that your partner reminds you of you—when you were young and whole.

Your partner turns out to be your finest mirror. In her or him you find reflected all that also exists in you. What you like in your partner, you value and accept in yourself. What you hate in your partner, you reject and are blind to in you. Your mate excels at what you think you can't do or be. Where your mate is overdeveloped, you are lacking. Where you are overdeveloped, your mate has growth challenges.

~ Becoming Whole ~

Together you and your partner add up to one whole. Your resources and deficits are complementary. They draw you to each other.

Early in your evolving relationship, you rely on each other to fill in your missing parts. Eventually, instead of relying on your partner to fill in your gaps, you are called to find in yourself what you imagine exists only in her or him.

What frustrates you in him, you must learn to recognize and accept in yourself. Where you overdo, you must let go and allow space for him to contribute. Where you underfunction, you are challenged to stretch into doing what does not come naturally. Where what you do doesn't produce the results you want, your task is to try the opposite. What you avoid, you must address. What you overuse, you must release. Becoming whole means finding both completeness and balance.

Your evolution into wholeness unfolds throughout the life of your relationship. With each life challenge you are called to stretch beyond your comfort zone into new dimensions of personal growth. Births, moves, losses, deaths, accidents, illnesses, successes, mistakes, and triumphs help you mature. They also deepen your connection with your partner, if you meet them head on. If you avoid the emotional, mental, and spiritual demands such life events bring—or try to deal with them by shutting your partner out—you abort their bonding potential and endanger your relationship's survival. But if you turn to your partner for support, your relationship will mature and become richer as each of you grows more whole through sharing.

Your Boundaries and Your Spirit

Involving the spiritual dimension of your being is vital to developing and sustaining healthy boundaries. With a strong sense of the divine presence within you and of your connection with God or a higher power, you are able to find the strength and comfort you need when human companions hurt, disappoint, or leave you. Your spiritual life—in whatever form you choose to practice it—empowers you to love yourself and others without trying to get from them what ultimately can come only from the realm of Spirit.

I often remind my clients and myself that all relationships in physical form will end eventually. Even partners in marriages that last a lifetime ultimately must release each other when one of them dies before the other. It takes great courage to enter an intimate relationship knowing that one day you and your mate will part. Even more courage is required to allow yourself to be as open and vulnerable to your partner as genuine intimacy demands. In order to do so we need to know we have the spiritual resources to help us through the times of grief that are inevitable when we live in profound connection with another.

With healthy boundaries that embrace body, feelings, mind, and spirit, we know there is much more to us than meets the eye. We also realize that we can easily forget the bigger picture when we become entangled in the fascinating dramas we create in this world of physical form. Caught up in our predicaments, we feel frightened, overwhelmed, and filled with anger about what others do and don't do that we cannot control. With our intimate partners we know we are especially vulnerable. What they choose affects us very directly, just as our choices affect them. If we get caught up in our fears we violate their boundaries and allow them to violate ours. On the other hand, when we choose to remember the larger reality and tune in to divine love, we empower ourselves to behave respectfully even when our life circumstances are particularly difficult.

It is my experience that healthy boundaries require a strong spiritual base. Loving our partner without losing our self demands that we stay in touch with the source of love that we cannot lose—except by tuning out our spiritual side. It is the loving spirit that enlivens our relationships, fills our hearts, and makes every day a time to celebrate living.

CHAPTER TWO

Safe Dialogue

M ike and Heather, a strikingly handsome couple, arrived in my office ten minutes late, with their two young children, a three-year-old girl and a four-month-old boy. Seating themselves at opposite ends of the sofa across from me, they began. "We're filing for divorce," Heather announced, eyes smoldering. "I can't take it anymore."

"*She* can't take it?" Mike broke in. "I've had it up to here!" he said, waving his hand above his head. "She's rude to me and always complaining about something."

"Oh, yeah?" Heather countered. "Well, you're always criticizing me—like I'm your child or something. I hate the way you act so superior—like I should bow down and worship you because you're so perfect! I just can't stand that!"

Five minutes into our session, and already they'd exhibited many of the classic signs of blurred boundaries. They interrupted each other, blamed each other, and seemed frightened and anxious. In addition, they had brought their young children along and were late for their first appointment—more signs of boundary deficits. They didn't appear to manage time limits well, and they failed to keep their children out of the middle of their marital conflicts. I glanced at the little ones and uttered a silent prayer for guidance in helping their parents. Then I did what I do first with couples whose boundaries need to be clarified. I began teaching them to practice what I call Safe Dialogue.[1]

Honoring Boundaries
When You and Your Partner Talk

Safe Dialogue is a structured communication process that allows two people to talk with each other and keep clear boundaries between them. Using Safe Dialogue, each person can say what she or he wants to and be heard fully and accurately by the other. My role as therapist is to act as their Safe Dialogue coach and referee, making sure each person plays by the rules and stays within the dialogue structure. This ensures that they can talk about even the most touchy subjects without escalating their discussion into yet another frustrating fight.

Safe Dialogue is basically a simple process, but it can be challenging to follow. Some people find it very frustrating and difficult at first. Others are relieved to discover just how good it feels to slow down their communication and take time to listen carefully to each other without reacting and becoming defensive.

I introduce couples to Safe Dialogue right away, even before listening to their litany of complaints. Experiencing a successful dialogue is far more healing for couples than for me to talk with them about what they ought to do to solve their problems. Helping them speak and listen respectfully to each other is the most effective way I know to interrupt the vicious cycles of boundary-violating behaviors.

In Safe Dialogue, I ask couples to follow two very important rules: The first is that each person speaks only about "I"—about his or her own feelings and experience. The second is that they avoid using the pronoun *we*. I urge the person who is speaking to reveal what is inside her so her partner can know and understand her more fully. Speaking only about "I" rather than "you" or "we" prevents boundary violations like critiquing or criticizing her partner or otherwise dishonoring him.

After one partner has had their say, the other then mirrors back to the speaker exactly what he heard. Like a mirror, which reflects everything it sees, he repeats only what he heard the other say, using the speaker's own words. This lets his partner know he really *got* what she said, whether or not he agrees with her. To act as a mirror, he has to empty himself so he can fully tune in to his mate. Instead of intruding on his partner with comments that deny her point of view, he honors her as a person separate from him—a person whose feelings and experience are just as valid and important as his.

After describing the dialogue process to Heather and Mike, I asked one of them to begin by speaking one or two sentences about what she or he was experiencing. Immediately Mike interrupted. "You need to understand that the only problem we have is Heather's bad temper. When she gets mad she says awful things to me, and I simply can't take that. That's why I left. She's got to learn not to be angry and talk so mean to me. That why we're here. So she can get better!"

Heather looked both hurt and angry. Raising her voice a bit, she jumped in to tell me, "Mike is impossible to live with. No matter what I do or how hard I try, he's always lecturing me and telling me what I do wrong. He never listens to me. That's why I get so furious! A saint couldn't live with him!"

I let them know I understood their frustration with each other; then I explained that the dialogue process would help them find their way through these hurtful episodes, keeping both of them safe so they would be able to speak openly and be heard fully by the other.

Gently but firmly, I guided them along. Heather spoke first. With a decided edge to her voice, she told Mike, "I am just so angry with you. I need you to listen to me and acknowledge what I say. I get so frustrated when you seem to ignore me. I don't know if you've even heard what I say." Mike reacted quickly and defensively. Rolling his eyes and sighing with disgust, he protested, "That's not true. I do listen to you, but what you say is wrong, and you're always so angry and stubborn. You're impossible!"

I intervened, asking Mike to hold on to his reaction, assuring him that he would get a turn to speak. His assignment now, I told him, was to mirror back to Heather exactly what he'd heard her say. He could say something like, "If I understand you correctly, you're telling me that you are so angry with me. You need me to listen to you and acknowledge what you say. And you get frustrated when I seem to ignore you. You don't know if I've even heard what you say." Mirroring, I told him, would help Heather feel that she had been heard, and it would help Mike tune in to her more fully.

Again Mike resisted, informing me impatiently, "You aren't getting it, are you? It's Heather's anger that is the problem here, not my listening."

I mirrored his words and told him I could imagine how frustrated he might feel with this process. Once more I asked him to simply repeat Heather's words so she could hear them coming out of his mouth rather than mine.

Finally Mike managed to repeat Heather's words, though not without a tone of impatience. I opted to let that pass and suggested that he invite Heather to "tell me more." This he did, but reluctantly. Heather then reacted, pointing out to me, "He doesn't really want to hear more. He isn't interested in what I think. Nothing is going to change that." Tears were starting to roll down her cheeks.

I mirrored her words and again encouraged her to talk to him anyway. Heather composed herself and continued, "I just feel so hopeless about our marriage, and I'm scared and lonely taking care of the children since you moved out."

With careful coaching each step of the way, Mike managed to reflect her words back to her. It was clear that part of him was moved by what she was telling him now about feeling scared and lonely. He could relate to those feelings much more readily than to her earlier angry and critical words. After he successfully mirrored and asked her to tell him more, Heather reported, "That's all for now." She looked relieved, sensing that Mike had connected with her feelings moments before.

Next I invited Mike to summarize all he had heard from Heather up to this point. He was to use her exact words as much as possible, and to put together what she had said so she would know he had really gotten it. He could end his summary with, "Did I get it all?"

Summarizing is one of the most difficult yet important parts of Safe Dialogue. It helps the listener really take in what is important to the other. This ensures that his partner's words penetrate his consciousness more fully so he understands her better and can relate to how things are from her point of view.

With a bit of further coaching, Mike was able to summarize what Heather had told him: "You are very angry with me, because I seem to ignore you when you try to talk to me. You need me to listen and acknowledge what you say. You are scared and lonely taking care of the children by yourself since I moved out, and you feel hopeless about our marriage."

Heather looked at him attentively and with an expression of amazed delight as she heard Mike accurately summarize her message. When he asked her, "Did I get it all?" she nodded her head and smiled. "Yes, you got it."

The last two steps of Mike's job as listener were also challenging for him. First I asked him to validate Heather's message. I suggested he say something simple like, "What you say makes sense to me." Or, "I think I can understand what you say because I've felt lonely and scared too."

Mike immediately protested, "But she doesn't make sense, and I don't understand her. I'm not going to sit here and lie about this."

Responding, I gently but firmly told him that validating her message would not mean that he either agreed or disagreed with what she said. Validation simply means that he realizes that another human being, separate and different from him, might possibly see and experience things differently from how he does. By validating Heather's message, he would let her know that he respects her point of view, even though it is not exactly like his.

Reluctantly, he rather quickly said, "I guess I understand what you're saying."

"Great!" I told him. "Now comes the final step." I asked him to tell Heather what feelings he sensed in her as he listened to her words. Feelings are described by single words such as *angry, sad, disappointed, confused, lonely, happy, excited, relieved, hopeful,* or *glad.* If Mike was right on, I told him, Heather would nod her head to let him know he really was in tune with her. If not, she would correct the feeling. I reminded Mike that Heather is the expert on what she feels, and Mike is only making a guess as he learns to tune in to her more fully.

"I guess you might be feeling a little better, maybe relieved even," Mike said. Nodding her head and smiling, Heather agreed. "I do feel relieved that you listened to me. Thank you!"

I congratulated both of them on successfully completing this segment of the dialogue process. I then turned to Mike and asked him to take his turn expressing what he was thinking and feeling. Heather was now on duty to listen and mirror for Mike.

Mike said how awful he felt when Heather got so angry with him. Heather had as much trouble reflecting Mike's words as he had had reflecting hers. Lots of coaching was required to help her tune in to him without allowing her reactions to escalate over what he said and fuel another angry reaction from him—a pattern they had been caught in for most of their marriage. But as I guided her and firmly insisted that she contain her desire to get out of the dialogue process, she relaxed a bit and began to mirror more readily.

By the time our session ended, both Mike and Heather told me they felt better and were encouraged that perhaps they could learn to understand each other better. I affirmed them for their courage in coming to couple's therapy and thanked them for their hard work in practicing this very demanding process for the first time.

As we left my office, I complimented their daughter on her excellent behavior during their session. Sitting on the floor, she had played quietly the whole time with a sack of hand puppets. I knew she was being too good, probably because she was afraid to do anything else. Their son, who was recovering from an upset stomach, had slept through the hour. He was waking up as Heather and Mike scheduled a second appointment for the following week. I suggested that it would be important for them to arrange for a baby-sitter.

A Near-Divorce Experience

Before Mike and Heather returned for their second session Mike called to cancel their appointment. He told me he was filing for divorce. Heather had had another angry explosion the night before.

I was not surprised. Couples often find a bit of success, such as Mike and Heather experienced in their first visit, quite scary. They're tempted to give up just when they sense there might be hope. But Mike would have none of my reassurances. "Heather will never be better," he complained.

I could have let it drop there, but instead I reminded him of their children and suggested that staying with their counseling would be a wise choice. Even if they divorced, the two of them would need to learn to cooperate in order to raise their children without harming them unnecessarily. Getting rid of Heather wouldn't solve his problems. A few years from now he would find himself in another relationship, frustrated by the same issues—only they probably would be even more difficult to handle then if he put off dealing with them now.

He said he would think it over.

It made sense to me that Mike—and probably Heather too—were angry after their first session. Anger is a natural reaction to being asked to behave in ways that do not come naturally. A near-divorce experience like they were having is really a wake-up call to grow into greater maturity and to learn how to relate to each other in more loving ways.

Heather and Mike did return for their next appointment, and without their children. Mike began their dialogue this time. His face was red, and his jaw vibrated with tension as he spoke. "I'm absolutely dismayed by Heather's terrible temper. You simply wouldn't believe how she acts and what she says to me. I just can't put up with her anymore!"

Heather reacted quickly and, forgetting to mirror, accused him, "You're just like your father—mean, critical, macho, and superior. I hate you when you act like that—like I'm your child or something."

I decided to be firm with them. I reminded them of the ground rules for dialogue: speak only about themselves, not about their partner, and mirror back to the partner exactly what he or she said, using his or her own words.

Like children relieved to know there was an adult in charge, Mike and Heather looked at me with interest. I think they sensed that I was neither afraid of their battle nor impressed by their finger-pointing. Both had failed in getting me to take sides.

That day, while I kept them in the dialogue structure and allowed no blaming or hiding behind "we," Heather and Mike managed a much more meaningful exchange. The beginners' boundaries created by the Safe Dialogue structure helped them relax and be less defensive. As each revealed more about himself or herself, the other responded more genuinely. It was refreshing for them to set aside their verbal weapons, remove some of their competitive armor, and be more real about their needs, fears, hurts, and hopes.

By their third appointment, Mike expressed his excitement about this boundaries thing. He and Heather still had lots of growing and healing ahead of them, but they were beginning to sense a glimmer of light. They weren't arguing as much, knowing they would be able to talk about what bothered them during their therapy session.

The fourth time I saw them, Heather reported that Mike had moved back home over the previous weekend. They were cautiously encouraged and anxious to continue learning what they needed to do to nurture each other and their marriage.

Preparing for Safe Dialogue on Your Own

The Safe Dialogue process I taught Heather and Mike is much more than a tool to enhance communication, though it does that most effectively. It can also be a deeply healing, profoundly connecting, and wonderfully practical way to establish the personal boundaries and clear identities couples need in order to be intimate. Though the process sounds simple enough, it is much more difficult to practice than at first glance it seems to be. For most couples a coach is necessary to help them stay within the dialogue structure as they learn to practice it.

When couples begin to use the Safe Dialogue process on their own, I suggest that they create rituals that are meaningful to them to mark their times of sharing. They may light candles before they begin to talk, play music they treasure as a background for their sharing, and even follow a prescribed form for addressing each other. Rituals like these are soothing and will help them feel safe. They may also assist them in establishing new habits and growing out of old dysfunctional patterns of relating.

Rituals calm fears when people are agitated. They offer order, consistency, and predictability. They also make change possible. When you know what is coming next, you can relax and shift out of instinctive fight, flee, or freeze reaction patterns. This helps you become more conscious, civilized, and loving as you respond to each other.

Before you practice Safe Dialogue at home, consider creating a dedicated space for your sharing. When you carefully craft a setting for dialogue, you establish a visual and physical boundary around the two of you and your dialogue experiences. You also help establish the safe context you need to open your hearts to each other.

There are many ways to create a beautiful setting. I keep pillows, stuffed lambs and bears, and even Silly Putty and strings of "worry beads" in my office so people can hold on to them and soothe themselves as they dialogue. I also have lots of plants and candles as well as a selection of relaxing music to help create an inviting, comforting space for sorting things out. Mike often picked up the Silly Putty when he felt himself getting tense, and Heather often went for the teddy bear.

You can experiment with aromatherapy to create pleasant and comforting fragrances to enjoy as you dialogue. Try candles as well—perhaps a large white one and two smaller ones of different colors to light before you begin to dialogue. Each person picks their favorite color and affirms an intention to do his or her part in creating a Safe Dialogue. Lighting your candle, you might say something to yourself like, "I center myself in love and affirm my intention to speak from my heart, to reveal my true self to you, and to listen with respect to what you tell me about yourself." Next, your partner lights her candle and makes a similar silent affirmation. Then together you could light a larger candle that represents your relationship and signals that you are ready to join in dialogue. Your individual candle represents you—the distinct person you are—while your relationship candle reminds you of the larger context you share.

When I suggested candles to Mike and Heather, their responses showed some of the differences between them. "That seems kind of weird—lighting candles and all that," Mike commented.

"I think it sounds real romantic," Heather countered.

I suggested that Heather mirror Mike's words and see if there was more he wanted to say about this seeming weird. It turned out that Mike's father, who was raised in a very conservative, fundamentalist church, often criticized his mother, who was Catholic, for lighting candles when she prayed. "I guess candles trigger scary feelings in me. They remind me of horrible fights my parents had about religion. I hated all that."

Heather reflected, "So your parents fought about candles, and your dad criticized your mom for lighting them when she prayed. It certainly makes sense to me that you might feel uncomfortable with the idea of lighting candles when we dialogue."

Mike looked relieved as he nodded his head, affirming Heather's new understanding of him. Then he added, "You know, now that I've remembered that and told you about it, I don't think lighting those candles with you will be any big deal. That was then and this is now. I can let go of it, knowing you understand."

Looking amazed, Heather mirrored Mike again and thanked him for letting her know him better.

What they had just shared was another step toward developing the healthy boundaries they needed to enjoy their marriage. By expressing themselves honestly and listening carefully, Heather and Mike were beginning to build the boundaries that would allow them to love each other without losing themselves.

Practicing Safe Dialogue at Home

Couples who come to my office have in effect made an appointment to dialogue with each other. At home it is also important to make a date for engaging with each other in the Safe Dialogue process. This ensures that you respect each other's time and emotional availability. When one partner requests a dialogue, the other honors the importance of that request by granting an appointment as soon as possible. You might dialogue immediately if both are willing and available, or make an appointment for a mutually agreeable time later.

When your appointment time arrives, meet each other in your dedicated space, and prepare yourselves for talking with each other. Observe a three- to five-minute period of silent preparation, and then practice any rituals you have agreed on together.

Finish with the following shared centering process: Invite an image of an open heart to come into your mind as you set your silent intention to create a satisfying dialogue experience. Join both hands with your partner and look into each other's eyes. Then close your eyes and focus on the area of your heart in the center of your chest. Feel loving energy flowing from your heart into the heart of your mate and from your hands into her hands. After a few moments gently squeeze each other's hands and open your eyes so you are again looking at each other.

Proceed by speaking and listening to each other, following the rules and structure of Safe Dialogue. When the speaking and listening phase of your dialogue is completed, you might celebrate your success by stating and mirroring what you appreciate about each other. End by celebrating your successful sharing with a hug and a kiss, by dancing, playing music, or in whatever way fits the two of you.

If you practice this dialogue process regularly, your interactions with each other will change. Each of you will become more aware of how you communicate. You will develop a stronger sense of yourselves as separate individuals who can love and trust each other without losing your uniqueness. As Safe Dialogue helps you take down your defensive barriers, you will understand each other more fully and be less frightened by your differences. By allowing each other to "see into me," you will experience the rewards of ever deepening intimacy.

EXERCISES

These exercises focus on practicing each step of the Safe Dialogue process. Because it is easier to first engage in these processes with people who aren't as important to you as your partner, you might choose a friend, coworker, or acquaintance with whom to practice your listening and mirroring skills. You needn't tell the other person what you're doing. Be aware as you do the exercises that you are preparing yourself for learning to dialogue with your mate.

When you dialogue with your mate, you may encounter feelings, fears, resistance, and reactions in yourself that will challenge you and make it more difficult to stay in the process with him or her than it was with others. Don't judge yourself or give up when dialogue is hard to do. Instead, stick with the structure and have compassion for yourself and your spouse. Dialogue is difficult to master and requires time, commitment, and growth in both of you.

1. Practice mirroring with a friend who is not your partner. Reflect back to your friend both his or her words and the gestures, breathing patterns, and body positions that accompany them. Notice the rapport you create with the person you mirror—a rapport that is usually unconscious. Notice how your mirroring communicates to your friend that she or he is visible and important to you. You affirm and honor that person as a distinct individual. Notice how mirroring allows you to understand your friend more fully and experience more directly what he or she may be feeling. Be mindful that your mirroring is respectful and does not degenerate into ridiculing mimicry. If you are subtle and intend only honor for the other person, your friend probably will not object or even notice what you are doing. If you are intrusive with your mirroring, your friend may tell you to stop. Remember that mirroring is a powerful art to be practiced with care and respect.

2. Tune in and consciously notice when other people mirror you. Be aware of how you feel when you are mirrored. You will develop a stronger identity and sense of self when other people who are important to you honor you by paying close and complete attention to what you say and do.

3. Practice validating what a coworker tells you. Tell this person that what they say makes sense to you or that you understand their meaning. This does not necessarily mean you agree with them. Notice how this person responds when you honor them in this way.

<u>**4.**</u> Explore your feelings about validating statements that don't agree with what you believe. How do you feel when you disagree with what you are validating? Notice how doing so requires that you stretch beyond your view of the world. Be aware of how you are allowing another person's reality to be meaningful to you even though it is different from your own. This helps you develop a much greater capacity to connect with others.

<u>**5.**</u> Practice the heart-centering ritual. Remember to take time for this very important personal preparation before you and your partner begin to dialogue. It also helps to practice this process each morning or at some special time during the day, whether or not you plan to dialogue with your mate. Building time for heart centering into your daily routine will bring you dividends in all of your relationships and interactions with others.

<u>**6.**</u> Invite your partner to join you in preparing a space in your home for Safe Dialogue. Be delightfully creative in adding decorative touches that are beautiful, comforting, and satisfying to both of you. Take before and after photos of the place you choose. Frame two of the after pictures. Give one to your partner, and keep one for yourself. Display yours in your office, dressing room, or other personal retreat. Let it be a frequent reminder of your sacred connection with your mate and of your joint efforts to nurture your committed relationship or marriage with beauty, ritual, and intimate sharing.

<u>**7.**</u> Make two copies of the Safe Dialogue Cue Sheet presented at the end of this chapter. Keep them handy for you and your mate in the special space you've chosen for dialoguing. Refer to the cue sheet as you learn to practice the process with each other. You also may wish to copy and refer to the Five Stages of Safe Dialogue, immediately below, for a more complete guide through the dialogue process.

The Five Stages of Safe Dialogue

STAGE ONE
Preparing for Safe Dialogue

MAKE A DATE FOR SAFE DIALOGUE

Express your desire to dialogue and suggest an appointment time.

If your partner is unavailable then, set a mutually agreeable time, within the next twenty-four hours, if possible.

PREPARE THE SETTING

Choose a pleasant space, visually attractive and physically comfortable.

Arrange comfortable seating for both of you so it is easy to look into each other's eyes and touch each other as you dialogue.

Have matches or a lighter and three candles available: one candle should be a color you choose to represent you; another should be a color your partner selects to represent him or her; a third, larger candle should represent your relationship.

Select quiet, soothing background music.

Turn off the telephone or allow it to be answered automatically so you are not interrupted.

Teach your children to respect your privacy when you dialogue. If they are very young, plan your dialogue for times when they are asleep or in someone else's care.

Agree upon a time frame for your sharing. Twenty minutes to an hour is quite challenging for beginners. Set a timer and agree ahead of time to stop when the allotted time is over—unless you both decide to continue for a specified additional time.

PREPARE YOURSELF

Share a short (three- to five-minute) period of silence.

Center yourself.

Close your eyes and take several deep, relaxing breaths.

Place one or both of your hands over your heart center.

Feel yourself filled with love and surrounded by it.

Visualize your heart opening.

Feel compassion, harmony, healing, and unconditional love flowing through you.

Silently repeat these or similar words: "With love as my guide, I share from my heart and listen with my heart. Moment by moment, I create joy in my marriage (or committed relationship)."

Will yourself to see and be seen; to hear and be heard; to feel and feel with; to touch and be touched.

Silently affirm your intention for Safe Dialogue: "I am grateful that my sharing with (your partner's name) is loving, open, honest, and joyful."

STAGE TWO

Connecting with Your Partner

Open your eyes and look into your partner's eyes. Continue to stay silent.

Join both your hands with both of your partner's. Close your eyes.

Turn your attention back to your heart by focusing on the center of your chest.

Feel love flowing from your heart into the heart of your partner.

Feel the energy of love also flowing between the palms of your hands.

Enjoy this loving connection that soothes your fears and transcends your differences, reminding you of the union of your souls.

After a few moments, gently squeeze your partner's hands and open your eyes so you are looking into your partner's. Gaze into each other's eyes for a few moments, feeling the love flow between you.

Light your individual candles. As you do, silently affirm your intention for Safe Dialogue.

Together, using your individual candles, light your relationship candle to signal that you are ready for Safe Dialogue.

STAGE THREE

Speaking and Listening with Open Hearts

ONE PARTNER SPEAKS WHILE THE OTHER LISTENS

Speaker:

Speak only about "I," not about "we" or "you."

Take full responsibility for what you say. Affirm to yourself, "I am responsible for my words, experience, behavior, feelings, choices, interpretations, and desires."

Be fully aware and conscious by listening to what you say as well as what you experience inwardly as you speak.

Do not criticize, blame, attack, analyze other people, predict doom, shame others, discount, use the past to undermine the present, tell others they are wrong, make worried comments about the future, or use guilt to manipulate.

If you notice yourself engaged in one of these fearful patterns, take responsibility for what you're doing. Say something like, "I notice that my fearful self is speaking. Please disregard my hurtful words. What I really want to say is _____." (See Chapter 8 for a discussion of the fearful part of you that violates boundaries when it is aroused, what I call the Internal Saboteur.)

Listener:

Open your heart and center yourself by silently affirming the following:

"I let go of any personal agendas for change, resolution, or outcome."

"I set aside my thoughts, ideas, reactions, and judgments."

"I open my ears, eyes, and heart so that I hear you and see you; I do my best to imagine what you feel."

"I focus on you and what you're telling me."

"I am aware. I notice my reactions, especially my fearful ones. I don't allow my fears to control me."

"I remember that your words are about you, not me."

"I remember that it's okay for us to be different and to experience the same things differently."

"My job is to listen and contain my reactions, no matter what you say."

THE LISTENER MIRRORS THE SPEAKER'S WORDS

The speaker pauses after making a two- or three-sentence statement. The listening partner then mirrors what the speaker has said.

Listener:

Mirror by repeating your partner's words, exactly as he or she said them, while making any necessary pronoun changes. For example, he says, "I am frustrated because you and I haven't talked in such a long time. I'm feeling distant from you and quite lonely." You mirror by saying, "You're frustrated because you and I haven't talked in such a long time. You're feeling distant from me and quite lonely. Did I get that?"

Do not paraphrase, change your partner's words, or offer your interpretation of what he or she says. Keep yourself out of the picture. The focus is on the speaker. Your job is to be a flat, nondistorting mirror of what you hear!

If your partner indicates that you did not get it, ask him or her to tell you again.

Speaker:

When your partner mirrors for you, listen to what you've said. Be open to hearing yourself as completely as possible.

Notice new ideas and doors of expanded awareness that open within you as your partner mirrors for you. Share what comes to you, and stay open to what continues to emerge as you are mirrored.

Recognize the fearful voice within that may object to staying in the dialogue structure. Consciously choose not to allow this fearful part of you to control what you say. Tell yourself, "That fearful, negative voice I hear hides my true feelings, which I'm denying or ignoring. I choose not to identify with that negative voice. I recenter myself in love and peace so I can notice what I'm really feeling and speak honestly about my emotional experience."

Let your partner know when he or she has gotten what you said.

EXPAND THE COMMUNICATION

Listener:

Invite your partner to tell you more. Do this by saying, with energy and enthusiasm, "Tell me more!" or "Is there more?"

Be sure the invitation you extend is genuine. Don't allow yourself to sound disgusted, bored, angry, or resentful. And don't attempt to direct your partner's next words by asking a specific question or steering the conversation in the direction you would like it to take. Keep your invitation open-ended and nonspecific so the message you convey to your partner says, "I am open, interested, available, patient, present, and willing to hear all you have to say."

Continue to listen and mirror small pieces of what your partner tells you until she or he indicates that there is no more at this time.

Speaker:

Continue speaking from your heart until you have said all you need to say at this time and your partner has mirrored it accurately so you know she or he has gotten it.

SUMMARIZE THE COMMUNICATION

Listener:

When your partner says he or she has no more to say right now, summarize all the speaker has said. This tells your partner that you have listened carefully and integrated what you have heard. Your summary also enables your partner to hear himself or herself more fully.

After summarizing, ask, "Did I get all that?" If you missed something, your partner will tell you what you missed. If he or she adds something new, mirror that as an addition to your summary.

Continue to mirror until both of you agree that your summary is accurate and complete.

VALIDATE THE COMMUNICATION

Listener:

Validate what your partner has told you by saying, "That makes sense to me" or "I understand what you are saying." Validation affirms your partner's integrity and sanity and expresses your respect for him or her as an equal and sensitive being with whom you can experience a common ground of understanding.

Remember that validation does not imply agreement. It simply recognizes that there are many ways to see and understand life experiences.

Remind yourself that validation—though sometimes difficult to give—helps the giver grow beyond self-centeredness, self-absorption, and destructive competitiveness.

EXPRESS EMPATHY FOR YOUR PARTNER

Listener:

Say to your partner, "Given everything you just said, I imagine you might be feeling _____."

Remember that whereas thoughts are expressed in sentences, feelings are described by only one word. Feeling words include: happy, sad, angry, frustrated, confused, helpless, powerful, concerned, excited, joyful, alone, lonely, lost, rejected, misunderstood, accepted, understood, anxious, dejected, frightened, jealous, betrayed, etc.

Empathy involves listening with your heart and *sensing* what your partner might feel—while remembering that your partner is the expert and final authority on what he or she *actually* feels.

If your partner's feelings are different from what you suggest, or if he or she elaborates on what he or she feels, mirror all that you hear.

STAGE FOUR

Changing Roles

When the first speaker is finished for the moment, the roles reverse. The speaker becomes the listener, and the process continues.

Participants take turns speaking and listening until their dialogue time is finished.

STAGE FIVE

Celebrating Your Genuine Sharing

Give one another joyful acknowledgment of the Safe Dialogue you have shared. Make statements of appreciation to each other and mirror them. Sing, dance, laugh, make music, give hugs, and celebrate your loving communication!

~ *Safe Dialogue Cue Sheet* ~

STAGE ONE: PREPARING FOR SAFE DIALOGUE

Make a date for dialogue
Prepare the setting
Prepare yourself through heart centering
Affirm your intentions for Safe Dialogue

STAGE TWO: CONNECTING WITH YOUR PARTNER

Feel the energy of the love connecting with your partner
Look into each other's eyes
Light your individual and relationship candles
Silently affirm your joint intention for Safe Dialogue

STAGE THREE: SPEAKING AND LISTENING WITH OPEN HEARTS

One partner speaks while the other listens

Listener mirrors—as exactly as possible—what the speaker says

Listener invites speaker to expand the communication

Listener summarizes all the speaker has said

Listener validates the communication

Listener expresses empathy for partner

STAGE FOUR: CHANGING ROLES

Speaker and listener change roles

Roles continue to alternate until the preagreed timeframe is finished

STAGE FIVE: CELEBRATING YOUR GENUINE SHARING

Make statements of appreciation to each other and mirror them

Sing, dance, laugh, make music, give hugs, and celebrate your success

CHAPTER THREE

Bonding and Boundary Blurring

By the time Heather and Mike came for help, they were so ensnared in their mutual frustrations that it was easy for them to forget that once, not so long ago, they had been hopelessly in love. Remembering that wondrous time of falling in love can be an important step in helping a stressed couple reconnect.

During an early therapy session I like to invite couples such as Mike and Heather to take a break from their battling to tell me how they met and began dating. This reminds all three of us of happier times in their relationship—times when hopefully they built a strong enough bond to help them weather the emotional storms they are now experiencing.

Reminiscing about the early romantic phase of a couple's connection creates a temporary shift in their perspective by allowing them to dip into some of the most potent and delicious of their shared memories. Once they recapture a bit of that early magic, I reframe their recollections in a way that allows them to feel less alarmed about their current problems.

I do this by telling them how the romantic stage of their attraction to each other was exactly the preparation they needed to motivate them to grow through their current relationship dilemma. I assure them that growth challenges such as they're experiencing are as inevitable and essential to the development of the relationship as their initial attraction stage was. And—I assure them—mastering these challenges will help them uncover new dimensions of romance and excitement about their commitment to each other.

I hope you too will enjoy reminiscing about the earliest phases of your relationship as you read this chapter. Intentionally recalling the joys of your coming together is a lovely way to shine the light of love into even your darkest times together.

"Blest Be the Tie That Binds"

Nothing quite compares with the overwhelmingly delightful joy of romance. In its bliss, you and your potential mate are attracted to each other by an energy too potent to resist.

The connection you feel in the warm embrace of your newly beloved is an essential first phase in the unfolding of an intimate relationship. This romantic bonding is the beginning of the "blessed tie that binds"— the growing attachment that inspires you and your partner to sustain the relationship you jointly create.

Every time you meet, touch, talk on the phone, think of each other, or fantasize about being together, you strengthen the connection you are building. As you grow closer and the tie you share becomes more firmly established, it inspires first tentative, and eventually formal, declarations of mutual commitment.

Your bonding is the groundwork on which you will ultimately build your lives together. Like a tiny bite of a delicious dessert offered as an appetizer before an ordinary meal, the bonding of romance gives you and your lover a taste of the joy that awaits you—if you manage to eat the meat and potatoes you must consume before dessert reappears. That dessert is the rich reward of experiencing a vintage relationship.

Just as a great wine matures gradually as it ages, a vintage relationship is one in which you and your mate mature gradually as your partnership ages. With each relationship challenge you meet successfully, you grow into ever greater wholeness as individuals. Gradually you recapture the romance you experienced initially—only now the joy and attraction you feel are lasting, because they rest on the secure foundation you have built together.

Romantic Boundaries

When you first meet, each of you perceives the other as having distinct boundaries that define you as unique, fascinating beings. You want to know and be known by each other. You thrive on the exciting energy you feel when you are together. Your personal boundaries seem whole and intact, because your lives are still quite separate.

You have what I call romantic boundaries. Romantic boundaries are not the same as the well-developed boundaries of a mature individual. They exist because your relationship is new. The circumstances of your lives are separate and distinct. You are still strangers to one another. Mystery, excitement, and anticipation combine to create lively—though temporary—boundaries around each of you that intensify your attraction.

Romantic boundaries are "virtual" boundaries as opposed to "real" boundaries. In the short run, they work as if they were real, mature, personal boundaries. In the long run they fade, leaving you and your partner to rely on the actual personal boundaries you bring into your partnership. While romantic boundaries exist, they disguise the personal boundary deficits you and your potential partner bring into your budding relationship.

Boundaries of romance are vitally important to the birthing of your intimate partnership. They allow you to bond as mysterious strangers. Romantic boundaries help you establish a connection that is strong enough to motivate you to stick together through the meat-and-potatoes growth challenges that await you once they begin to fade.

~ A Chemical Attraction ~

Romantic boundaries often ignite the chemistry that fires your initial attraction. This potent chemistry arouses your bodies, your feelings, your minds, and your spirits

At the physical level your bodies are busy sending rushes of a potent chemical, phenylethylamine (PEA), through both of you.[1] PEA is a mood-altering drug that creates euphoria. It stimulates all your senses with the delicious juiciness of being together. You feel delightfully alive—able to see, hear, taste, smell, and touch subtle pleasures that previously escaped your notice. Your emotions are on fire too. You're in love, and you want more and more of the heady feeling that hits you whenever you're in your potential partner's presence.

You have incredible bursts of energy. You don't need to eat, but when you do, food tastes especially good. Sleep apparently is no longer necessary. Everything looks brighter and more beautiful than you've ever noticed before. Ordinary experiences take on a special glow.

Meanwhile, your mind is busy imagining fabulous things about this amazing person you've met. Because you don't know him or her well yet, he or she is like a blank screen on which you can project all the qualities you want in a partner. You interpret your shared experiences in the most positive light. In your enthusiasm about who you imagine him or her to be, you forget that he or she is a person separate from you. Absorbed in your own projections, you tend to ignore any evidence that might spoil the ideal image you've created.

Meanwhile, the other person fits you into his or her ideal image for a partner, too. Ignoring the fact that neither of you knows the other as she or he actually is, the two of you are stunned by your delightful illusions. You marvel at how "right" you are for each other.

At the emotional/psychological level, each of you unconsciously reminds the other of Mom or Dad.[2] You embody enough of their positive and negative qualities to set each other's bells chiming. The bliss you experience when you are together is like what you sensed as infants when your needs for love, nurturing, safety, and security were fully met by your parents. You feel as if you've known each other forever. You comment on how at home you feel when you're together.

You forget that though your partner reminds you of people who are very familiar to you, he is not those people. In your entrancement—enhanced by the boundaries of romance—you discount his unique identity and the *actual* boundaries that define him as separate from you and your family.

~ Your Souls Rejoice ~

Beyond the physical, mental, and emotional dimensions of bonding, your soul—the eternal part of you—is deeply touched, too. Part of the bliss you feel is a spiritual opening. Your hearts open to each other and rejoice in your deep connection. In your ecstasy you experience a temporary state of spiritual liberation. All your personal boundaries—both romantic and actual—dissolve in the joy of spiritually merging with your mate. You glimpse who you truly are.

Your bliss appears to rely upon your connection with one another. For the time being, your frightened self drops out of the way. The spiritual connection you feel overrides fear.

You are capable of amazing acts of selflessness and devotion. Your beloved becomes a representative of the divine. You worship the beauty and wonder you behold in her, not fully realizing that what you see "out there" in your magical other is also "in here," within you. Opening your heart to the one you love simultaneously opens your heart to the truth of who you are.

In your passionate connection you experience a great paradox. The boundaries of romance that seem to define you as separate and distinct also allow you and your partner to enjoy moments of spiritual merging. When this happens, you "know" that you are not two, but one in your love for each other. At these moments, you transcend your separateness, experiencing you and your beloved as unique manifestations of the same whole—like two cups of water drawn from one ocean of possibility.

With your fearful self temporarily out of the picture, you feel the bliss of what in Hinduism is called *Sat Chit Ananda. Sat* is the eternal truth that is the root of all that is. *Chit* is full consciousness of that oneness—the peace that resides beyond all fear. *Ananda* is the bliss of that consciousness.[3] You know that you and your partner are created of the same stuff—like two cookies cut from the same dough with different-shaped cutters.[4] You feel your common God Source and the indescribable pleasure of reunion with Spirit.

Bonding and Release

If only it could last—this amazing, passionate springtime of being in love, in Spirit, one with each other! But since movement and change are the flow of life, this early time of idealized unity can't endure.

The very bond you create catapults you into *the* major challenge of intimate relating. That challenge is to keep the breath of life moving rhythmically and freely in the relationship you are building. The breath of life keeps your connection fresh. It keeps your relationship alive. It is the regular pulsing rhythm of both bonding and release.

Just as each inhalation of your breath must be balanced by a full exhalation, bonding must be followed by release. You bond and experience your oneness in Spirit; you let go and are separate beings again. You connect once more; you release each other. You breathe in; you breathe out. You come together. You move away. You are one; you are two again. This is the rhythm of life and the ideal rhythm of intimate relating.

Romantic boundaries allow you to bond. Yet they don't allow for the necessary release. How well you are able to release each other depends upon how well developed you are as individuals and how healthy your already existing personal boundaries are.

If your personal boundaries are not yet well developed, you may have trouble with the releasing phases of relating to your partner. Instead of letting go naturally and easily, you cling to him, avoid telling the truth, run from him, or freeze him out.

Because you aren't able to release fully and balance bonding experiences with relaxed free times for being separate, your relationship becomes stagnant. Your difficulty letting go of your partner is like failing to exhale completely when you breathe. It is as if your relationship develops asthma. Your partner feels as if he or she might be smothered by your clinging. Or if you run from your partner or freeze your partner out when you feel stressed, he or she feels abandoned and rejected. This intensifies his or her clinging reaction and magnifies your determination to flee. Your relationship begins to feel like a roller-coaster ride with highs and lows that exhaust your patience.

Love You...Love You Not

At this point, one or both of you may decide to escape. Many are unwilling to do the growth work that lies beyond the initial addictive high of romance. They go away, making excuses, saying they are no longer "in love," or announcing they have found someone new.

When relationship clouds start to gather, it is tempting to look for another delicious fix of PEA with a new romantic interest. Becoming addicted to the chemistry of romance is a convenient way to avoid the personal growth that must take place to sustain a relationship. In the short run, settling for a series of romantic liaisons may feel more attractive than sticking around to master the fine art of mature loving. In the longer run, there is no escaping the life lessons committed relationships teach.

Bonding Doesn't Stop with Romance

Powerful and important as it is, the early romantic phase of your relationship is not the only source of the bonding necessary to sustaining your commitment. Lasting relationships are marked by rich bonding and rebonding experiences that are woven through all the days and seasons partners share.

Some of these bonding experiences are intentional and planned, like pregnancies, births, anniversary celebrations, trips, new homes, and personal successes. Many are spontaneous and delightful experiences like shared moments of fun, times when you laugh together, surprises you create, and the simple joys of daily living. Others are painful times of grief, disappointment, illness, and redirection.

Inherent in each of these potential bonding experiences is the challenge of intentionally facing the feelings they trigger so you can express them and let them go. This emotional letting go occurs as you talk together, hold each other, cry, laugh, and help each other digest what happens in your life.

Every shared experience can deepen "the tie that binds" you to each other—or it can be the final straw that eventually breaks your connection. Your tie deepens if you stay connected with each other as you live your experiences, assimilate them, and let them go. Your bond suffers and may even break if you fail to acknowledge and express your feelings about what you encounter along the way. This is why many divorces and breakups occur within a couple of years of a major success, a big change, or a painful loss. Great successes and devastating losses as well as the more ordinary ups and downs of life must be shared, processed openly with each other, and fully digested.

As you integrate your experiences, you let them go and move on with your life. The more skilled you and your partner become with the art of emotional digestion and letting go, the more you are able to have fun together. You respect each other as separate people with distinct and different emotional responses to life events when you share your feelings through dialogue, touching, and holding each other. Your emotional honesty helps keep your personal boundaries intact and sustains your attraction to each other. It also helps your sexual relationship remain lively.

But knowing yourself, feeling your feelings, and revealing them openly with your mate is hard to do. It demands emotional maturity, personal security, faith, trust, wisdom, and spiritual development—resources that evolve slowly through ongoing experiences of intimate relating. The temptation is to take the easy way out—to ignore what happens, refuse to talk about what is difficult, avoid your feelings, isolate, or go outside your relationship to find someone else who will listen.

Inevitably, to sustain the bonds built by romance and the sharing of life, you must risk being vulnerable—again and again. You must reveal yourself, deeply love and connect with your mate, and then release her—knowing you cannot control her choices or force her to do your bidding. You must tend to the business of discovering the complexities of the real person she is. At the same time, you must continually rediscover yourself, changed and enhanced as you are by walking the path of life paired with your partner.

When Romantic Boundaries Begin to Fade

Each of you brings to your potential partnership the personal boundaries you have developed through all of your prior relationships. If you are mature, fully differentiated adults, you have healthy personal boundaries that continue to define you when the boundaries of romance fade.

You are at ease sustaining a joyful rhythm of connecting and releasing and prepared to handle whatever conflicts and challenges lie ahead. Your mature boundaries allow you to keep love flowing freely in your relationship, nurturing the two of you and your connection in loving, mutually satisfying ways

If the personal boundaries you bring into your partnership are blurred and incomplete, your boundary deficits reveal themselves when the boundaries of romance fade. Unconsciously you often violate your partner's boundaries and allow him to violate yours.

Blurred boundaries feel sticky and uncomfortable. They disallow the blissful merging you felt when as two people with separate life circumstances you and your partner first connected. With inadequate personal boundaries you feel frightened because you don't know how to protect and support yourself. Important parts of you are missing—resources you need to relate successfully to your partner. Often you find yourself feeling caught, captured, somehow lessened by your connection. This is in sharp contrast to how you feel when you and your partner merge in Spirit. Connecting spiritually frees you, enraptures you, leaves you feeling expanded and blissful.

You know your and your partner's personal boundaries are blurred when you sense that something vitally important is missing in your relationship. You realize that things have changed between you. One or both of you may be turning to addictive activities to avoid dealing with the other. You may be anxious and depressed, physically ill, or focused almost exclusively on work, children, or your parents. Parts of both of you are lost and hidden—parts that must be reclaimed to bring you into a mutually satisfying and sustainable connection with each other. Other parts are overdeveloped and overused.

You may notice yourselves hiding the truth—or leaving out details you imagine might upset your partner. When you feel angry, you pretend all is well. Instead of revealing your feelings, you act them out in subtle and not so subtle ways. Or you find yourselves trying to control each other with anger or tears. Sex becomes less spontaneous and more often a subject of concern. You disagree about how to spend time together and apart. Money issues surface and feed your escalating anxieties.

Your emerging fears serve to cool down the intensity of your attraction. Along with fear, *need* intrudes on your awareness. The more time you share, the more your lives become entwined—and the more you have to lose should your relationship fail.

At times you treat your mate as your parents treated you—attempting to mold, control, nurture, correct, criticize, scold, or praise him, as if you were in charge of making him into the person you think he ought to be. On other occasions you behave with your partner as you behaved in response to your parents when you were a child—attempting to charm, con, get your way, rebel, please, pout, or cajole in the ways that worked for you early in life. Eventually you realize that living with each other feels a lot like living at home with Mom and Dad.

~ *"Protecting" Your Connection Can Destroy It* ~

The ways you violate each other's personal boundaries are unconscious efforts to protect your relationship boundary. You want to preserve your connection by not rocking the boat. Consequently you attempt to control what happens between you and your partner, much as your parents tried to control your behavior when you were small. Without being aware of it, you start sounding a lot like your mom or your dad when you correct your partner's behavior. He or she in turn reacts with resentment or compliance. Unexpressed angry feelings pile up between you.

You expect your partner to change in the ways you want while also demanding that you be accepted by him—just as you are. You hide your true self behind attacks, blame, and criticism of her. You don't listen, you lecture. You lie to avoid upsetting him. You avoid each other. You shut each other out.

By trying so hard to preserve and protect your relationship, you are likely to create the ultimate loss you fear. Your efforts to control each other ultimately may destroy what you treasure. Even if you manage to stay together and tolerate your blurred personal boundaries, you lock yourselves into painful power struggles and relationship paralysis— hardly what you dreamed of when you met.

Incomplete, blurred personal boundaries create a lifeless, enmeshed relationship. You and your partner feel bound together like two people trying to function as if they were only one entity. You imagine that your very survival depends upon sustaining your connection. You feel yourself losing your Self—becoming like a dependent child absorbed by your partner, or like an anxious, controlling parent obsessed with remodeling your mate.

The Enmeshment-Making Process

Nicole and Reed, a couple who consulted me after five years of marriage, were caught in a stifling enmeshment that was threatening the life of their partnership. The picture they presented when they began couple's therapy is an excellent example of how what I call the enmeshment-making process evolves.

If Nicole told Reed she was angry, Reed thought she was being critical of him and reacted to defend himself from what he perceived as a personal attack. When Reed tried to let Nicole know he was angry and upset, she became frightened and cried like a child who had just been scolded for being bad. Reed then felt guilty for upsetting her. It wasn't long before they both learned to hide their true feelings from each other.

Instead of being honest and allowing "release," they replayed "holding in" patterns of behavior they had learned in their families. Reed held in his emotions, much as his father had when he was angry with his wife, Reed's mother. Nicole then tried to get Reed to talk to her. If he refused or only pretended to listen to what she said, she became furious and exploded in rage—a pattern she had absorbed from her mother who used anger to try to control Nicole's behavior when she was a child. Hurtful fights ensued; angry accusations were tossed back and forth. Sometimes threats were made. Reed often left for hours at a time, trying to escape Nicole's anger and regain his composure.

Though they fought and seemed to be expressing anger, they were not addressing the real issues that concerned them. What came out was distorted by fear and disguised by hurtful behavior. They replayed their favorite fight patterns frequently—whenever honest communication failed and their frightened reactions to each other escalated into full-scale battle.

They went around and around fighting about issues related to time, money, and sex. These three potent subjects were the focus of many of their relationship frustrations. Though they fought endlessly about these topics, they made little significant progress addressing them. In effect, time, money, and sex were like a smoke screen that diverted attention away from Reed and Nicole's more basic challenge of differentiating themselves from one another. (See Chapter 4 for a more thorough discussion of this phenomenon.)

Eventually, they accumulated a number of small and large unacknowledged resentments, which became bricks that they piled into a wall of painful trivia that gradually grew into an unseen barrier between them. Hiding behind this barrier, they lost touch with their loving feelings of connection. Their wall of trivia made it increasingly difficult for them to bond and connect. They didn't listen and hear each other accurately. Instead of trying to understand one another, they both treated each other as though they were extensions of themselves. Each behaved as if the other should automatically know their thoughts, feelings, and needs. Each held on to the belief that his or her perspective on what happened between them was *the* correct perspective. Their communication focused on persuading and convincing each other that the speaker was right and the listener was wrong about whatever they were discussing. They forgot that they were separate people with equally valid but frequently different thoughts, feelings, and needs.

Frustrated at being treated as an extension of the other, they fell into painful power struggles. They attacked, blamed, and criticized, not realizing that these ABCs of power struggle and control simply don't work. The more they pointed their fingers at each other, the more entrenched they became in the very behaviors they hated.

Attacking (*A*), blaming (*B*), and criticizing (*C*) reinforced and encouraged them both to continue doing what drove the other one wild. They hadn't yet discovered the great paradox of healing—that genuine change comes only through acceptance of "what is" with their partner. Instead of offering the soothing balm of "I love you just as you are," each tried to remodel the other to fit his or her notion of how their partner ought to be. They both behaved as if they were an all-knowing parent to the other, charged with the responsibility for molding a misguided child into an acceptable adult.

Both had X-ray vision for the other's shortcomings while remaining blind to their own part in their problems. They projected their shadow sides onto their partner, convinced that they themselves were the innocent, helpless victim of a defective, bad, and sometimes evil spouse. They did their best to try to erase in the other what their own parents tried to erase in them when they were small. Neither of them realized that what they criticized and rejected in the other was a criticized, rejected aspect of themselves that their mother and father refused to allow when they were children.

Because they did not know how to release and accept each other in loving ways, they tried to cope with their pain by escaping from each other. Nicole worked longer and longer hours at her job and generated a busy schedule of social and community activities to absorb her time and attention after work. Reed devoted himself to making a fortune. When he wasn't at his office, he was on the golf course, cultivating contacts and making deals. Their time together was spent at high-profile social gatherings. They seemed like the perfect couple—beautifully groomed, extraordinarily successful, financially secure, and happy on the surface. But when they were alone, their mutual pain overwhelmed them and they fought or became numb, trying to tune the other out. Their arguments were often about money and their different approaches to handling it. Reed wanted to invest as much as possible. Nicole wanted to enjoy their prosperity. She longed for a beautiful home, travel, and fun to share with Reed.

Their sexual relationship suffered, too. They took turns being unavailable and fought about who was to blame for what was wrong. Both of them knew their marriage was in trouble, but they were afraid to seek help. They held on to the belief that they ought to be able to handle their problems on their own. But they had long since stopped feeling safe enough together to be honest about the real issues that troubled them.

This enmeshment process took them into an ever-deeper spiral of painful fighting, threatening, intimidation, and self-effacement. They became more and more discouraged. Eventually they almost completely lost touch with the love that lay hidden behind their personal barriers and beneath their mutual pain. In desperation they might have separated and divorced. Or they could have adapted to their pain and settled into living distant but parallel lives while sustaining the appearance of being happily married.

Instead, after a particularly terrible fight, they decided they had to seek help to grow beyond their impasse. Their pain, combined with their courage, intelligence, and love for each other, ultimately outweighed their fears and kept them working together in couple's therapy to create the healthy boundaries that are the foundation of what is now a consciously loving marriage.

~ The Enmeshment-Making Process ~

Mates often hide their true feelings—especially anger, hurt, and disappointment—from each other.

Unexpressed resentments become bricks in a wall of trivia that they unconsciously build as a barrier between them.

This barrier makes it increasingly difficult for them to listen to each other and hear each other accurately.

Both begin to treat the other as an extension of themselves, assuming they know what the other thinks, feels, and needs, and assuming also that the other knows their own thoughts, feelings, and needs without being told.

They both focus their communication on convincing and persuading the other of the correctness of their own perspective and position.

They forget that they are separate people with different thoughts, feelings, needs, experiences, and perspectives.

Both resort to attack, blame, and criticism (the ABCs of power struggles) in efforts to remodel the other to fit their own notion of how the other should be. Each behaves like a controlling parent attempting to mold a difficult child into an acceptable adult.

In effect, each says to the other, "You change so I won't have to."

Both project their shadow side onto the other, seeing the other as the "bad guy"/"villain" and themselves as the "innocent victim."

They fill their time with addictive behaviors that numb their hurts and help them avoid each other.

They fight about time, money, and sex—potent issues that distract their attention from their deeper hurts.

Their struggles gradually escalate in a pattern of hurtful behavior that leads to either divorce and resignation or necessary growth.

If you see your relationship reflected in the outline above, refrain from judging yourself or your partner. Instead, congratulate yourself for waking up and noticing your enmeshment. The exercises that follow will help you review your relationship history and clarify some of the differentiation challenges you now face. They will also show you how to use breathing to enhance your ease in connecting and letting go.

EXERCISES

1. If you don't already keep a journal, purchase one. It can be as simple as a looseleaf notebook. In it, record the history of your romantic bonding experiences with your partner. Address your physical, emotional, mental, and spiritual experiences during the early romantic phases of your relationship.

2. Ask your partner to record his/her romantic bonding history as well. Share what you write with each other.

3. Using the Safe Dialogue process, talk with your partner about how each of you handles close times and times of being separate. Reveal your feelings about connecting and releasing. Avoid the temptation to analyze your partner.

4. When your romantic boundaries began to fade, how did your personal boundary deficits contribute to creating enmeshment in the relationship? Write about what you discover and/or dialogue with your partner about your personal boundary challenges: What subjects do you tend to avoid raising with your partner? What experiences do you fear? How do you deny your true self as you interact with your mate?

<u>5</u>. Practice breathing. Learn to be consciously aware of inhaling and exhaling and using your breathing to help you relax. Whenever you find yourself becoming tense and anxious, remind yourself to breathe, paying particular attention to exhaling fully. Your breath is your steady ally and ready resource. As long as you are breathing openly and comfortably it is impossible to remain anxious and frightened. This will help you calm yourself during stressful times with your partner. Yoga classes and relaxation tapes are great resources for learning to breathe openly and let go.

The balancing breath is especially helpful. To practice it, sit in a relaxed posture with your spine straight and your feet flat on the floor. Bring your right hand to your face, placing it over your nose with your thumb touching your right nostril, your second finger just above and between your eyes, and your third finger touching your left nostril. Close your eyes. When you are ready to begin, press your thumb in to close off your right nostril. Breathe in through your left nostril in a slow steady inhalation to a count of seven. Then close your left nostril with your third finger. Hold your breath for a count of seven. Release your right nostril and exhale slowly to a count of seven. Then hold for another count of seven. Now, breathe in through your right nostril to a seven count. Close your right nostril with your thumb. Hold for a count of seven. Release your left nostril and exhale to a count of seven. Hold again for a count of seven. Repeat the sequence for a total of seven rounds. When you are finished, noticed how balanced and relaxed you feel.

CHAPTER FOUR

Breaking Out
of Enmeshment

Blurred and inadequate personal boundaries eventually create enough pain to motivate you to build healthy ones—or else to leave your relationship in body or in spirit. The only way to breathe life back into an enmeshed relationship is by differentiating yourself from your partner while also sustaining your connection.

Breaking out of enmeshment is not a one-time event. It is a process that evolves as you gradually come to know and reveal your true self to your partner while also opening your heart to listen to and understand him. It requires both self-understanding and understanding of how your partner sees and experiences you.

As you differentiate yourself from your partner, you grow beyond being absorbed in yourself and begin to develop and express genuine interest in her. You become curious about how she thinks, what she feels, how she interprets life, and how she experiences both herself and you. You also begin to realize that there is more than just one way of seeing "what is" in the world and in your relationship.

You want to change the ways you behave that are hurtful to you both. You decide to address important relationship issues that you previously avoided. You begin to consciously choose to do what is hard for you rather than perpetuating old habits that come naturally. In doing so, you discover the joy of reclaiming the lost or denied parts of yourself.

Emotional Digestion

Breaking out of enmeshment requires strengthening one's emotional digestive system. We all recognize that a well-functioning digestive system is vital to our physical health. But usually we are not taught that it is equally important to be able to digest life experiences.

Just as our bodies must assimilate the food we eat in order to keep us alive, we must assimilate both our feelings about our experiences and the lessons we learn from them in order to maintain our mental and emotional health. Our well-being and the well-being of our relationships depend upon mastering this art.

People who don't develop an adequate mental and emotional digestive system often suffer from depression, relationships problems, anxiety, and repeated episodes of self-sabotage. Eventually, their physical health may deteriorate as well. Life, left only partially digested, becomes more and more difficult. Unassimilated experiences may fester within us and gradually poison our lives.

All the processes and exercises presented in this book are designed to strengthen your mental and emotional digestive systems. Assimilating life as you share it with your mate means consciously accepting the whole range of your feelings, learning how to express your feelings appropriately, and learning from your experiences.

With good mental and emotional digestion, you can integrate your experiences so they become a part of you. And by sharing them with your partner, you can nourish yourself, strengthen your personal boundaries, and begin to break free of enmeshment. As you become more whole, both of you may grow into richer maturity.

When boundary violations occur, you and your partner need a safe way to digest what transpires between you. The material provided in this book is intended to provide a structure to help you do this. It can assist you in keeping healthy boundaries, healing your hurts, feeling empathy, and deepening your commitment as you work through the difficult times you and your partner share.

Beginning the Enmeshment-Breaking Process

I help couples begin the enmeshment-breaking process by offering them a safe way to talk about the feelings of anger they've repressed or denied. For many people, anger is a forbidden, frequently misused, and misunderstood emotion. Partners who do their best to ignore it often explode in periodic volcanic eruptions of rage, or they may use anger (and its first cousin, guilt) to try to intimidate and control their partner. In neither case do they talk about the real issues that concern them. Because they don't know how to address their angry feelings successfully, they feel numb, stuck, frustrated, or victimized by their partner.

To help them break through this stalemate, I teach them the Anger/ Appreciations Exchange, which provides a safe way to acknowledge angry feelings. The exchange helps clear the air between partners, allowing them to open up about subjects one or both of them have avoided or given up on. Once they admit their anger and get to a point where they feel that those feelings are accepted and understood by their partner, some of the tension between them melts. Then it becomes easier to remember and express as well what they appreciate about each other.

This chapter presents the Anger/Appreciations Exchange so you can practice it with your partner. It also explores smoke-screen issues—such as time, money, and sex—subjects that are often a focus of battles between couples caught in enmeshment. As we saw in the preceding chapter, fights about these topics can go on and on—usually without generating any real change, resolution, or release.

The Anger/Appreciations Exchange

Both Liza and Tony are advertising executives in their early thirties. They met while working together on a project for a local charity and had been married for three years when they started couple's therapy. This was a second marriage for both of them. They had no children.

When they described the concerns that led them to making an appointment, I could see that they were firmly entrenched in defensive, boundary-violating styles of relating. Hiding their true selves from each other, they had created massive misunderstandings between them. They couldn't genuinely connect because of the unspoken anger that was seething in them both.

Early in their first session I described Safe Dialogue to them. After a few frustrating rounds of trying to mirror, validate, and empathize with each other, I saw that communication between them was so completely blocked that they couldn't even begin to practice the dialogue process successfully. So I intervened to simplify the process by introducing them to the Anger/Appreciations Exchange.

In the Anger Exchange, partners take turns completing the statement "One thing I feel angry about is _____." The person listening then mirrors that statement by saying, "One thing you feel angry about is _____. That makes sense to me. Thank you for telling me." The roles of speaker and listener are repeatedly reversed as the partners tell each other about their anger, a bit at a time.

I ask partners to observe one important rule during this exchange: that they don't respond defensively to what they hear their partner say. If the listener is angry about the same issue, he or she waits a few turns before addressing that subject. This practice ensures that they won't escalate this exchange into yet another hurtful fight.

The Anger Exchange allows them to put their anger cards on the table so both can hear and understand the other. The object is not to resolve problems or assign blame. It is simply an exchange of information.

~ Practicing the Process ~

Liza spoke first. "I feel angry when you walk away and ignore me when I'm talking to you. I get really upset, because I feel so shut out. I just want you to listen. What I say to you is important to me."

Tony mirrored Liza and thanked her for telling him this. Then, on his first turn, he told her, "I feel angry when you tell me how to do things that I am perfectly capable of doing on my own. I hate it when you sound just like my mother." Liza mirrored and thanked him for telling her this.

Once they began their exchange, the energy in the room changed almost immediately. It was satisfying to me to watch their faces light up with newly kindled interest in each other as they discovered they could talk about their feelings and be heard, respected, and safe as they did so.

As they continued and the tension between them lessened, I could sense their deep love for each other emerging. Though there were still obstacles to be faced, they had shared many major frustrations. After about twenty minutes, I invited them to shift gears and focus on what they appreciated about each other, using the same dialogue structure.

To help them make this shift I invited them to take a couple of deep breaths, clear their minds, and let go of the angry feelings they had heard and shared. Then I suggested they put one hand on the center of their chest and focus on the love they felt for each other.

Next, I instructed them to tell each other, "One thing I really appreciate about you is _____," naming a quality they saw in their partner that they valued. I pointed out that when sharing an appreciation, it's important to talk about more than just the fact that he's a good cook or that she earns a good living. I asked them to talk also about their mate's more personal attributes. "I appreciate how you look at me with your beautiful brown eyes. I love your smile, the way you laugh at my jokes, and hug me sometimes when I come home." The person listening then mirrors what he heard by saying, "One thing you appreciate about me is _____. That makes sense to me. Thank you for telling me."

After a space of silence, Tony began this new round of exchanges. "One thing I really appreciate about you, Liza, is that you take good care of yourself and of me. You always look terrific, and I'm proud to be with you when we go out."

Liza skipped the mirroring step and immediately thanked Tony for telling her this. I intervened to remind her to reflect his appreciative words just as she did his angry ones. This step makes it more likely that she will remember his words and allow them to affect her.

She did so, though directly acknowledging his kind words was not as easy for her as acknowledging his anger. Then Liza looked at Tony and said, "One thing I really appreciate about you is that I can count on you to do what you tell me you'll do. I trust you, because you are so re-liable. That means a lot to me." Reaching out to touch her hand, Tony mirrored Liza and thanked her for telling him this.

They continued exchanging appreciations for the last ten minutes of their session. Before they left that day, each of them acknowledged that they were encouraged and hopeful about their relationship for the first time in many months.

~How the Anger/Appreciations Exchange Helps ~

Through practicing the Anger/Appreciations Exchange, Liza and Tony discovered that, despite their conflicts, the bond of love between them remained strong—even when they felt divided by differences. Conflicts need not displace love. They can call partners to address what they've been trying to hide.

A safe way to speak honestly about denied thoughts and feelings is fundamental to breaking out of enmeshment. Talking about their frus-trations helps couples begin dismantling the walls of unexpressed re-sentments and hurtful trivia that they have erected between them. These walls—built with bricks of buried anger—serve as substitutes for the healthy personal boundaries intimate partners need.

The Anger/Appreciations Exchange encourages mates to develop several habits that I believe are vital to taking down defensive walls. The first of these essential habits is expressing themselves honestly while also taking full responsibility for what they think and feel.

You can do this by using phrases like "I feel angry about _____" or "I feel angry when _____" or "I think _____." These sentence stems help you reveal yourself and take ownership of your emotional responses to circumstances, events, and interactions.

Unlike statements beginning with "You make me so mad" or "You should be _____" or "If you really loved me, you would _____," "I" messages do not attack your partner, blame her for your feelings, or criticize her for her choices, her behavior, or what she shares. When you speak in "I" language you take responsibility for your thoughts, for the interpretations you make, and for the feelings you have about what you experience.

Another habit necessary to breaking out of enmeshment is mirroring your partner's thoughts, interpretations, and feelings whenever she shares them with you. Mirroring lets her know you have heard her accurately. It also opens your mind and heart to the realization that your mate is different than you—her perspectives, interpretations, feelings, reactions, and responses are what make her unique. You cannot know what they are unless she tells you. By consistently mirroring her you tell her you care about what she thinks and feels. This creates the safety she needs to allow you to come close enough to see inside her.

A third vital habit that the Anger/Appreciations Exchange helps instill is thanking your partner for what he shares. By adding, "Thank you for telling me that," you communicate both your appreciation and your acceptance of him. You let him know that you are mature enough to respect all his feelings—his anger and frustration as well as his love and appreciation. Your "thank you" honors him by affirming that he is important to you and that what he thinks and feels matters to you.

Giving gratitude gracefully minimizes enmeshment. It reminds you and your partner that what you both give, you give out of choice, not obligation. Neither of you can afford to take the other for granted, or assume that you are the other's prisoner for life. In today's world, relationships don't necessarily last a lifetime. People who are not appreciated and valued often opt to seek new mates.

Thus, it is smart relationship insurance for you and your partner to nurture an attitude of gratitude. You might begin by telling each other at least three things you appreciate each day. One lovely time to do this is before falling asleep at night. Rerun your day in your mind, looking for all the contributions your partner made to your comfort and well-being, as well as to your home, your children, your extended family, and your friends. Tell each other what you noticed and liked.

Expressing your love verbally is also important—even if it wasn't done often, or at all, in your home when you were a child. If saying "I love you" is hard for you, that is all the more reason to stretch into learning to both give and receive these words gracefully.

Often I request that couples begin their dialogue sessions by first centering themselves in the loving spirit of the heart and then by sharing appreciations. I ask them to review the past week and dialogue about new behaviors they have noticed and liked in themselves and their partners.

At first, a person may tend to be more aware of what the *other* has done than of their own efforts to change. It is easier to see the other—and to want them to change—than it is to see yourself and the choices you make. I encourage both partners to increase their awareness of what *they* do that makes a difference in the relationship. Of course, maintaining awareness of the other person's contributions is also vital.

Noticing positive behaviors reinforces them and helps couples break out of enmeshment. It also helps each partner take responsibility for what he or she can do to improve the relationship. Instead of waiting for the other to change, both partners own up to their own growth progress and their growth challenges.

~ The Anger/Appreciations Exchange ~

Partner A states: "I feel angry when _____."

Partner B mirrors: "You feel angry when _____. I can understand that. Thank you for telling me."

Partner B then states: "I feel angry when _____."

Partner A mirrors: "You feel angry when _____. I can understand that. Thank you for telling me."

Partners A and B continue taking turns expressing their anger, listing only one grievance per turn.

Remember this rule: Neither partner reacts to what the other shares. If Partner A says he is angry about a particular issue, Partner B does not react by saying she is angry about the same thing. Partner B waits at least three turns before saying how she feels about it.

After five to ten minutes of exchanging angry feelings, partners center themselves in the spirit of the heart—placing their hands over their hearts and looking into each other's eyes. After releasing their angry feelings, they take turns as follows:

Partner A states: "One thing I appreciate about you is _____."

Partner B mirrors: "One thing you appreciate about me is _____. I can understand that. Thank you for telling me."

Partner B then states: "One thing I appreciate about you is _____."

Partner A mirrors: "One thing you appreciate about me is _____. I can understand that. Thank you for telling me."

The appreciations exchange continues for five to ten minutes. Ideally, partners practice this process once each day—either in the morning before they begin their day or in the evening before they go to bed.

The Smoke-Screen Issues: Time, Money, and Sex

Blurred, incomplete personal boundaries create a host of relationship troubles. None are more highly charged emotionally than those that concern time, money, and sex.

When mates in enmeshed partnerships violate each other's boundaries in ways that affect their time, their finances, or their sexual relationship, they often stir up deep fears and other strong feelings. Typically, they blame each other for their pain and wait impatiently for the other person to change in the ways they desire.

This is because conflicts over time, money, and sex may disguise more basic growth challenges. In order to handle money well, use time wisely, and enjoy their sexuality fully, adults must rediscover and reclaim parts of themselves that they were taught as children to hide and deny. In order to relate to each other freely, openly, joyfully, and responsibly, they need all their available resources and attributes—not just the ones that were acceptable to their parents. Only when they are able to embrace all their inner selves can they resolve time, money, and sex issues in lasting and satisfying ways.

When partners in a committed relationship keep their attention focused on smoke-screen issues, they blind themselves to the more basic need to establish healthy personal boundaries within the context of their relationship. Time, money, and sex issues—though important—may camouflage a deeper challenge: differentiating themselves from each other as two unique individuals.

~ *Time* ~

People who are clear about who they are and where their boundaries lie are usually also clear about honoring the limits of time and space. They are prompt in keeping appointments and allow ample time for leisurely living and relating. This is because they have a well-developed, nurturing parent ego state that enables them to structure their time in reasonable ways.

People whose personal boundaries are blurred have trouble respecting the constraints of time and the necessity for personal space. They lack an adequate parent ego state and are therefore incapable of structuring their time effectively. In today's busy world, it is easy for them to ignore the need for leisure, space, and consistent attention to nurturing each other and their relationship.

How relationship partners invest their time affects both of them directly. One may want more time together while the other wants more space. One may be in constant motion, bent on accomplishing something with every available second. The other may be a confirmed couch potato, intent on relaxing with the remote control. Clashes are frequent and heated if both struggle to change the other rather than accepting their differences and thus growing as individuals which would create a greater mutual capacity for investing their time wisely.

Many couples—especially those who work for themselves—allow their professional activities to consume a disproportionate amount of their daily time. This leaves them little or no margin for enjoying each other, creating a nurturing home life, parenting their children, and having fun.

To help such couples learn to create adequate time boundaries, I encourage them to keep regular working hours and stop their office and home duties at an agreed-upon quitting time. Reminding them of the old adage that work expands to fill whatever time is available, I point out that they can accomplish more by using their work hours effectively than by continually extending their time on the job and feeling overwhelmed because they lack time to rest and relax.

I also suggest that they establish a weekly date night for just the two of them—with a regularly scheduled baby-sitter if they need one. I invite them to take turns planning their evening outings. The one in charge is challenged to be creative in finding interesting and entertaining activities to explore. I recommend that they pretend they have just met and design dates that will be delightful surprises for their partner—even if what they do is a big stretch for the one making the arrangements.

Regular date nights bring lots of benefits. Couples look forward to this time and quickly become accustomed to spending it together. Even when they are rushed during the rest of the week, they can count on being able to talk, play, and enjoy surprising each other at least one night out of seven. Their children benefit from a parents' night out as well. It helps them feel secure about the strength of Mom and Dad's relationship. They also enjoy a night on their own with a sitter and special routines they may establish.

In addition to a regular date night, it is important to set aside time each day—even if only fifteen or twenty minutes—to devote to talking to your partner and practicing the Anger/Appreciations Exchange and the Safe Dialogue process. I suggest that you make this an essential dimension of your commitment to each other. While you may not use the dialogue structure each time you talk, you can introduce the process when either of you feels unsafe or wishes to discuss what may be a difficult issue. You also can begin to mirror, validate, and empathize when either of you senses that it would be helpful because of the nature and sensitive content of what the other is sharing.

Daily rituals are great ways to establish adequate time boundaries. One wonderful couple I know, whose forty-year marriage is a tribute to the possibilities of vintage relationship, spends the first hour of their day together—watching the sun rise over the ocean, having their morning coffee, journal writing, and meditating in each other's presence.

Others enjoy special customs that help them reconnect with each other after a busy day at work. They may share a cup of tea, sit together outside, take a walk, ride bicycles, or cook together while talking about their experiences when they were apart.

Bedtime rituals are important too. Praying with each other, reading a meditation together, or settling down to watch a favorite TV program or read before going to sleep are habits that create comforting, stabilizing results.

All these experiences help adults develop the strong, firm, and loving inner parent they need to care for themselves and to nurture their relationships and their children. Consciously taking the steps necessary to create a healthy parent ego state is part of becoming the whole person you are meant to be.

~ Money ~

In some homes, money reigns as another terrifying household god. Different values about money and styles for handling it fuel intense fears about control and physical security. Talking about finances can be even more difficult than talking about sex. Both trigger joys and terrors that can turn even the most rational people into emotional basket cases. (See also the section titled "Sex," immediately below.)

There is either too much or too little or none at all. One person is a flirt or a ready spender; the other is jealous or staunchly conservative and on a constant lookout for any possible signs of potential rejection, abandonment, or financial ruin. One is absolutely monogamous, reliable, and cautious; the other ambivalent, prone to secret liaisons, or a secret spender. One is adventurous and openly expressive; the other shy, reserved, and reluctant to experiment. They are vulnerable to each other, deeply bonded, and so intensely enmeshed that their differences seem like survival issues, and their fights about money and sex seem like life-and-death struggles for the relationship.

Without a clearly agreed-upon system for handling finances, money is a minefield, waiting to explode into damaging, repetitive fights. Fears about addressing money issues often result in years of procrastination before they take rational charge of financial matters.

Good money management requires that a person have a well-informed, clear-thinking adult ego state and the courage to do what needs to be done to handle financial issues successfully. Developing such an adult ego state can help create better personal and relationship boundaries.

Just as establishing rituals helps people create adequate time boundaries, establishing rituals also helps them meet the adult challenge of handling money effectively. Deciding upon a regular routine for reviewing the budget, paying bills, discussing money issues, and making financial plans is essential for sound money management. Such structures calm fears about finances. They also assist you in taking charge of this aspect of your relationship.

Both you and your partner should have access to all the available information about your financial standing—jointly and individually. Each of you should be responsible for your own money choices and for honoring a jointly agreed-upon budget for family expenses.

Many couples prefer separate rather than joint checking accounts. Their personal boundaries remain clear when each person handles their own bookkeeping, contributes their fair share of the common expenses, pays their own bills, and manages their own accounts. Computers make these tasks easy to manage and even fun to do.

If finances are a loaded subject for you and your mate, I suggest that you both use the Safe Dialogue process to explore what you were taught about money by your mother and father. You will find helpful questions to consider in the exercises at the end of this chapter. It is essential that you understand the programming you absorbed as a child about money and finances so you can make any necessary updates of your internal money software.

You also need to educate yourselves about money and how it works in today's world so you can overcome any deepseated fears you might have about having and handling it.[1] There are many institutions—banks, investment firms, colleges and universities, and adult education centers—that offer courses in money management.

Becoming informed is vital to developing the savvy adult self you need to be able to care for yourself financially. Education helps you fulfill your identity and establish the healthy personal boundaries you need for both financial success and intimate connection.

~ Sex ~

Loss of personal boundaries in the presence of sexual passion is at the root of many marital difficulties. Romantic boundaries—as long as they are in place—help newly connected couples meet the challenge of enjoying passionate lovemaking and then releasing each other after being sexually intimate. Once romantic boundaries fade, each person's personal boundary deficits come into play and disrupt their previously shared sexual pleasure.

Many couples sadly report that their sexual difficulties began soon after they made a lasting commitment to one another. This is because lasting, wholehearted sexual intimacy between life partners requires mature boundaries and healthy personal wholeness. Some young newly-weds have a lot of growing to do before they are capable of sustaining a richly sensuous and deeply committed sexual partnership.

We come into committed relationships with undeveloped potential and wounded, rejected parts of ourselves absent from our lives. We may have learned that we shouldn't move our bodies freely, relish our senses, or be passionate about what we feel. Our natural desires for moving, sensing, and feeling in the world and while experiencing sexual pleasure are blocked.

These blocks constitute gaps in our sexual identity that become obvious once romantic boundaries fade. They diminish our capacity for wholehearted sexual sharing. These identity deficits may also feed deeply buried fears of being overwhelmed or consumed by a sexual partner.

We compensate for our repressed sexual resources by overdeveloping and overusing other aspects of ourselves that we believe are more acceptable and useful. Our overfunctioning parts tend to invade our partner's boundaries and cause them to pull away, afraid of being absorbed, controlled, consumed, or misused.

Meanwhile, our underdeveloped sensual and sexual resources are like vacuums in our own identity. They attract boundary-violating sexual behaviors and cause us to pull away, afraid of being used and abused or lost and consumed by a partner who appears to be excessively dominating and controlling.

Only well-differentiated, whole people with healthy boundaries can fully connect sexually, release completely, and keep the breath of life flowing freely in a lasting, committed relationship. Those with inadequate personal boundaries usually experience sexual havoc, confusion, distortion, or avoidance.

SEXUAL AVOIDANCE AND SEXUAL DISTORTION

Many couples substitute avoiding each other sexually or distorting their sexual experiences for the personal boundaries they need in a committed relationship. By doing so, they manage to keep some sense of their separate identities, even though they remain emotionally enmeshed with each other.

Some enmeshed couples totally avoid sex. Others put a distinct boundary around their sexual experiences. This allows them to keep their sexual sharing separate from what they experience in the rest of their lives.

They are wounded sexually—either because of actual sexual abuse suffered in childhood or because of emotional, mental, and spiritual abuse that convinced them that sexuality is bad, evil, shameful, and distasteful. They coped with such abuse by moving away from their natural view of sexuality. In order to experience sexual pleasure they must put themselves in situations that are synonymous with rebellion. Only when they are being "bad" can they feel sexy, act sexy, and experience erotic delights.

They develop rebellious rituals to mark their entry into a sexually expressive space. Drugs, alcohol, cigarettes, and unusual circumstances create an aura of mystery and defiance that heightens sensuality and is titillating and exciting. They also remove sexual inhibitions. While under their influence, couples feel free to express themselves in ways their sober minds won't allow.

Some couples fight fiercely—become charged with adrenalin—then have angry, aggressive sex. Others fall into the "Let's just hurry up and get it over with" mode of perfunctory, nonengaged sex. They calculate how often they "ought to" have sex and do their best to seem normal sexually.

Those who were sexually wounded as children often lose their boundaries almost completely when they enter a sexual relationship. They are easily overstimulated by the intensity of their sexual feelings.

In the heat of passion, they might flash back to the past and relive the overpowering emotions they felt when they were sexually abused. When this happens, they regress to the ages they were when they were violated.

Their behavior mystifies and frightens them and their partners. Many don't consciously remember their abuse experiences and don't understand why they hurt as they do. Neither partner understands the source of the sexual troubles they are having.[2]

Some adults who were physically, emotionally, and sexually abused as children use sex to try to satisfy their unmet needs for love and nurturing. This distorts their sexual sharing and often puts excessive pressure on their mate to engage in sex more frequently than they may wish.

Others shut down sexually and do their best to shut their partners out. Some use sex as a temporary fix for emotional pain or to distract themselves from feelings that are overwhelmingly intense. They may fight intensely then make love to soothe themselves and make up. Or they may act out sexually by having affairs with others, rather than talking openly and honestly with their spouse about what troubles them.

Couples who fall into patterns of distortion like these often sustain a sexual relationship. But when they have sex, it is not fully engaged, "whole-being" sex. Satisfying though it may be, it is primarily physical— with an added bonus of emotional release. Each person is absorbed in their own world and their own pleasure—often with eyes closed, shutting their partner out.

Open-eyed, "I–Thou" sexual union eludes them. They are unable to experience the physical, emotional, mental, and spiritual merging that is possible for people who are fully differentiated, whole individuals with healthy boundaries. Sadly, they don't realize what they are missing. Like people who eat only fast food, they don't know how much they might enjoy a leisurely gourmet feast of transcendent sexual sharing.[3]

Lost Selves

Ellie and Tyler are a lesbian couple who consulted me after a twenty-year relationship and almost as many years of ineffective therapy. Their relationship is an excellent example of how distorted boundaries and lost selves create relationship tangles that manifest as problems with time, money, and sex.

Ellie is a relaxed woman who enjoys reading, gardening, painting, writing, and other solitary pursuits. She is sensitive, emotional, and expressive. Though she made some money as an artist and writer, she was not well oriented to business and professional pursuits and didn't manage her finances well. This alarmed her partner, who did her best to keep a tight rein on money.

Ellie had trouble getting things done and finishing what she started. She wasn't particularly concerned about making the most of every second of her time. She liked a leisurely life pace—and didn't mind leaving household chores to be done when and if she felt like doing them. This really bothered Tyler, who tried to take efficient advantage of every spare moment. Ellie, in turn, complained that Tyler ignored her need for them to spend time together and enjoy a relaxed pace of living.

Tyler is a very successful attorney. She is intense, focused, competitive, and demanding—and was usually unaware of her inner life. Tyler overfunctioned in business and at home. She saw what needed to be done and did it, rarely taking time to relax and play. Secretly, she resented Ellie, who seemed to be enjoying life more than Tyler did.

Tyler pushed Ellie to be sexually intimate with her without taking time to connect with her emotionally. Tyler's intensity, drive, and urgency tended to send Ellie scurrying off in the need for privacy and space. Tyler pursued. Ellie got angry and told Tyler how she felt. Tyler was frightened by Ellie's strong feelings and tried even harder to please Ellie so she wouldn't be mad—and so she might want to have sex. Yet the more Tyler pushed for sex, the more Ellie pulled away.

Tyler's boundaries were overinflated or overdeveloped where Ellie's were collapsed or deficient, and vice versa. Neither of them felt whole, loved, and fulfilled. Each wanted the other to change to better accommodate her needs. They fought about time, money, and sex when their real issues went much deeper. The only way they could achieve the relationship they desired was through developing the balanced and complete personal boundaries both needed in order to relate fully with the other.

Ellie's collapsed boundaries around personal power invited boundary-violating behaviors from Tyler. Tyler's collapsed boundaries around play, relaxation, and emotional sensitivity invited boundary violations from Ellie. Both of them reported feeling used by the other—though in different ways.

Ellie's challenge was to discover and reclaim the active, powerful, effective sides of herself that would balance and complement her more passive, artistic, expressive talents. Tyler's challenge was to discover and reconnect with her sensitive side, and learn to relax, play, be aware of and express her feelings, enjoy her own company, work a lot less, and place less emphasis on sex. As each of them grew into greater wholeness as individuals, their relationship grew into greater intimacy and they experienced deeper satisfaction with each other.

Their relationship challenged them both to develop the personal aspects they needed in order to become more of who they were. As they reclaimed their lost and rejected parts, their boundaries became less distorted and more balanced and whole. Their capacity for intimate contact was greatly enhanced. They also settled into a more satisfactory balance in their relationship with regard to time, money, and sex.

~ How Ellie and Tyler Developed Healthy, Balanced Boundaries ~

An important part of their healing work was seeing that the qualities that were missing in one were amplified in the other. Each of them realized that what irritated and even enraged her about her partner was what she denied and repressed in herself. This helped them move beyond their smoke-screen fights about time, money, and sex.

To become whole as individuals, they had to embrace both their passive and active sides; their vulnerable and powerful parts; their light, loving selves as well as their dark, fearful shadow sides. In doing so, they discovered and learned to use and enjoy the whole range of their personal potential for successful living—their capacities for thinking, feeling, sensing, and acting. Some of these resources they were encouraged to develop as children. Others they were instructed to limit or avoid.

We examined both Ellie's and Tyler's childhood histories in order to understand how each of them had lost touch with parts of themselves. This meant taking an honest look at their parents and honoring the anger and sadness as well as the compassion they felt for the imperfect human beings their mothers and fathers were.

Tyler realized she had cut herself off from her playful side, because she saw how overdeveloped and overactive her dad was in this area. Her mother had supported the family and kept the household going, filling the same roles that Tyler assigned herself in her relationship with Ellie.

She acknowledged that she was deeply afraid of being anything like her father, who shirked his adult responsibilities and never realized his potential as a talented, creative man. Consequently, Tyler cut herself off from the parts of herself that reminded her of her dad and overidentified with the parts of herself that were like her mother, whom she respected and valued. Like her, Tyler was a clear, sharp thinker, a great problem solver, and she knew how to take action and get things done.

Ellie was much more highly developed in the realms of sensing and feeling. She was in tune with her emotions—though she did her best to hide and deny her anger, because she'd been severely punished for showing it when she was small. The artist in her relished what she could see, touch, taste, hear, and smell. She needed her own space and was very sensitive to any behavior from Tyler that seemed invasive or overpowering. She tended to have chronic health problems and felt as if she were a helpless victim of her body.

Ellie acknowledged that she'd been sharply criticized by her parents and frequently found wanting in their eyes. She discovered early in life that no matter how hard she tried, she rarely succeeded in pleasing them or in receiving any sort of acknowledgment for her well-intentioned efforts to be the person they wanted her to be.

In the course of our work together, Ellie saw that she protected herself by withdrawing, rather than by confronting—until she became overwhelmed by her repressed anger and exploded in rage when she felt victimized. She limited her powerful, effective self because she received criticism rather than appreciation for her attempts to function competently and think clearly. As a child she had been a victim of her parents' harshness. As an adult her passivity fed her feelings of being victimized in her relationship with Tyler.

She frequently felt criticized, even when others—especially Tyler—had no intention of judging her or finding her lacking. In therapy she became aware of how hypersensitive she was to words that sounded the least bit invasive. Gradually she learned that she could control these reactions and choose not to retreat into the safety of her own world of solitary pursuits when she felt threatened.

Both Ellie and Tyler were deeply bonded with their parents. Both had received strong "don't feel" injunctions when they were children. This made it difficult for them to risk acknowledging and expressing grief about their relationships with their parents. To do so, Tyler had to reconnect with her lost and neglected emotional self. Ellie needed permission and guidance so she could learn to reveal and express her anger in constructive, appropriate ways.

As they gradually grew more honest about emotions they had previously denied, they also gradually differentiated themselves from their parents. This helped them develop more appropriate personal boundaries in their relationship. Eventually, each of them got the divorce she needed—not from her partner, but from her enmeshment with her family.

Ellie worked on developing her reasoning abilities—a resource she had neglected in the face of her parents' harsh criticism when, as a child, she asked questions and tried to figure things out. She realized that, as an adult, she had allowed her emotional reactions to at times distort her thinking.

When she was upset, she made dire predictions about the future, got confused, told herself she was bad, wrong, and guilty, which escalated her already intensely uncomfortable feelings. As she learned to recognize these self-sabotaging thought patterns, she was better able to release them. She also learned to change fearful, critical thoughts into loving, empowering ones. By sharpening her thinking and reasoning abilities, Ellie found it easier to take action, and she began doing things she wanted and needed to do.

Ellie remembered that as a child she'd learned she wasn't supposed to call attention to herself by moving her arms, hips, thighs, and pelvis. At church she'd been taught that dancing was evil. She was to sit still and be quiet, no matter how restless she felt. On the playground at school she hadn't enjoyed running and playing, because she believed she was not gifted athletically.

Practicing her commitment to take action, Ellie enrolled in dance and yoga classes and decided to take tennis lessons. Gracefully moving her body in space gave her a wonderful new sense of herself as a powerful person. This helped her be less intimidated by Tyler and better able to stay in contact with her instead of retreating into solitude.

Meanwhile, Tyler concentrated on opening up emotionally and expressing the sensitive side of her nature. She began keeping a journal and recording her dreams. In her sleeping adventures she encountered her sensual self—a long-denied part of her that she had cut herself off from because it reminded her too much of her dad. She dreamed of fragrant gardens and lavish feasts. She woke up with ideas and insights that surprised her—but were, as she subsequently discovered, quite helpful in her personal growth.

She made a conscious effort to slow down and be attentive to her senses—to get out of her head and into her body. Not only did she "stop to smell the flowers," she also now fully appreciated birds singing and the pleasure of walking on grass with her bare feet. She started listening to music at home and at work. In her car she found a jazz station she enjoyed rather than listening to talk radio.

Expanding Tyler's awareness of her senses helped her discover the slow, sensual side of lovemaking, which created a much deeper rapport with Ellie, whose sensuality was more well developed. Ellie felt much less intruded upon as Tyler expressed more of her softer side. Both of them were delighted to report that Ellie now more frequently initiated their lovemaking, enjoying her newly discovered freedom to be a more active sexual partner.

Throughout their therapy, Ellie and Tyler focused on core issues rather than continuing to fight about time, money, and sex. Both developed healthy personal boundaries and established a more complete personal identity.

They did this by learning to recognize their boundary-violating patterns of behavior and working to correct them (see Chapter 5). They practiced the Safe Dialogue process regularly and talked with each other whenever they became aware that they were reenacting hurtful behaviors they'd experienced with their parents when they were children. They also learned to laugh at themselves and appreciate the humor in what had previously been overwhelmingly difficult struggles with each other. Their old conflicts about time, money, and sex disappeared as Ellie and Tyler began to relate to each other as fully developed individuals.

EXERCISES

1. Each evening before you go to bed, make a list of any times you may have felt angry during the past twenty-four hours. Keep an anger record for the next three weeks.

   After writing about your angry feelings, make a list of all that you have appreciated about your partner during the past twenty-four hours. Keep an appreciations record for the next three weeks.

2. Use the Anger/Appreciations Exchange to share with your partner what you have realized through your journaling.

3. Notice with heart-centered, loving awareness when you use attack, blame, and criticism to distance yourself from your partner, instead of revealing yourself by expressing what you truly feel. You don't have to change. Just be aware of these attitudes without judging them.

4. Using the Safe Dialogue process with your partner, design a time-structure plan that ensures the two of you adequate time to nurture yourselves and your relationship. Be sure to include a weekly date as well as daily times to talk and vacation times to get away together.

5. Consider your financial structure. How might you establish rituals to help you both deal with money issues more effectively? Use Safe Dialogue to share ideas and concerns.

6. Write a letter to your mate expressing your feelings about what you most enjoy, need, appreciate, and desire in your sexual relationship.

7. Consider reading a book together about enhancing your sexual sharing. I suggest Pat Love's *Hot Monogamy* and Lonnie Barbach's *For Each Other*. Take your time—perhaps reading one chapter a week—and dialogue with each other about what you discover.

8. Think about a quality or trait in your partner that irritates or upsets you. Practice the heart-centering process. Once you feel centered and loving, focus on accepting that aspect of your mate. In your journal, invite the part within you that possesses similar qualities or traits to speak to you. Write a note to yourself from this rejected part of you.

9. Consider how you learned or decided that this part of you was unacceptable. How might this part of you bring useful resources into your life and your relationship?

10. Write a note of healing and acceptance to this previously rejected aspect of yourself. Invite this part of you to join you when you need its input and assistance.

CHAPTER FIVE

Boundary Violations

They happen so easily! Unconsciously and unintentionally you cross that imaginary boundary line with your partner. You're not thinking, because you're busy, on automatic pilot, distracted, angry, sad, scared, tired, or tense. Before you know it, you've said or done something that dishonors you both. Such painful slips cause sometimes small, sometimes big tears in the fabric of a relationship.

Boundary violations are hurtful, disrespectful... and human. They come from fear; they create distance. When we feel violated, we react by hiding behind defensive walls built of criticism, attack, blame, silence, rebellion, demanding, preaching, and lying.

When Our Boundaries Are Violated

Our natural state of being is relaxed and joyful. When we are in touch with our essential spirit, we let go of cares and worries. We breathe deeply, feel warm and alive, and enjoy all our senses. We are like young babies whose need for love and nurturing is met consistently by affectionate parents. With nothing to fear, we simply *are* in the moment that is, deeply relaxed and joyful as we experience the bliss of being in loving synchronicity with all creation.

But when we are disturbed by another person who somehow intrudes upon us, or neglects us, or avoids us in ways that threaten—or seem to threaten—our survival, we react. The most primitive part of our brain receives any actual or perceived violation of our boundaries as a danger signal. This old, "reptilian" base of the brain is cold-blooded and quick. It immediately leaps into action to protect us from harm. We feel physiological reactions such as tightening muscles, adrenalin pumping through our body, an accelerated heartbeat, shallow breathing, elevated blood pressure, or disturbed sleep and digestion. In this aroused state of red alert, we are ready to react instantly to dispel the real or imagined threat to our survival.

With our "old brain" in charge and our bodies charged up, we have only three basic choices: fight (with ourselves or the one who intrudes), flee (by running or engaging in addictive behaviors), or freeze (by distracting ourselves, denying the problem, or going numb). The choice we make is a natural reaction to the boundary violation we experience or perceive.

Three Types of Boundary Violations

Boundaries can be violated in three different ways.

I. **Intrusions** into our physical, mental, emotional, or spiritual space threaten our safety and personal identity. When we intrude on others, we are, in effect, **rejecting** them by pronouncing them defective, weak, or misguided, implying that they would be a more acceptable person if they were the way we think they ought to be. We behave as if they are inferior to us and need our advice and constructive criticism in order to be acceptable.

The old brain reacts to **intrusive/rejective** boundary violations by constricting the body, causing it to pull away from the source of danger. Like turtles going into their shells, we retreat when we feel intruded upon or rejected. Our emotional and psychological reactions are often consistent with our physiological response. Both distance us from the person who is invading our physical or psychic space. Alternately, we may behave in ways that disguise our fear and belie what is happening inside us. With our bodies tensed and on guard, we may counterattack, trying to protect ourselves. Looking far more fierce than we feel, we are like a frightened cat who pulls its body into a small, tight ball, while its hair stands on end, making it appear larger than usual as it hisses at an enemy.

If we don't counterattack or retreat, we may try to placate our partner by giving in to their demands or pronouncements, although we are filled with seething, secret resentment inside.

2. When we **neglect** our physical, emotional, mental, and spiritual needs, we devalue ourselves. We are left feeling unimportant and impoverished. When we neglect others, we, in effect, **abandon** them by breaking or discounting our connection with them. They are left alone, feeling devalued, and wondering why we behave as we do.

   When we feel neglected or abandoned, we often respond by expanding our boundaries. We try to reach out to reestablish contact and connection. This behavior may be perceived by the one moving away as frightening and intrusive—perceptions that only exacerbate the difficulties between us. If our pursuit of their attention fails repeatedly, we eventually give up in frustration. We accept our abandonment and, in turn, distance ourselves from them. When this happens—if we truly let go emotionally—our partner naturally senses the change and may then seek to reestablish contact and connection.

3. **Freezing** like a frightened animal is a way of **denying** our needs, feelings, behavior, and ideas in order to hide from ourselves and others. We stop cold in our tracks, block our genuine interac-

tions, and camouflage what we truly feel and think. This crip-
ples us and violates other people's boundaries by putting our
relationships on ice. In the resulting chill, those we freeze out
may experience painful periods in anticipation of possible future
rejection or abandonment.

When we freeze up, we not only deny the importance of our
own experience, but also we deny our partners the privilege of
knowing us and feeling close to us. In reaction they may freeze
up too, in order to numb themselves to the hurt and loneliness
we have created between us. At times they may make heroic
efforts to warm the atmosphere and create a thaw, reaching out
to try to make contact. If they are unsuccessful, eventually they
may resort to more drastic means—a serious illness, deep depression, increasing anxiety, or addictions. Or they may violate our
relationship boundary by turning to someone else to talk about
their pain. An affair—emotional and/or sexual—is often a loud
cry for comfort and relief from an emotionally frozen relationship or marriage.

BOUNDARY VIOLATIONS	RESPONSE
Intrusive/Rejective	Restricting boundaries, constricting the body, placating, or counterattacking
Neglecting/Abandoning	Expanding boundaries, reaching for contact and reconciliation, or withdrawing
Freezing/Denying	Freezing also, intruding by pushing for an open response, or abandoning efforts to connect

Four Levels of Boundary Violations

Each of these three types of boundary violations affects us on one or
more of our four levels of being: physical, emotional, mental, or spiritual.

Physical boundary violations impact the body in unwelcome ways. They are hurtful, disrespectful, and dangerous to our safety and physical survival.

Emotional boundary violations involve using feelings as tools for manipulating others. They also include making unwarranted assumptions about other people's emotions, and then believing and acting upon what we imagine.

Mental boundary violations are attempts to force ideas and beliefs on others without regard for the integrity and value of their thinking and reasoning. They may occur when one person, assuming that he knows what another is thinking, insists that his way of seeing things is accurate and that the other person is not telling the truth about what he really thinks.

Spiritual boundary violations take place when a person or a group condemns the beliefs of another, acting as if only they are authorized to speak for God. Any who do not embrace their truth as *the* truth are defined as evil. The inverse can be another form of spiritual boundary violation, that is, a person insists the material world is the only bona fide reality, thereby discounting others' beliefs in an inner realm of the Spirit. In short, any refusal to respect and honor others' beliefs about the nature of reality constitutes a violation of their spiritual boundaries.

Let's look in closer detail at the three types of boundary violations, and at how each operates on the four levels of our being; physical, emotional, mental, and spiritual.

Intrusive/Rejective Boundary Violations

"He hit me!" Donna announced in a grim tone when she and Wesley came for their first couple's session.

"You provoked me until I did. You wanted me to hit you!" Wesley retorted.

"No, I didn't! You're always blaming me for everything. Why can't you just take responsibility for being abusive. You're just like your stepfather, and you know what a brute he is."

"You're impossible. You're never satisfied with anything I do. Who do you think you are—my judge and jury? Get a life and get off my case. Besides, you provoke me into hitting you. You hit me sometimes too. Don't pretend you're so innocent in all this!"

"Whoa, guys!" I said to interrupt their rapidly escalating battle. "It makes sense that both of you are scared and upset. You're intruding on each other's boundaries and trying to protect yourselves at the same time. Let's slow things down a bit and find out what's beneath the emotional and physical abuse you're describing."

I told them that the first order of business was to stop the hitting. They simply could not allow it to continue. I referred them both to a Compassion Workshop, a twelve-week program designed to help people who were wounded early in life.[1] (If a Compassion Workshop is not available in your region, I suggest anger-management classes, which are offered by various local organizations.)

Because Wesley and Donna didn't bond securely with their first caretakers, their parents, they had trouble trusting and being close to others later in life. Intimate relationships were a particularly difficult challenge. When they felt unsafe—especially when they feared being rejected or abandoned—they tended to become violent and abusive in their efforts to control their partner and avoid being hurt.

Compassion Workshops teach couples to feel compassion—not pity—first for themselves, and then for their partners. The workshops help partners learn to calm themselves when they feel threatened, so they can interrupt impulses that cause their fears to escalate into abusive behavior. The couples practice methods that enable them to consciously develop their capacities for feeling empathy.

The workshop experience, when combined with couple's therapy, is strong medicine. Given such an antidote, if couples fail to put a stop to hitting, I advise them to separate, so that they can establish their personal boundaries independently of each other. Sometimes a separation in the service of healing is an excellent way for couples to grow into the maturity and self-control they need to build a lasting, healthy intimate relationship.

I acknowledged to Donna and Wesley that I knew they probably didn't want to separate—so I advised them that they would have to practice faithfully everything they learned both with me and in the workshop. I told them I would teach them Safe Dialogue, which would help them talk calmly and honestly with each other without becoming abusively reactive. And I emphasized the importance of using it absolutely *every* day. Developing and practicing the self-discipline that Safe Dialogue teaches seemed the best way to make sure they dealt with the conflicts that occurred between them while they were fresh and before they festered. Otherwise, tensions would gradually build, and before they knew it one or both of them would feel so frightened and anxious that they would be in danger of having the situation escalate into violent behavior.

I acknowledged that they might not like making the effort Safe Dialogue requires. It wouldn't be easy for them to really listen to each other and restrain their reactions until it was their turn to speak. But I didn't think they'd like the alternative either. Though dialogue can be difficult, it is lots easier and less expensive than separating or getting a divorce.

Donna and Wesley seemed relieved that, though I was firm about the seriousness of their situation, I didn't get caught up in their fears or pass judgment on them. Like many couples who finally decide they need help, they simply didn't know how to stop their hurtful patterns of relating. Their style was to hide their genuine feelings by attacking each other. Rather than calming themselves when they felt unsafe because of strong feelings like anger, sadness, success, closeness, or excitement, they covered their fears by acting tough. In this "macho" mode, they invaded each other's boundaries with escalating rounds of critical, rejecting words and provocative behavior. Each created a protective facade to defend them as they battled with the other. Neither revealed what they actually felt beneath those heavy shields of defense. Instead, both shot wounding arrows of judgment and blame at the other.

Donna saw Wesley as the problem and maintained her innocence and helplessness in the face of his difficult behavior. She invaded his boundaries by placing responsibility for her behavior on him, blaming, criticizing, and sometimes hitting him. Wesley invaded Donna's physical boundaries by striking her; he invaded her emotional and mental boundaries by attacking her with rejecting words. He claimed she was responsible for his behavior because she provoked him.

Both Donna and Wesley invaded the other's boundaries with hurtful verbal assaults. Both defined the other as impossible, or even crazy, as they competed for superior status and pleaded with each other to change so their relationship would work properly. Neither took responsibility for their part in the difficulties. But they did stick with couple's therapy and enrolled in a Compassion Workshop.

Halfway through the twelve-week workshop, they had a particularly intense fight. In the heat of anger they fell into their accustomed practice of hitting each other. At their next couple's therapy session, they agreed that a separation was necessary to help them establish the personal boundaries they needed to relate to each other safely and respectfully.

~ Recognizing Intrusive/Rejective Behaviors ~

It is obvious how Wesley and Donna violated each other's physical boundaries. Physical boundary intrusions are easy to identify. They include observable actions like hitting, slapping, pinching, and shaking. Unwanted tickling and other kinds of unwelcome touch are a more subtle form of violation and intrusion. There are also cruel and blatant criminal intrusions, such as intentionally inflicting injury with cigarette burns, cutting, stabbing, twisting limbs, striking with a fist, rape and other forms of sexual intrusion, as well as stealing or destroying treasured possessions. Murder is the ultimate boundary intrusion.

It is more difficult to identify the ways Donna and Wesley violated each other's emotional boundaries. Emotional boundary intrusions

Table ~ INTRUSIVE/REJECTIVE BOUNDARY VIOLATIONS

Physically Intrusive/ Rejective Behaviors	Hitting, slapping, pinching, shaking.
	Unwanted tickling.
	Intentionally inflicting injury (e.g., burning with a cigarette, cutting, twisting limbs, pushing down, striking with a fist, or killing).
	Rape and other forms of sexual intrusion.
	Stealing or hiding valuable possessions.
Emotionally Intrusive/Rejective Messages	**Emotionally Manipulating Messages**
	Name-calling.
	Because I feel the way I feel, you should change (or give me what I want).
	You are responsible for how I feel.
	You should feel _____ (bad, guilty, ashamed, embarrassed, responsible for me).
	If you really loved me you would _____.
	I'm your victim (said directly or indirectly).
	I'm a victim of _____ (illness, depression, abuse, anxiety, helplessness, misunderstanding, etc.), so you (and the world) should _____ (excuse me, make it up to me, give me special privileges, overlook my misbehavior).
	I've done so much for you, you should _____ (the martyr stance).
	If you won't _____, then I will _____.
	You're all I've got. I can't survive without you.
	Emotionally Projecting Messages
	I know how you feel better than you do.
	I know how you feel even if you don't.
	I feel what I imagine you feel, but I'm unaware of my own feelings and assume they are coming from you.
	You *make* me feel _____.

Table ~ INTRUSIVE/REJECTIVE BOUNDARY VIOLATIONS (CONT'D)

Mentally Intrusive/Rejective Messages	This is *the* truth. This is what you ought to think.
	My ideas count. Yours do not.
	I know what you think.
	I can read your mind accurately, all the time.
	My interpretation of you is correct.
	My interpretation of what happened *is* what happened.
	Don't dispute my authority.
	Only what *I* think, want, say, or do counts.
	I know what is best for you.
	I know what you ought to do.
	I'll ____ (threat of whatever kind) if you don't do what I want you to do.
	What you think is bad, wrong, misguided.
	You just don't understand how it really is.
	Your perceptions don't count.
	You didn't see what you think you saw.
	Don't ever tell anyone our family secrets.
	If you ever tell, I'll ____ (threat of whatever kind).
	We don't talk about that subject.
	Don't think that.
	Don't think for yourself. Let me think for you.
	You're stupid, dumb, wrong, misguided.
Spiritually Intrusive/ Rejective Messages	I (or we) speak for God.
	You'll go to hell if you don't follow our rules.
	There is only one way to believe and this is the way.
	Don't question your faith.
	Don't explore other points of view.
	Anything other than our way is the devil's way.
	Your sexuality is bad.
	Your feelings are bad.
	Your thoughts are bad.
	You are bad.
	God wants to punish you.

aren't as obvious, though they can be equally painful. The wounds and scars they leave are not readily visible.

Emotional manipulation is an intrusion that involves one person who uses her feelings to try to get another to do what she wants him to do. Guilt trips are a well-known example of a method of manipulation that is used by people who want to present themselves as martyrs. Others use anger, helplessness, and pain to manipulate their partners. Name-calling is another example: one partner denigrates the other with a harsh epithet in an effort to intimidate him into behaving in a nonthreatening way. Posturing as an innocent victim is also a manipulative tool; it implies that our mate should rescue us or relieve us of our problems.

Emotional projection violates boundaries when one person "projects" or sees something in the other that is actually within himself—although beyond his conscious awareness. He may say something like "You are such a critical person," failing to notice that he is being critical himself. Or she may make statements like "I know how you feel even if you don't" or "I know how you feel better than you do," imagining that her feelings are not her own but instead are taking place within her partner.

Mental intrusions are one person's attempts to force his views and ideas on another. "This is *the* truth. This is what is right and what ought to be obvious to you." Mind reading—when I tell you that I know what you are thinking better than you do—is another form of mental intrusion. Overprotective efforts to tell others what they ought to do or what is best for them are also invasive—unless the other person has deliberately requested our input. Blanket, discounting pronouncements like "You're dumb, stupid, wrong, or misguided" are especially hurtful intrusions. But perhaps most damaging of all are a person's threatening commands that we keep guilty secrets at the expense of our own needs and perceptions. Statements like "Don't you dare tell!" or "You don't know what you're talking about" or "You didn't see what you think you saw (or hear what you think you heard)" can be debilitating to the recipient, especially if she or he is a child.

Spiritual intrusions are grandiose attempts to speak for God, or to imply or threaten eternal damnation to anyone who dares to believe differently. Such intrusions are, in effect, injunctions not to think, question, or explore either one's own spirituality or faith, or other points of view. Often they are accompanied by definitions of beliefs other than the speaker's as the work of the devil. They frequently include pronouncements that amount to saying, "You are bad. Your feelings are bad. Your thoughts are bad. Your sexuality is bad. God is an angry father who you must dread and fear."

~ Transforming Intrusions by Connecting with an Open Heart ~

It takes loving awareness and courage to transform boundary intrusions. Doing so requires consciously stepping out from behind our defensive walls and owning up to what we truly think, feel, want, and need. Instead of attacking our mates, we must reveal our authentic selves. This means revealing our vulnerability and trusting our ability to handle whatever response we receive.

I believe that the self-confidence necessary for such revelation comes with knowing that God's love always supports us when our hearts are open to receive it. Calling upon our spiritual resources helps us nurture and accept ourselves, even if our partner fails to meet our needs for listening, validation, and empathy. Whatever your spiritual practice is, having a sense of connection with a reality that is greater than your immediate circumstances can provide an inner strength that will support you when things are difficult with your partner.

The atmosphere between Donna and Wesley changed dramatically as they learned to talk about what they felt in their hearts instead of expressing their negative assessments of each other. By using the Safe Dialogue process, Donna could acknowledge that she was lonely and terribly sad about their separation. She wasn't sleeping well and missed Wesley. She also was brokenhearted when she saw how much their two little boys missed their father. When it was his turn to speak, Wesley told her how frightened he was by the possibility of losing her. He missed his sons, and he missed her. He now realized that he had hidden himself, as if behind a protective wall, because he was afraid to let her know what was really happening inside him and how important she was to him.

The Safe Dialogue process provides a necessary and safe way to transform boundary-violating behavior. It enabled Donna and Wesley to connect with each other within a structure that ensured they would be accepted and heard as they spoke from their hearts and revealed their true feelings. Instead of making unwelcome, intrusive comments about our partners, we speak about and reveal our innermost selves when we practice Safe Dialogue. Instead of reacting to hurtful remarks, our spouses then respond by mirroring what they have heard us say. Instead of dishonoring what we have said, they validate what we have told them. Instead of denying or rejecting our feelings, they gift us with expressions of acceptance and empathy.

In receiving all this, we are blessed by the healing balm of love. With repeated practice and consistent experiences of such loving connection with our partners, we grow into the confident, secure adults we are capable of becoming. And through our maturing we are more and more able to sustain heart-centered connection with one another and therefore less and less likely to resort to immature, invasive styles of relating.

Neglecting/Abandoning Boundary Violations

"I can't stand the way she's always calling me at work—like she's checking up on me. I've told her not to, but she does it anyway. Now I let my voice mail answer so if it's her I don't have to talk. She just doesn't get it!" Thus Barry opened what he intended to be their first and only therapy session in an angry tone. It had taken months for his wife, Frances, to persuade him to come to meet me.

I asked Barry to direct his concerns to Frances, who was looking very uncomfortable. I wanted them to enter the dialogue process, not tattle on each other.

Barry restated his position, addressing his wife directly. With my help, she listened carefully and successfully mirrored him, validated his concerns, and expressed empathy for his feelings.

When it was her turn to speak, she told him, "No matter how I try to tell you that I am unhappy and very concerned about our marriage, you ignore me. Or if you do respond, you tell me there is nothing wrong at all. It's all my imagination, I should be grateful for all the stuff you give me, and you're comfortable with things just the way they are. But I don't want all that stuff. I want someone who wants to talk to me and to be with me—who is interested in me and cares how I feel. No matter what I tell you, you ignore me. When I try to talk to you, I end up feeling crazy—like I don't even exist in your eyes. I just want you to care about me," she concluded as she started to cry.

Frances was trying her best to get Barry's attention. The more he ignored and neglected her, the more anxious she became and the harder she tried to get through to him. Barry felt invaded and smothered by her phone calls at work and efforts to talk to him at home. He kept his protective walls up to ward off what he considered invasions of his privacy. The thicker his walls became, the more Frances tried to cling to him to ward off feeling abandoned.

After Barry had mirrored, validated, and expressed empathy for Frances, I asked if they were open to hearing my observations. Both of them eagerly agreed.

"Each of you is doing what drives the other to do more of what you like least!" I told them. "It's no wonder you are both angry and upset. You are violating each other's boundaries, and that really hurts. Boundary violations cut through your emotional skin and wound you just as deeply as a knife that cuts your physical skin and causes you to bleed."

Barry violated Frances' boundaries by neglecting and ignoring her. She felt as if she were invisible to him—as if, when he discounted her importance and her very existence, he was abandoning her. Frances violated Barry's boundaries by invading his space, as she tried hard to get him to notice her. Neither of them felt safe, and in defending themselves so diligently, they damaged the very heart of their relationship by eroding their trust in each other.

I told them I would teach them to connect safely so they wouldn't have to resort to neglecting or intruding on each other. The Safe Dialogue process helped Frances make contact with Barry instead of invading his space. It allowed Barry to be attentive to Frances instead of ignoring her and neglecting her needs.

~ *Recognizing Neglecting/Abandoning Behaviors* ~

In an intimate partnership neglect means not doing something that is necessary or desirable. Because it is more difficult to notice what is missing than what is present, neglect is less visible and harder to identify than boundary intrusions are.

A partner who ignores his mate may appear blameless and reasonable while the other seems overly demanding or even crazy. The distance between them that this disparity creates frightens his partner. She feels abandoned and reacts with sometimes frantic efforts to get his attention. Her behavior, in turn, scares him. He feels invaded and smothered by her demands. He reacts by pulling himself more tightly into his shell. The greater the vacuum he creates, the more she is drawn to fill it with even more intense efforts to get him to respond to her.

Neglect is a passive way to express feelings, especially anger. His neglect is a distress signal, a silent manifestation that something is wrong. Perhaps he comes home late without calling, leaves his clothes strewn all over the bedroom, forgets to pay the bills, or ignores his usual chores. Or perhaps he simply doesn't respond to her when she speaks to him. Maybe he disappears for a while without letting her know where he is. By failing to function responsibly, he sets the stage for her to take up the slack in the relationship, to do his share as well as her own. His neglectful behavior also acts as an unspoken invitation for her to guess what he is upset about. When she reacts in frustration, she expresses the angry feelings he has chosen not to share.

Examples of physical neglect include refusing to attend to your own physical needs or your partner's. These can include not eating, sleeping, or resting. It can also mean failing to care for your body with adequate exercise, nutrition, health care, or personal hygiene. Ignoring sexual needs is also neglectful behavior, as is not touching, hugging, and giving and receiving physical comfort, warmth, and attention.

Table ~ NEGLECTING/ABANDONING BOUNDARY VIOLATIONS

Physically Neglecting/Abandoning Behaviors	Refusing to attend to physical needs. Not eating, sleeping, or resting Not caring for one's body via exercise, nutrition, adequate health care, personal hygiene. Not dressing appropriately. Ignoring sexual needs in adult, intimate relationships. Ignoring needs for touch, hugs, physical comfort, and attention. Having an affair.
Emotionally Neglecting/Abandoning Messages	Don't feel what you feel. Don't feel what you feel in response to what I tell you. Don't feel anger; it's a sin. Don't cry. Boys don't cry. Girls should never show anger. I don't like you when you cry (or are angry). Let me tell you how you ought to feel. I'm ashamed of you. You don't belong in this family.
Emotionally Neglecting/Abandoning Behaviors	Ignoring your feelings and the feelings of others. Intellectualizing emotional experiences. Refusing to care about your mate's family and friends. Not responding to what you say.

Emotional neglect is commonplace in our culture. Many of us were trained in childhood to ignore feelings and discount their importance. We often intellectualize our emotional experiences and give "don't feel" messages to ourselves and others. A comment I hear frequently in working with couples is "I want to tell you this, but I don't want you to be

Table ~ NEGLECTING/ABANDONING BOUNDARY VIOLATIONS (CONT'D)

Emotionally Neglecting/Abandoning Behaviors (cont'd)	Interrupting you when you speak. Ignoring what you tell me. Not following through with what I tell you I will or will not do. Turning to others to fulfill emotional and/or sexual needs while cutting off from one's partner.
Mentally Neglecting/Abandoning Behaviors	Refusing to acknowledge what you think. Changing the subject when you share your ideas or thoughts. Not responding to your ideas. Making a joke of what you say. Not speaking to you. Not acknowledging your presence. Disagreeing with you, no matter what.
Spiritually Neglecting/Abandoning Messages	The physical world is all there is. A belief in God is self-indulgent and self-deceiving. You are alone. Look out for number one. Only scientifically determined evidence is valid. Competing with others is a way to feel good about yourself. Worry and fearfulness insure you against pain and loss. Always be prepared for the worst. This is a scarce, unfriendly universe. Abundance is an illusion.

angry or hurt by what I say." In effect, the speaker attempts to dictate that his partner should not feel so he can reveal his real feelings. He asks his mate to protect his emotional state by neglecting her own.

Other instances of emotional neglect include refusing to care about a partner's family and friends, or attempting to get him to cut off contact with people who are important to him. Not responding to what a partner says or interrupting her when she speaks are also ways of neglecting her needs. Ignoring what a partner tells us or failing to follow through with what we say we will or will not do also constitute emotional neglect. Refusing to talk to a mate while turning to a substitute partner for an emotional and/or sexual affair is another example of emotional neglect.

Mental neglect occurs when one partner refuses to acknowledge the importance or validity of what the other thinks, even though he disagrees with her ideas. Changing the subject when a spouse shares his ideas or thoughts or not responding to what he says are other hurtful examples of mental neglect. Making a joke of what a mate reveals, not speaking to her or acknowledging her presence, constantly disagreeing with a partner, no matter what he says or does—all are forms of mental neglect that wound and violate the partner's dignity.

Spiritual neglect is epidemic in today's world. We are taught to value power, money, material possessions, and financial success. Instead of seeking connection with others, we learn to compete to determine who is most valuable. We resort to worry and needless fear, trying to insure ourselves against pain and loss. We focus on being prepared for scarcity and disappointing outcomes instead of expecting joy and abundance. We look for the worst in others and are horrified when we find what we seek.

In all these instances we neglect the invisible dimension of being that gives us meaning, connection, hope, bliss, and the confidence that we are more than merely what meets the eye. Only by quieting ourselves and opening our hearts to love can we experience that we are more than just bodies, more than the mind can conceive, more than our limited perspective allows us to know. When we take time to honor our spiritual source—by whatever term we call it—we lift our hearts beyond our bodies and honor our eternal, timeless union with all that is.

In intimate relationships, spiritual boundaries are violated when one partner discounts or ridicules the spiritual life of the other, or when one mate insists that his spouse adopt his beliefs, whether or not they feel right or make sense to her. When we neglect prayer, meditation, music, grace, holiday rituals, and shared times of worship or contemplation, we ignore our spiritual needs and deprive our relationships of opportunities for deepening experiences of love-filled intimacy.

~ *Transforming Neglect Through Nourishing Connection* ~

Neglecting yourself and neglecting your partner go hand in hand. It is impossible to be genuinely nurturing with another person if you starve yourself of the nurturing you need.

If you ignore your needs and neglect yourself, you also will ignore and neglect your partner. When she protests and tries to get your attention, she is mirroring the neglected parts within you that cry out to be included in your life.

You can ignore your needs and feelings, sacrificing yourself and appearing to be unselfishly generous with your mate, and, in the short run, all may seem rosy. But in the long run, you will resent her for being the recipient of the necessary attention and consideration you deny yourself. Inevitably your resentment eventually will emerge. You may resort to passive but hurtful ways of indirectly expressing your anger. Or you may erupt periodically like an angry volcano. Later you make contrite resolutions to submerge your feelings even more completely in the future.

To neglect yourself is to be disconnected from the parts of you that need nourishment in order to thrive. Transforming neglect requires awareness of and sustained contact with a spiritual source, with yourself, and with your partner.

The first step is noticing that you are ignoring your needs and feelings and are disconnected from your inner self. The second step is responding—tuning in to your body, mind, and emotions while opening your heart to love. In doing so, you vastly expand your capacity to tune in to and authentically respond to your partner.

Jean Houston, Ph.D., teaches a powerful way of helping partners tune in to themselves more fully so they can also more fully understand each other. She uses "mesmeric passes" to create a relaxed state of consciousness in which it is possible to connect with one's deepest truths.[2]

One person lies on the floor on his back, arms at his sides, and legs uncrossed. The other centers herself and releases any personal agenda she may hold that pertains to her partner. When she is in an open, relaxed state, she begins making "mesmeric passes" over her mate's body and through his energy field.

She does this by using her dominant hand (her right hand if she is right-handed), which she holds about six inches away from his body. Starting at the crown of his head, she moves her hand over the center of his face and down the middle of his body to his knees. When she reaches his knees, she brings her hand toward herself and away from him. Then, making sure her hand does not move over his body, she moves it back to the crown of his head.

She continues to make these silent, loving passes through his energy field while he relaxes and moves into an increasingly deeper, peaceful state of consciousness. When she senses that he is ready, she may ask him a question, calling his name gently and saying something like, "Barry, what are the parts of you that feel neglected and want to be more fully included in your life?" He responds with whatever spontaneously comes to him—even if it does not seem to be a direct response to her inquiry.

Amazing truths often emerge through this process. It is helpful for the person who does the mesmeric passes to make notes for the partner who is their recipient. She can discontinue the passes and do this as he speaks or continue the passes and make notes when the process is completed.

When the person receiving the passes is ready to come back to his ordinary state of consciousness, he does so gradually and gently, allowing all the time he needs to make the transition. The partners can then change roles so both of them experience being giver and receiver, facilitator and subject in this inquiry into their inner worlds.

In addition to this process, journal writing, dialoguing with your partner, meditating, praying, relaxing with music, painting and other expressive arts, dancing, spending time in nature, and reading literature are powerful ways to connect with neglected aspects of your self. The keys to transcending neglect/abandonment are consistent attention to your inner world and your spiritual life as well as daily practice in making meaningful contact with your mate.

Freezing/Denying Boundary Violations

Jon and Katherine came for their first therapy session, bringing their seventeen-year-old daughter Haley with them. I began by asking them to tell me what they would like to accomplish by working together as a family. Katherine deferred to Jon, telling me he should be the one to begin. Jon gladly stepped into the role of family storyteller.

I watched Katherine and Haley as he spoke. Katherine was attentive, but appeared to be drawn tightly inside herself, with a tense expression on her face and a noticeable throbbing in her jaw. Haley closed her eyes and appeared to be sleeping—except that her foot was swinging back and forth and her rage was palpable, though silently expressed.

Jon droned on and on with a detailed account of their family history. I decided not to interrupt him but rather to observe the scene that was unfolding before me. I took special note of his statement that Haley had been their perfect child—a stark contrast to their two older children, who were both troubled teenagers. One had run away repeatedly; the other had been a rebellious underachiever. But Haley they saw as the golden child—the one who did things right, was polite, made good grades, and never caused trouble—until she turned fourteen and was arrested for arson. They were dumbfounded to discover that their "perfect" child was in terrible trouble. Now, three years later and after eighteen months in a locked facility for delinquent girls, she was back at home and starting to exhibit behaviors similar to the earlier ones that had gotten her in trouble.

As he told his story, Jon showed little emotion. Though he spoke of terribly painful experiences and was obviously concerned about his family, there was no anger, no tears, no passion. Occasionally, he used harshly critical words to describe Haley and her behavior, but he uttered them without feeling. As I listened with all my senses to this troubled family, I realized that Jon left no room for anyone else to speak or even to be. Katherine and Haley seemed accustomed to his controlling behavior and to his talking about them as if they were absent. I could feel Haley's seething rage and see the energy Katherine devoted to staying quiet and avoiding challenging her husband's dominance.

I was in the presence of a marriage that had been in the deep freeze of emotional denial for years. All three of this couple's children had acted out their frustration in angry, vengeful ways—expressing through their destructive behavior the powerful feelings that went unrecognized and unacknowledged in the family. It was as if the teenagers were saying, "Wake up, Mom and Dad! Things aren't as perfect as you claim. You are lying about what's happening. We're here, and we want to be noticed. We are not you. We have feelings. We have thoughts and ideas. We won't let you freeze us out! We don't fit the perfect molds you've been trying to put us in. We're going to force you to notice how angry and hurt the people in this family really are."

I suggested couple's therapy for Jon and Katherine and individual sessions for Haley. I wanted to teach Jon and Katherine the Safe Dialogue process to help them find the safety they needed to begin to speak more honestly with each other. I knew it would take time to help them gradually experience a thaw in their frozen marriage. Attending to what needed healing between them would also help get Haley out of the middle. I wanted to get to know her as a person separate from her parents and to assist to her in discovering and honestly expressing who she truly was.

Freezing our feelings and denying our thoughts, needs, ideas, and impact on others may appear to buy peace and avoid conflict in the short run. But, like using credit cards instead of cash, when the bill comes due, there are finance charges to pay. Our emotions and needs may be well hidden, but they do not go away. Instead, they mount up inside and require more and more energy and effort to keep them contained. Eventually they erupt—sometimes in ugly temper explosions or open rebellion, other times in more subtle, better-disguised forms such as illness, hurtful comments and behavior, depression, anxiety, and destructive addictions.

In intimate relationships, partners violate each other's boundaries when they freeze each other out and refuse to tell the truth. They may continue along this way for years—until life events or their children, especially when they become teens, throw the hot waters of long-suppressed rage on the icy surface of Mom and Dad's relationship. Then, as Jon and Katherine discovered, parents are challenged to face themselves and each other in order to come to terms with the children they love. (See the table of Freezing/Denying Boundary Violations on pages 102 and 103.)

~ *Recognizing Freezing/Denying Behaviors* ~

Freezing, denying, and avoiding are physically evident in the person who looks as if he were holding himself under tight control. There may be an area of vibration just below his cheekbone that reflects the amount of energy he puts into clenching his teeth and keeping his mouth shut.

People who freeze up and avoid expressing themselves are often thin and seem tightly strung. Or they may be obese, inflated by the pressure of what they hold inside. They tend to refuse or deflect hugs, may be uncomfortable with touch, and often are cut off from their sexuality. (Some, however, use sex as a drug to help keep their genuine feelings on ice.) They tend to avoid being with their partner, and may change plans abruptly, leave unexpectedly without notice or discussion, or fail to show up for a date or appointment.

Emotional freezing and avoiding appear as tuning out and cutting off from others by isolating and refusing to connect. Addictions mask emotional freezing, as does compulsive activity like overspending, intense cleaning, obsessive thinking, and ritualized activities that are used to quell anxiety.

Depression, often evidenced by excessive sleeping, neglecting necessary tasks, and procrastinating, is also a sign of emotional freezing and

Table ~ FREEZING/DENYING BOUNDARY VIOLATIONS

Physically Freezing/Denying Behaviors	Walking away in the middle of a conversation. Avoiding sexual contact in a marriage or committed relationship. Refusing or deflecting hugs or caring touch. Leaving unexpectedly without notice or discussion. Changing plans without notice. Not showing up for a date or appointment. Having an affair.
Emotionally Freezing/Denying Behaviors	Tuning others out or cutting them off. Isolating oneself and refusing to connect with others. Cutting off feelings by numbing or disconnecting from them. Using addictions to bury feelings (eating, drinking, smoking, drugs, TV, computer). Compulsive activity (spending, cleaning, obsessive thinking, and other ritual-like activities used to quell anxiety). Depression (sleeping, avoiding necessary tasks, procrastination). Provocative behavior (being late, setting others up to be angry, making careless mistakes, forgetting). Bouts of anxiety and avoiding feared situations (refusing to leave home, phobias about certain objects or activities, anxiety attacks). Changing the subject when feelings are expressed. Making jokes to diffuse feelings. Not responding to a message, letter, or request. Not returning phone calls. Avoiding contact with friends, relatives, or one's mate. Having an affair.

Table ~ FREEZING/DENYING BOUNDARY VIOLATIONS (CONT'D)

Mentally Freezing/Denying Behaviors	Talking excessively so there is no chance for others to speak.
	Interrupting others when they are talking.
	Changing the subject to avoid responding to what another person says or does.
	Turning what others say into a joke.
	Talking over others.
	Not responding to another person's overtures.
	Not talking about what needs to be discussed or acknowledged.
	Allowing only "small talk."
	Putting other people's ideas down.
Spiritually Freezing/Denying Behaviors	Constant activity.
	Avoiding quiet time.
	Not noticing what is good.
	Not appreciating what one has.
	Not expressing love and gratitude.
	Not appreciating other people.
	Not seeing the good in others.
	Not recognizing the spirit in others.
	Always be prepared for the worst.
	This is a scarce, unfriendly universe.
	Abundance is an illusion.

avoiding. Anxiety and frequent illness are common in those who avoid connecting emotionally. They tend to change the subject when feelings are expressed, make jokes to diffuse feelings, and fail to respond to messages, letters, requests, or phone calls. Their agenda—though often unconscious—is to keep their feelings under tight control by avoiding potentially emotional situations with partners, relatives, and colleagues.

Mental freezing and avoiding are evident in people who talk non-stop, disallowing a chance for anyone else to speak. By controlling the airwaves, like Jon, they make sure nothing is said that might be painful or difficult for them to handle.

People who freeze and avoid are quick to interrupt, to change the subject, to talk over what others are saying, or to allow only "small talk." Many are masters of making a joke of whatever someone else says, so they can avoid talking about what needs to be discussed.

They fail to use their intelligence to solve problems they could address effectively. Instead, they often judge others for what they are blind to avoiding themselves.

Money issues like those discussed in Chapter 4 are a good example. Mental freezing and avoiding locks partners into blaming each other for financial problems. One acts like a righteously indignant parent lecturing a rebellious child. The other silently collects resentments, then secretly, like a guilty kid, does exactly what his mate hates and fears. They exchange parent-child roles frequently in this repetitive drama. Their power struggles over money keep them absorbed and assist them in avoiding personal growth challenges. Meanwhile, they silently collude to sabotage their finances instead of thinking creatively and supporting each other in finding genuine solutions to their money problems.

Spiritual freezing and avoiding are evident in people who stay absorbed in constant frantic activity that allows them no space for quiet times of prayer, meditation, and reflection. Those who avoid the spiritual aspect tend not to notice the good in their lives and fail to appreciate their blessings. They have trouble expressing love and gratitude and appreciation of other people, especially their intimate partners. They don't see the good in others or the loving spirit in themselves. Their lives—though they may appear successful in material terms—are empty of meaning and fulfilling purpose. Their relationships are placed on hold, drained of the vital energy necessary to nurture them with the gifts of love, peace, joy, and contentment.

~ *Transforming Freezing/Denying Behaviors* ~

The same strategies that help us to transcend neglecting/abandoning boundary-violation patterns are also useful in creating the warmth and connection necessary for thawing frozen personal resources. Self-nourishing is essential to the cultivation of the warmly accepting attitude that is vital to melting feelings, needs, and desires that are locked away in cold storage.

Addressing frozen grief is especially important. Too often couples try to ignore the depth of their feelings when one or both of them experience a profound change or loss. Their relationship suffers—sometimes for years or until another crisis brings their icy pain into sharp focus.

If frozen grief has created an uncomfortable chill in your relationship, take the time to do some exploring. Meditate and visualize yourself as healed. Though your fearful self may do its best to sabotage your efforts, call upon your wise higher self to stay in charge and make sure you do what you need to do.

Like defrosting an old-fashioned refrigerator, thawing frozen feelings takes time and patience. Begin by making a list of the major changes and losses you have experienced in your lifetime. Don't forget moves, graduations, big successes, job losses, deaths, and major growth transitions (like children being born, evolving through their developmental stages, and then leaving home after high school or college).

In your journal, write about each of these experiences—allowing as much time as you need to address them fully. Describe the whole range of emotions you feel or might feel as you face your grief. Each time you work through a layer of frozen feelings you will feel lighter and more alive. But remember that healing is a process, not an instantaneous fix. What is important is that you remain committed to your healing path—knowing that though your journey may require weeks, months, or even years, every step takes you closer to your destination.

Start with anger and express it as completely as you can. Then delve into your sad feelings, letting your tears flow as the ice within you starts to melt. Visualize the warm sunlight of universal loving compassion shining on you as you consider the impact each event had on you. When your sadness is exhausted, explore the fears you feel as a result of the experiences you grieve. Then move on to what you regret and what you appreciate about your difficult times. As you move through the layers of your emotions, you will uncover bit by bit the gifts of freedom and peace hidden at the core of frozen pain.

The warm sunshine of loving acceptance gradually thaws frozen feelings. It melts your icy places and frees you to express what you previously kept hidden. Regular practice of a variety of expressive behaviors like journal writing, Safe Dialogue, drawing, painting, dancing, and making music promotes healthy boundaries and an open flow of feelings within you and between you and your intimate partner.

Boundary Violations Are Defensive Styles of Relating

Boundary-violating styles of relating are defensive. They serve to hide your true feelings and experience from your partner. Instead of openly revealing yourself, you attack, withdraw, or deny your feelings. In doing so, you appear to be powerful, but this is merely a defensive mechanism that conceals how vulnerable you really feel.

By violating your partner's boundaries, you try to shift your vulnerable feelings onto him. If he takes your words or behavior at face value, he will feel angry, hurt, violated...and vulnerable. Because he does not know what is really bothering you, he can't respond to you effectively. Instead, he is likely to react to your boundary-violating behavior with defensive boundary-violating behaviors of his own. Your exchange may well escalate into a raging battle or a cold emotional standoff. In the end you both feel shaken, sad, and sorry.

Stopping boundary-violating patterns of behavior is the subject of Chapter 8. Before we address that challenge, it is important to understand how boundary-violating behaviors trigger you and your partner into unconsciously reenacting with each other what wounded you when you were children. Becoming conscious of what I call reenactment trances is the next step on the road to creating healthy boundaries.

EXERCISES

1. Create a relaxing environment for yourself, putting on music that is soothing and pleasant. Take time to center yourself in love. With your journal in hand, reflect on the following questions and record what comes to you. Do not judge yourself or your parents, but rather open yourself to the importance of knowing and accepting the truth of your personal history.

   How were your boundaries violated when you were a child? Remember to consider your physical/sexual boundaries as well as your emotional/mental/spiritual boundaries.

   What are the reactions you learned in order to protect yourself as a child? When you fight now, how do you do so? When you flee, what is your *modus operandi*? When you freeze, what is your strategy?

   How do you tend to violate your partner's boundaries? How does your partner react?

   When and how do you feel violated by your partner? How do you react when you feel violated?

   What present-day patterns do you see between you and your partner that remind you of your childhood home?

2. Set aside time for quiet reflection. Center yourself in love, and relax, releasing any cares and concerns that may vie for your attention. When you feel ready, allow yourself to notice any times in the past twenty-four hours when you felt that your boundaries were violated. Then reflect on the following questions, recording your responses in your journal or using Safe Dialogue to share them with your partner.

Part 1: Reflect upon the times when you felt your boundaries were violated.

Identify each violation as an example of intrusion, neglect, or denial.

How did you react to each violation?

What feelings did each violation stir in you?

How did you express or not express your feelings? Would it be helpful to you to reveal your feelings to your partner or to the other person involved?

Part 2: Continuing to reflect upon the past twenty-four hours, notice any times when you may have violated someone else's boundaries.

How did each person react to your boundary-violating behavior?

What feelings did you sense in the other person?

How did that person express or attempt to hide his feelings from you? How did you feel or would you feel if he talked with you about his feelings and responses to your behavior?

Part 3: How might each situation you identified above have been handled differently so that no one's boundaries were violated?

3. In your journal write a short note to each of the other people involved in the boundary-violating experiences you noticed in step 2 above. These notes are for you, not to be sent to the others involved unless you decide to do so. Express yourself as honestly and responsibly as you can, telling each person who violated your boundaries or whose boundaries you violated what you might have revealed about yourself if you had spoken openly instead of intruding, neglecting, or avoiding discussing the truth with them.

4. While still in a relaxed, centered state, open yourself to receiving an image or symbol of yourself with the personal boundaries you currently have. Make no conscious effort to generate this image. Simply allow one to pop spontaneously into your mind. When that image is clear, open yourself to receiving an image or symbol of yourself with the healthy boundaries that are optimal for you. When these images are clear to you, describe them in your journal, and draw or paint them or create a collage that represents them.

5. Follow the same process to visualize an image of your mate with the boundaries he or she currently has. Then open to receiving an image of your partner with the healthy boundaries that are optimal for him or her. Record these images in your journal.

6. Follow the same process to visualize an image of you and your partner with your individual boundaries and surrounded by your relationship boundary, as they currently are. When that image is clear, open yourself to receiving an image of the two of you with optimal personal boundaries surrounded by an optimal relationship boundary that embraces you both. Record these images as well.

7. Select music to symbolize you with your optimal, healthy boundaries in place. Listen to that music while holding the image of yourself with your optimal boundaries. Play this music frequently when you read, meditate, pray, write in your journal, and relax, as well as when you need to bolster your boundaries and strengthen your sense of self.

8. Also select music that symbolizes the boundary that defines your relationship. Share this music with your partner and tell your partner about its symbolic significance. Play it frequently, especially at times when you need to strengthen the connection you feel with your mate.

9. Take ballroom-dancing lessons with your partner. Notice how each of you must learn to carry your own weight and manage your footwork and body position even as one of you leads and the other follows. Let your dancing together become a metaphor for your sharing the dance of life.

10. Together, learn to play tennis doubles or another sport or game. Choose an activity that you both enjoy and that involves teamwork or joint effort. Explore how you are able to work together with healthy boundaries as you support each other, encourage each other, and improve your game without allowing your fears, criticisms, or competitiveness to derail you.

CHAPTER SIX

Reenactment Trances

S usannah, a beautiful five-year-old with enormous, bright blue eyes and long dark lashes, headed straight for the play area in my office. By now, she was familiar with me and with the toys available to her. This was her sixth session, and she made a beeline for the shelf with a selection of family dolls.

"This is the mommy and this is the daddy," she informed me as she carried them to the kitchen of my open-roofed dollhouse. "And this is the big brother and little sister."

"The mommy and daddy and big brother and little sister," I mirrored and nodded my head. Watching her play unfold, I knew she would show me more by what she created than words could possibly tell about her perspective on life with her mother, father, and older brother.

As she arranged the dolls, she became more intent. The mother doll was preparing a meal while the children played together on the floor near the kitchen table. Susannah started to hum "Row, Row, Row Your Boat," establishing a pleasant relaxed feeling among the three dolls.

Suddenly her humming stopped and her attention shifted. Quickly she went back to the toy shelf to get a red car—transportation, it turned out, for the father doll, who was on his way home from work. When Susannah brought him into the kitchen, the mommy doll came toward him to greet him with a hug. He appeared to ignore her and said hello to the children instead. Then he left the room, and Susannah turned the mother doll back to her work, but with stiff, jerky motions now and a tense, angry look on her little face.

Shifting her attention back to the children, Susannah directed them into a fight over the toys they had been quietly sharing. "That's mine. Give it to me!" the little boy shouted. "No, it's not. You know better than that. You can't have it!" the smaller girl retorted.

Grabbing the mother doll, Susannah shouted as she rushed her toward the bickering children. "Stop that right now," the mother doll screamed. "Stop! Stop! Stop! Stop bothering him!" she ordered the little girl. "Troublemaker! Bothering brother...bad girl!"

Now with her little face contorted in rage, Susannah had the mother doll repeatedly spank the little girl, shouting at her all the while, "Troublemaker! Leave good brother alone!"

Still holding the mother doll, Susannah picked up the father and rushed him into the kitchen, shouting, "What's going on? Stop! Stop! Stop bothering me!"

The mother doll, turning away from spanking the little girl, shouted back at him, "Help me! Help me! I can't do it all! You don't care!" Then lunging at him, she attacked him, raging and continuing to shout. An intense fight ensued with Susannah bashing the two dolls together until she was exhausted by her efforts.

"Susannah is angry, sad, and scared," I commented quietly. "Your feelings make sense to me." Looking up at me, she seemed relieved that I recognized her feelings. After a few moments, she crawled over to the place where a teddy bear waited in a small rocking chair. Reaching up, she clutched him to her chest and climbed into his chair, cuddling with him to comfort herself and soothe her pain.

Re-Playing Family Dramas

Susannah had reenacted for me a painful and probably all too familiar scene from life with her family. Her effort to re-create what hurt and frightened her was an attempt to express her grief and to find a way to release her terror. She used the dolls available in my play area to tell me her family's secrets without violating any command she might have received from her parents to keep quiet about what happens behind their closed doors.

Adults also reenact traumatic scenes from the past, much as children in play therapy do. But instead of using dolls to re-create the family dramas that harmed us, we use ourselves, our mates, and our children. The reenactment dramas we create are unconscious efforts to communicate about our hurts and express our buried grief. They are automatic, trance-like behaviors we repeat without knowing why, and they trouble us as much as they trouble the people we love.

Our reenactment dramas are unconscious, automatic replays of what we experienced while trying to differentiate our child selves from our parents. We fall into them when we are attempting to differentiate our adult selves from our partners.

Discovering who we are within the context of a committed relationship is essential to our maturing as individuals and relationship partners. In trying to establish the healthy personal boundaries we need as a mate, we inevitably rely upon the patterns of relating that we experienced with our parents—whether or not we liked the results. Encounters with Mom and Dad—even the most difficult ones—taught us to relate to our spouses and children as our parents related to us.

As adults we reenact what we learned from these encounters. Our partners do the same. Some of the patterns we bring into the mix of our relationship are complementary. Others generate terrible clashes. If our relationship is to evolve into maturity, each of us must grow beyond the limits of what we learned as children. Our challenge is to discover who we are now within a chosen relationship with an intimate partner, rather than in the context of a relationship between parent and child. Reenactment trances help us do so.

~ How Reenactment Trances Differ from Discounting, Enmeshed Patterns of Relating ~

The discounting patterns of relating that are typical of the enmeshment-making process described in Chapter 3 are habitual and more or less continuous styles of interacting. Like reenactment trances, they may be replays of styles of relating learned in childhood. What distinguishes them from reenactment trances is their familiar, almost easy feel. Like old, well-worn shoes, discounting patterns of relating are comfortable. They are culturally supported and generally accepted as normal. Often they fit old sexual-role stereotypes and are so well programmed into us that they are difficult for us to notice or question.

Reenactment trances are more specific, distinct, and usually more intense. They are replays of old scenes from our specific families, set off by a triggering behavior—a word, a tone of voice, a gesture, a facial expression, or an accent. These triggers echo some element of a past hurtful experience. When they occur, they cause a flashback to that old scene. We step out of the present into the past and immediately go into an entranced state of consciousness. In our trance we are on automatic pilot. Our reactions are subconsciously controlled replays of our original, emotionally hurtful experience.

Triggering behaviors are like posthypnotic suggestions. Perhaps you remember seeing a stage hypnotist give his entranced subjects a posthypnotic suggestion. He might say something like "When you hear the word *go*, you will drop to your knees and sing 'Twinkle, Twinkle Little Star.'" His intention is to entertain and amaze his audience with the power of the hypnotic spell he casts over his subjects.

Parents and other authority figures unconsciously induce equally powerful trance states in children by yelling at them, hitting them, threatening them, and otherwise trying to overpower them. Once they have frightened their kids sufficiently, they give them potent posthypnotic suggestions through certain looks, tones of voice, accents, gestures, words, and facial expressions. Later, when children hear or see these behaviors, they react to them by obeying their parents' trance-induced demands.

When they become adults, they continue to react to triggers that are similar to the posthypnotic suggestions their parents used to control them. When their mate says or does something that reminds them of their parents' threatening behavior, they react automatically—either as they reacted to their parents or as their parents acted toward them.

~ *Serving a Purpose* ~

Reenactment trances serve several purposes. The first is to defend us and ensure our survival. We go into reenactment-trance states in automatic attempts to protect ourselves and to cope with hurt when our partner intrudes on us or when we feel neglected, abandoned, misunderstood, frozen out, or otherwise discounted and violated.

It is as if a frightened or frightening monster within us emerges to defend us from what we perceive to be a threat. One face worn by this defensive monster self is that of an enraged or critical, intimidating parent. Its agenda is to correct the situation we are in by employing tactics that the monster parts of our moms and dads used. The other face our defensive monster wears is that of a hurt, manipulative child who is trying to defuse our parents' monster tirades.

In addition to being defensive, reenactment trances are also unconscious calls for help. We use them to try to work through the pain we experienced when our boundaries were violated in childhood. Through reenactment trances, we try to resolve in the present what was hurtful to us in the past so we can reclaim lost and denied parts of ourselves.

They are subconscious attempts to get our own attention and create conscious awareness. It is as if the subconscious mind says, "Look here! Pay attention! Your monster is out! What does this remind you of? Is this how you tried to protect yourself as a child? Are you acting like the monster parts of your mom and dad—replaying a hurtful role they once played with you? Wake up and notice what is happening here. There is a lesson to be learned and a wonderful healing opportunity at hand."

Although unaware of it, in these situations we are hoping for a response from our partner that is different from the way we reacted to our parents. Inside, we are crying, "Stop me! Show me how to do this differently! I don't like being at the mercy of this kind of behavior any more than you do. This is what it was like for me as a child. Help me find a way to escape this awful drama!"

Through reenactment trances, we give our partner a direct experience of what it was like to live in the family we grew up in. If our mate is frightened and gives in to what we demand, part of us is pleased with the apparent success of our manipulative behavior. But another part is disappointed. Our mate's acquiescence is not what we truly desire. Subconsciously, we are looking for new responses that model different, potential responses that we might learn to use.

We want our partner to say something like "Stop that. I'm not available for verbal attacks and criticism." Or we want to hear a calm, clear statement like "I'm not afraid of your threats and your temper tantrums. They don't work well with me. Tell me what you really feel and want. I'll listen and be sensitive to what you need." We want our partner to show us a different way. We are looking for the boundaries we needed as children—for limits when we violate them and for the capacity to hold firm ourselves when someone else's behavior is an attempt to violate us.

Our challenge is to wake up to what is happening so we can change our monster appearances into opportunities for developing healthy boundaries. Rather than judging ourselves for having a monster inside, we are called to learn to love it and take responsibility for its actions as our wounded teacher. Though reenactment trances are difficult and painful, they allow us to know ourselves more fully. Our monster appearances expose the fearful, shadowy sides of us. They are our unconscious cries for the light of love and healing.

Each reenactment episode offers an opportunity for us to grow beyond our typical reaction patterns. When we replay our parents' hurtful behavior, we are challenged to see ourselves acting like them—without judging what we see.

When we are on the receiving side of hurtful behavior, we are challenged to overcome our fear of manipulative, boundary-violating behavior. We must learn to center ourselves and respond as loving adults rather than as fearful children—even when our partner is behaving in difficult, discounting ways.

Our goal is to stop automatically reacting as if our mate is our parent or our child. We can begin by using the process described at the end of this chapter, in the section titled "Waking Up from Entrancement." It offers a structured way to talk about what you learn about yourself by noticing the roles your monster self likes to play. Honestly and openly acknowledging the hurt that drives your difficult behavior helps you stop compulsively re-creating it.

To accomplish this growth you need to express yourself consistently— honoring feelings you originally repressed or were not permitted to acknowledge. This helps clear your mind so you can think more effectively and relate to others in more loving, appropriate ways. Ultimately, it also allows you to release your grief and to fully forgive your family for the very human ways they harmed you.

Initially, your confidant may be your journal or a therapist, but ultimately, you must risk revealing yourself to your mate, as well as to your parents and others whose behavior harmed you. By speaking honestly and courageously, you empower yourself to stop blindly and repeatedly re-creating the pain from your childhood in your present-day relationship.

Reenactment Trance Patterns

Reenactment trances involve a variety of possible interactions between intimate partners. To illustrate some of them, we will imagine that we are invisible observers in the home of Lynette and John, a couple who came for therapy after eight years of marriage.

TRANCE PATTERN ONE
Critical Monster Parent vs. Critical Monster Parent

In the first reenactment trance pattern, John is nervous about company coming. Although unaware of it, he reacts to a visual trigger—a small detail that is out of order—and sees that as the cause of his anxiety and anger. This tiny bit of imperfection causes him to replay his mother's angry behavior when he created disorder in what she tried to maintain as a "picture book" home.

John's tone of voice and angry words, in turn, trigger Lynette's reaction. She flashes back to hearing her father rage at her when she tried to assert herself with him as a child.

In the scene that follows, Lynette and John violate each other's boundaries just as their own boundaries were violated when they were small. They attack, blame, criticize, and judge each other in an unhealthy competition to gain the upper hand. Their battle escalates quickly as they try to protect their positions of innocence and disown any personal responsibility for the difficulty at hand.

John: (*Sounding like a critical, exasperated parent.*) Lynette, what will it take to get you to fix the cushion on that chair? I don't know how many times I've asked you to do that one simple thing. Now we're about to have guests over and it is still sitting there looking disgraceful and embarrassing. You know how hard I work. And you're here all day every day. Taking proper care of the house is your job— I certainly don't just neglect doing what is expected of me. I don't know what's wrong with you.

Lynette: (*Also adopting a critical, exasperated parental tone.*) You have no right to talk to me like that! You don't know what I do, keeping this house running and taking care of the kids and driving car pools and doing all the thousands of things I do every day that you never notice. And you come along and have the nerve to criticize me because I haven't fixed that...that chair cushion. Just how important can it be in the whole scheme of things! I can't believe how picky and ungrateful you are. Just because you're already in a bad mood gives you no right to attack me. Fix it yourself if it's such a big deal to you. I've got plenty of other things to do so you won't be "embarrassed" when we have guests!

Neither John nor Lynette is being honest about what their real concerns and feelings are. Instead of revealing those, they respond to each other as they were once responded to and attacked by their parents. In doing so John and Lynette hide what they are afraid to reveal about themselves. Were they to be open and real with each other, their conversation might sound something like this:

John: You know, Lynette, I'm feeling really anxious about having guests over tonight. I find myself picking our home apart, looking for anything I can find that might be out of place or imperfect. And I'm remembering how tense my mother used to get when she entertained. It would be so easy for me to just go off on you right now, instead of owning up to what's really happening with me.

Lynette: I really appreciate your telling me that, John. It makes perfect sense to me, because I'm a little tense too. I know it will be okay and we'll have a great party, but right now, with all there is still to be done, I'm wondering if we really will be ready with everything in order by seven o'clock tonight.

TRANCE PATTERN TWO

Critical Monster Parent vs. Angelic or Rebellious Monster Child

In the second reenactment trance pattern, one partner behaves as one of her parents did when they were upset with her. The other responds as he did when he was a child scolded by a parent. He responds either like an angel, sweetly complying with her demands, or as a rebel, steadfastly refusing to submit to her control. If he rebels, he may do so silently and subtly, or in blatant, unmistakable ways.

In the following scene, Lynette reacts to seeing John wearing mismatched clothes. This visual cue triggers memories of her mother's obsession with proper dress. She launches a manipulative attempt to get John to change his clothes. Her approach is a reenactment of her mom's efforts to get her to dress as she thought her daughter should.

Lynette's tone of voice and slightly patronizing attitude trigger, in turn, John's memories of *his* mother's style of manipulating and controlling him. In one possible response pattern he simply acquiesces. In the second, he takes a passive-aggressive tack and reappears wearing an even more mismatched outfit.

Lynette: (*Sounding a bit shrill and harsh.*) John, you surely aren't going to wear that shirt with those pants. Can't you see they don't go together at all? And besides, this is a fairly formal occasion. I really think you ought to be in a coat and tie.

John: (*Taking an angelic child's posture while secretly feeling resentful.*) Okay, dear. I guess I didn't realize how dressy I'm supposed to be. I really do so much better when you pick out my clothes for me. I must be color-blind!

OR

John: (*Adopting a rebellious child's attitude.*) Okay, dear, I'll change. (*Five minutes later he reappears, wearing a tie he knows Lynette hates with a green sport coat and plaid golf pants that are predominantly red and blue.*) I'm ready to go, babe! How about you?

Once again, neither John nor Lynette is being honest about their real concerns. Were they to reveal those, rather than reenacting scenes from their respective pasts, the conversation might go more like this:

Lynette: I'm excited about this party we're going to tonight. In fact, I'm so excited and nervous that I find myself wanting to numb my feelings and distract myself by criticizing you and what you're wearing. Actually, I think you look great, and you seem more relaxed than I feel.

John: I think it's going to be fun! I know I'm not as dressed up as you are, but I like what I'm wearing, and I love the way you look. I think it's great that we don't have to look like two peas in a pod.

TRANCE PATTERN THREE

Angelic or Rebellious Monster Child vs.
Critical or Fearful Monster Parent

In this pattern, the initiating partner reacts to a situation in which he feels vulnerable because of events that are beyond his control. Instead of taking an active approach by addressing the problems at hand, he acts as he did when he was an unhappy child, unable to express himself directly and honestly. The manipulative style he adopts was probably modeled for him by one of his parents, who used it for similar purposes.

He may whine, beg, complain, pretend illness, or become overly compliant. His words, looks, or behavior are intended (consciously or subconsciously) to trigger predictable patterns of reaction from his part-ner. She is likely to be provoked to anger, anxiety, threats, or tears. If so, she becomes his emotional surrogate—expressing the feelings he re-presses. This affords him temporary relief from the inner emotional pressure created by his denial of his feelings.

In this example, John's nonverbal communication triggers an old re-active response pattern for Lynette. She flashes back to a particular scene from her past when her father arrived home from a trip obviously feeling ill but denying that anything was wrong. Later that day he died of a heart attack. Lynette still harbors a lot of buried grief over losing him. She is especially angry because she believes that, had her dad ad-mitted he was ill, he might not have died.

Here is the reenactment scene that unfolds:

John: (*Enters the house after a day at work. His shoulders are slightly slumped, he has a worried look on his face, and he barely mumbles hello.*)

Lynette: What's wrong, John? You look miserable. Are you okay? Has something terrible happened? Are you feeling sick? Please tell me what's bothering you.

John: Nothing, really. I don't know.

Lynette: Nothing! What do you mean, nothing. It's perfectly obvious that you're upset. I hate it when you come home like this! Anyone can see that something is wrong, and you act like a dummy, pretending not to know what the problem is. What am I supposed to be anyway? A mind reader! You make me furious when you do this!

John: I can't believe you. I simply come in the house, looking for a little peace. I don't do or say anything, and the first thing I know, you're angry—jumping all over me and telling me I'm the one who's upset. You're impossible. Just leave me alone.

With healthy boundaries in place and awareness of their potential reenactment patterns, Lynette and John might have interacted like this:

John: (*Enters the house after a day at work, looking tired, discouraged, and upset. He greets Lynette with a limp hug.*) I've had a terrible setback at the office. My assistant—you know, Ken, the one I just got trained and like so well—comes in this morning to tell me he's accepted another job with lots higher pay. I'm disappointed and really angry about it. Just when he's starting to be able to do the job I need, he bails out on me! What a bummer!

Lynette: That is a bummer! You must be discouraged and angry after all the effort you put into training him.

John: Yes, I am. But it helps to be able to talk with you about it. I need to think through what I'm going to do next. But first I want to change clothes. Maybe we could go for a walk before dinner.

Lynette: Sure. I'd like that. You can tell me more when you want to.

TRANCE PATTERN FOUR

Unhappy Monster Child vs. Unhappy Monster Child

In this pattern both partners reenact behavior patterns they used when they were overwhelmed and displeased as children. Their parents may have used these patterns, too, modeling their manipulative power and effectiveness.

The trigger that sets off the reenactment trance in the following illustration is a frustrating day. This creates anxiety in Lynette because it reminds her of how her mother behaved when she felt overwhelmed. In reaction, Lynette revisits childhood, feeling and acting as she saw her mother behave then. Instead of responding by assuming a parental mode as Lynette did in the previous example, in this reenactment John also comes from an unhappy child position. They compete to win the prize for being the most miserable, afflicted person of the day.

Lynette: (*Looking tired, haggard, and overwhelmed.*) I haven't done anything about dinner. The house is a mess. The kids have been fighting upstairs. You'll have to take care of it. I'm beyond coping with anything.

John: I've had it too. Nothing has gone right today and now you're in a bad mood too. I don't know what I'm supposed to be able to do about all this. I'm not up to it either. You just don't understand how stressful my job is. If you did, you'd know I can't manage to be in charge at work and at home. It's too much for any one person. No one seems to care how I feel around here.

Lynette: (*Bursting into tears.*) You're not the only one with feelings, you know. My day has been just as awful as yours, yet you seem to expect me to take care of you, no matter what happens to me. I'm sick with a headache. My hormones are raging, and you want me to feel sorry for you. Who's supposed to care about me?

John: Take care of yourself if you're so miserable. You sure don't take care of me, and I'm getting sick and tired of coming home to a crying, pathetic wife. I give up. I'm going to bed.

Lynette: (*Still crying.*) So you're just going to leave me with no understanding and no help! I can't believe this. The one night I really need some support and you're abandoning me. How can you be so mean!

Both Lynette and John respond from an overwhelmed child stance, competing for the misery crown. They try to appeal for help but do not ask directly for what they need. Neither has learned to draw on adult resources for coping with a difficult day. Each wants the other to be a magical parent who automatically comes to the rescue of a child in distress and makes everything better.

With expanded consciousness and healthy boundaries in place, this exchange might sound more like this:

Lynette: (*Looking tired and a bit frazzled.*) This has been a really awful day. I woke up with a pounding headache. Then traffic was backed up for miles on the expressway, and I was thirty minutes late for my first appointment. By lunch I was practically in tears, and it didn't get any better. I just couldn't seem to do anything right. It's a relief to be home—though the kids are fussy and stressed out too. I suggest we order a pizza and make things as easy as possible for all of us tonight. I'm in no mood to cook or do anything very taxing.

John: A pizza sounds good to me. I've had an awful day too. Things were falling through right and left and people were snapping at each other and being generally unpleasant. I don't feel like doing anything demanding either. I'll call for the pizza.

Lynette: Thanks. You do that, and I'll set the table and round up the kids. Maybe we'll all feel better when we get something to eat and have a little time to relax together. I think there's even an interesting movie on TV tonight. I'd love it if you'd watch it with me and maybe just cuddle with me on the sofa.

John: You've got a deal. Pizza and a movie sound like just what I need too. It's great to come home and recover from the rest of the world. I need some cuddling too!

Seeing Partners as Parents

Some of these reenactment trance patterns involve projecting old pictures of our parents onto our partners. We see them as we saw Mom and Dad when we were children, and then we react to what we've projected.

In other instances we see our partners as the children we were, and then we treat them as our parents treated us.

In our entrancement we forget that our partners are separate from us. They are distinct from our history—rather than exact replicas of our parents or of us. Though they may have many traits and behaviors that remind us of mom and dad or of ourselves when we were small, they are not the people our parents were or the children we were then. Their behavior and intentions may even be quite unlike what we imagine.

Unfortunately, we may become so completely convinced of the truth of our projections that we fail to know our partners as they actually are. We thus deprive ourselves of the pleasure of being with them, and we deprive them of the respect they deserve. All too easily we forget that they know who they are better than we do, and they may be quite different from the ways we imagine them to be.

Let's rejoin John and Lynette to see another example of parental projection in action. They are dialoguing with each other during a therapy session in my office.

Lynette: John, I am so angry and frustrated because I see you acting just like my father—cold and aloof and impossible to really connect with. It's lonely being married to you. I long for a man I can really share with—a man who is warm and open and accepting.

John: (*Reaches for Lynette's hand and mirrors her words.*) You're angry and frustrated because you see me acting just like your father—cold and aloof and impossible for you to really connect with. It's lonely for you, being married to me. You long for a man you can really share with—a man who is warm and open and accepting. Did I get that?

Lynette: Yes, you did.

John: Tell me more.

Lynette: Daddy was such an interesting man! But he never had anything to do with me. He was too busy writing his books and teaching his classes to be bothered with a little kid like me. Mother tried her best to make up for what he didn't give me, but she relied on me too much. I guess she was really lonely too, like I am now. I know how she felt. I've been married for eight years to you and you're just like him. I can't believe I was so blind when I met you. You seemed different then—like you really were interested in me and warm and caring. But now you're cold and caught up in your own world. You don't want to be with me or be close to me. It's so sad, and I'm so disappointed.

John: (*Continues to hold Lynette's hand and mirrors her words.*) Did I get that accurately?

Lynette: Yes, you got it. That's all for now.

John: Well, it makes sense to me that when I seem aloof and caught up in my own world, I remind you of your father, and then you feel as lonely as you did when you were a child and sad and disappointed because you think I don't want to be with you or be close to you. I imagine you're also angry about this and frustrated with me and with your dad.

Lynette: (*Nods her head in agreement.*)

John: I feel so sad and frustrated myself when I hear you say all that. I understand that your dad was aloof and caught up in his own world. I see that in him, too. And I know that sometimes I get absorbed in what I'm doing and probably really do remind you of your father. But that's as far as it goes. I do love to be with you, and I want to be much closer to you. That really is my deep desire. And I do my best to let you know that. Yet it seems to me that you push me away and don't want to be with me. No matter what I tell you to the contrary, you insist that you know what's true about me better than I do. That really angers me. You don't know what's true for me unless I tell you!

Lynette: (*Dropping his hand, looking away, and allowing a long pause be-*

fore she begins to mirror in a flat tone of voice.) You feel sad and frustrated when you hear me say all that. Sometimes you are aloof and absorbed in your own world. And you understand how that reminds me of my dad. But you think that's as far as it goes. You really do want to be close to me. (Then she turns to me in frustration.) I can't believe he's lying like this. I can't just sit here and mirror what I know is wrong. He just drives me crazy pretending like this and sounding so nice while he does.

I mirrored Lynette's comments to me and told her I could understand how frustrated and angry she felt. Then I suggested that perhaps some of her feelings relate more to her father than they do to John. "When John is busy or distracted or absorbed in his own world, I'm sure he really does remind you of your dad—so strongly that you probably feel all the loneliness and despair you experienced as a child, wanting him to notice you and relate more to you," I told her. "Your feelings make sense to me, and it makes sense to me that when John tells you he wants to be close, it's hard for you to believe, given that he reminds you so much of your father."

Lynette nodded her head in agreement, and I continued. "But I do believe John when he says he wants to be close, and I see how warm and caring he was with you when he was listening to you, holding your hand, and mirroring what you told him. Those things probably were hard for you to notice a few minutes ago."

"That's right. I really wasn't aware of what he was doing when I was talking to him," Lynette affirmed.

I explained to Lynette that when a partner does something that reminds us of our parents, we tend to flash back to the past so we feel and experience now what we felt and experienced then. It is as if we put on magical glasses that change our vision by filtering out anything that is different from what we remember. We become blind to everything else. I call these "enchantment shades." When we put them on we become enchanted. They transport us to different times and places that are totally real to us though they may fail to make any sense to others.

"I must have a really good pair. And I suspect I may wear them more than I've realized," Lynette commented. Then turning to John, she told him, "Maybe I do push you away sometimes when I've got my shades on and am so convinced that you don't want to be close to me. I tell myself that I don't want to be disappointed again. But maybe I am afraid to find out how good being close to you would feel. If I let myself do that, I suspect I might be really furious with my father and that would be scary...especially since he's so old and seems so frail now and I guess I keep hoping he'll finally give me the warmth and love I've always craved."

Looking very relieved, John mirrored Lynette's words and then responded by opening his arms and asking if he could give her a hug. Lynette hesitated a bit. Then like a shy child with eyes down and head slightly bowed, she moved into his arms, where she gradually relaxed into enjoying a warm, healing embrace.

Waking Up from Entrancement

The process I am about to describe is designed to assist you and your partner in waking up to how reenactment trances sustain symbiotic enmeshment where couples act as if they have no personal boundaries. It will help open your eyes to the old scenes you replay in the present and allow you to release your buried feelings about them. By acknowledging and sharing your grief, you will strengthen your personal boundaries. You will also expand your capacities for empathy and forgiveness as you also gradually free yourselves from repeatedly replaying old pain.

STEP ONE

Identify your entranced behaviors without judging yourself for them.

Think about the fights you have with your mate. What repetitive patterns do you notice? What actions, words, sounds, touches, songs, looks, or experiences tend to push your emotional buttons and trigger you into past entrancement? Begin paying attention to these things, remembering to look with loving, compassionate eyes at what you see. Your intention is to know yourself more fully and understand yourself more completely so you can accept yourself. **Remember:** *You are not guilty or bad for being exactly as you are. You are not trying to change yourself. You are creating more choices for yourself as you relate to your partner.*

STEP TWO

Snap out of it! Then reflect on what just happened.

When you notice you are in a trance pattern, snap your fingers or use some other nonverbal gesture to get your attention and snap yourself back into the present. Take a few deep breaths and say to yourself, "My breath brings me back to my true self and the new choices I have as a conscious adult."

Interrupting a familiar trance pattern may feel a bit strange and disorienting. If so, remind yourself that you are exploring new territory by stopping in the midst of an old entrenched sequence of behaviors. It is not surprising that you don't know what to do next.

It may help to decide ahead of time on a set of actions that will fill in the blank places when you interrupt an old, familiar mental program. You might do something like ask your mate to excuse you for a moment, go to the kitchen for a glass of water, drink it, shake out the kinks in your body, roll your neck three times to the right and to the left, and then rejoin your partner. Or you could excuse yourself, go to the bathroom, wash your face, do five push ups (or other exercises), shake out your body, and then return to your mate. The idea is to break up your old pattern as completely as you can by using your body to interrupt your accustomed mental pattern.

Once you have interrupted your old reactive pattern, reflect with an open heart on what just happened between you and your mate. Acknowledge and express gratitude—to your higher self, the universe, or God—for any insights that you had. If you want to continue your exploration, work with the first question in the exercises at the end of this chapter.

If nothing comes to you or you feel confused, simply accept yourself where you are. In time you will find greater clarity.

STEP THREE

Reveal yourself to your partner.

Instead of hiding behind your old defensive modes of interacting, consciously choose to reveal your inner self to your partner. Your first statement is an affirmation of your love and the strength of your attachment to her or him. It also reminds both of you of your growth challenge: becoming separate, fully evolved people within the context of your relationship. Now set the stage for safe sharing by asking your partner for time to use the Safe Dialogue structure.

STEP FOUR:

Address your feelings from the past.

This is an essential step in freeing yourself from entranced patterns of behavior. It is important to write about your feelings and to talk about them with your partner using the Safe Dialogue structure. As you write and speak, address your anger first. When you have exhausted that layer of emotion, move into the sadness you feel. What you fear comes next. Then state your regrets, and finally what you appreciate about the difficult experiences you are facing.

STEP FIVE

State your intention to forgive and release the past.

Now state your intention to forgive yourself and your parents for the hurtful times you had with them. Forgiveness is the ultimate outcome of healing and growth. It is a process, not a single event, and it evolves as you release your grief—one experience at a time.

I like to reverse the syllables in the word *forgive* so that it then becomes "give for." That helps me think of forgiveness as "giving for" my need for emotional release when I feel hurt, intruded upon, misused, or misunderstood by someone who is important to me. "Giving for" my feelings means I accept and express them so I can digest and release them. Having done so, I can forgive whoever has harmed me by releasing the painful emotional burden I was carrying. Forgiving is a gift I "give for" myself.

I think you will find too that as you gradually "give for" your tears and your anger—again and again—your "giving for" releases you from emotional burdens you may have carried since you were a child. It helps complete your differentiation from your parents. Forgiveness does not imply condoning hurtful behavior. Rather it reflects your maturity and healing from the wounds of the past.

> **You:** Ultimately, my intention is to forgive myself and my parents for all that was hurtful between us. Thank you for helping me take this step of healing and release.

> **Partner:** You are welcome. Your work and your healing also help me heal and grow. Thank you for trusting me and honoring me by revealing yourself to me. I appreciate knowing you more fully, and I will hold what you have told me in confidence and respect in the sacred privacy of our relationship.

> **You:** Thank you! I am available now (or later) to hear from you about whatever you want to share.

> Continue your dialogue, using the Waking Up from Trance process if it is appropriate.

RECAP ~ *The Waking Up from Trance Process at a Glance*

Step One: Identify your entranced behavior without judging yourself for it.

Step Two: Snap yourself out of it! Then reflect on what just happened.

Step Three: Reveal yourself to your partner using the Safe Dialogue structure.

Step Four: Address your feelings from the past.

Step Five: State your intention to forgive and release the past.

EXERCISES

1. Ask yourself the following questions after you snap yourself out of a reenactment trance:

    What does the scene I was replaying remind me of from the past?

    Was I behaving like someone from my original family? If so, whom?

    Was I behaving as I did when I was a child? If so, how?

2. Ask your subconscious mind to take you back to a scene from the past that parallels in some way what just happened between you and your partner. Let go of any effort to control or direct this search. Simply close your eyes, take a few deep breaths, relax as completely as you can, and notice what spontaneously pops into your awareness.

    When you have a scene in mind, replay it as if you were rerunning a segment of a movie. Notice what happened just before and just after the interaction you remember. Let your present-day self watch the younger you in the role she or he played in this family movie. Next, allow yourself to be in the body of your younger self and to feel the whole range of that self's feelings. Are you angry, sad, scared, confused, overwhelmed, anxious, regretful, excited, appreciative? Experience the emotions as fully as you can.

    Now see yourself as you are today—with all the strength, wisdom, and adult power you possess—entering this past scene to comfort and protect the younger you. Imagine your present-day self comforting and embracing your younger self while encouraging that self to tell you how she or he feels and how this scene affects her or him. Listen with an open heart and hear yourself mirroring your younger self's feelings and validating her or his experiences. You as your adult self are her or his trusted ally, confidant, and healer.

In your mind's eye, change the movie you have been watching so the outcome is different for you. For example, you might see your adult self entering an old painful scene, picking up the child that is you, holding and comforting you, while also bringing in a skilled relationship and family counselor to help your parents learn to listen to each other more effectively and to parent their children in a more mature way.

3. In your journal, record what you have discovered.

4. Set an appointment to use the Safe Dialogue format to talk with your mate about your discoveries.

5. When you suspect your partner may be in a reenactment trance, take a few deep breaths and pray for strength and guidance as you practice reacting differently from how you've reacted in the past. Begin to mirror for him, validate his experience, and express empathy. As you do so, he may emerge from his trance state and rejoin you in the present. This is possible when you are able to contain your fearful reactions and give him the loving, healing response he needed as a child but lacked from his parents.

6. When you feel yourself in a reenactment trance or about to be drawn into one, play music that makes you want to dance. Dance alone or with your partner, moving your body as freely as you can, to interrupt your threatened or actual entrancement.

7. Pick a particularly potent scene from your history that you tend to reenact frequently with your partner. Draw or paint pictures of that scene and pictures of you as your adult self changing its outcome and impact on you.

8. Visualize a symbol to represent a painful scene from the past that you reenact in the present. Make no conscious effort to create this symbol. Simply let it spontaneously pop into your mind, and when it does, express gratitude for receiving it. Then open your awareness to receiving a second symbol to represent the new choices you now have for interacting in loving rather than fearful ways with your partner. Express gratitude for this symbol as well. Then see the symbol that represents your old ways of reacting being absorbed by the new symbol that represents your freedom from the past. When you find yourself in or about to enter a reenactment trance, remember the old symbol being absorbed by the new one and helping you change your part in the traditional drama.

CHAPTER SEVEN

Creating Healthy Boundaries

R osie has a Ph.D. in educational psychology and is a tenured profes-
sor at a local university. When she entered my office, I saw a young
woman in her mid-thirties whose pretty features were well disguised by
an unflattering hairstyle and dowdy clothes. I sensed her depression and
anxiety before she said a word about the desperate situation she was in
with her third husband.

As we got acquainted, she told me she couldn't imagine why she had
chosen the marriage partners she had. Inevitably, the men she fell in love
with turned out to be disastrous losers.

With tears brimming in her big blue eyes, she acknowledged that she
was facing a humiliating third divorce. She was on the brink of financial
disaster, having used her savings and income to underwrite her husband's business ventures. He was away from home most of the time.
When he did show up, he was verbally abusive if she tried to talk to him
about his absences and their problems. He failed to keep the financial
commitments he made to her and left her to deal with their rapidly
mounting bills. Yet he was an expert at sweet-talking her into believing
that he was on the brink of a great success—despite all evidence to the

contrary. She told me she was waking up to the harsh reality that he was in fact a criminal—and was angry with herself for having been so naive and stupid.

Over the next few weeks, as Rosie shared more about her marriage, it was clear that she had overlooked lots of warning signals early in her relationship with Slick. He had pursued her as she was getting over her second divorce. She admitted that his nickname, when she first heard it, had struck her as unusual, but she assumed it referred to his being a dapper dresser. She recalled that she had felt a strangely unpleasant prickly sensation up the back of her neck the moment she met him. Though that had bothered her, she told herself it was a sign that he and she were meant for each other. Even when Slick admitted that he had been in prison for stalking his ex-wife, stealing her car, and kidnapping their child, she bought into his story that he had been the victim of an angry woman's exaggerated and false claims. Rosie wanted to help him recover from the trauma of that unfortunate experience and saw herself as uniquely suited to assisting him in getting back on his feet.

Now, looking back on all these clues, she realized she had ignored a number of danger signals when Slick began to pursue her that should have told her to run—not walk—in the opposite direction. But she was still hurting from her second divorce, feeling down on herself and less than desirable. When this handsome guy showed such an interest in her, she was flattered and grateful. All too soon she was hooked by his charm. He had an amazing capacity to make even ordinary things seem exciting. By the time they had their third date she knew she was in love.

She now wonders forlornly how she could have been so foolish. When they met Slick, her friends warned her to beware. But strangely, her parents liked him and encouraged their relationship. After she and Slick were married, they loaned him a large sum of money to pay off his debts and start a new business.

Obviously, Rosie and her parents suffered the same blind spot when it came to dealing with Slick. As I listened, the image of Rosie and her mom and dad wearing only bathing suits in a potentially lethal blizzard popped into my mind. They needed to be warmly dressed for maximum protection, instead of blindly trusting in the face of obvious indications that Slick was dangerous. Yet all three of them discounted their instincts in order to accommodate him.

Neither Rosie nor her parents had the boundaries they needed to protect themselves from a con man on the make. They operated with a "love as self-sacrifice" relationship model, failing to realize that they were giving their power and responsibility for self-protection over to someone who had already demonstrated that he abused others.

When Rosie and I talked about her relationships with her mother and father, she spoke of them in the most glowing terms. They were wonderful people who had always been loving and generous with her. She saw nothing in her family history that might help her understand the difficulties she'd consistently experienced in her relationships with men.

I told her that my experience has taught me that no matter how loving and good parents may be, there is no way they can teach us everything we need to know about how to nurture ourselves, protect ourselves, and relate to others successfully. They do the best job possible—but even the finest parents have deficits in their learning that affect what they are able to teach their kids. When we become adults, our job is to augment and complete the education we received from our parents during our growing-up years.

It seemed clear that Rosie's parents had a blind spot when it came to recognizing conning, manipulative behavior. They weren't equipped to teach her to notice signs of danger that could alert her to the possibility that someone was trying to take advantage of her. Nor had they been able to teach her to notice when she was fooling herself.

Now that she is an adult, her job is to fill in the missing pieces in their parenting, so she can protect herself adequately in the future. I suggested that she start by reading *The Gift of Fear*, by Gavin De Becker, an excellent resource for learning to recognize potential danger and identify people who may intend to harm you.

Updating the Inner Parent

Augmenting and updating the inner parent is a challenge and responsibility for all adults. It is essential to creating and sustaining the healthy boundaries we need for successful relationships.

No matter how much we may have enjoyed childhood and adored our families, there is still lots to learn about life—more than any parents can possibly teach us. What they omit, distort, or are mistaken about is our adult job to find out and correct. Problems in our relationships with others alert us to the areas where we need information, education, practice, and healing.

Like Rosie, I had lots of blind spots that made it difficult for me to see other people—especially men—accurately. My blind spots were related to the idealized picture I clung to of my parents and the abuse I learned to tolerate as a child.

By unconsciously creating amnesia for the ways my mother and father crossed my physical, emotional, and sexual boundaries, I protected myself from seeing their shadow sides. I prohibited myself from remembering how their behavior hurt me. Nor did I realize that healthy relationships do not include such hurtful behaviors.

What I failed to notice about how my parents violated my boundaries I also failed to notice in the people I met as an adult. Consequently, I inadequately assessed their shadow sides. My inner parent—which I incorporated from my observations and experiences with my mother and father—was severely impaired. I trusted too naively. I did not recognize boundary-violating behaviors—my own or those of others. I also made myself much too vulnerable, seeking the love and acceptance I craved from people who were incapable of giving what I needed.

As I became aware of these major deficits in my inner parent, I realized that it was my challenge as an adult to fill in the gaps. Gradually, I taught myself to create and maintain the healthy boundaries I needed to define and protect myself as I related to others. This required seeing my mother and father clearly and remembering my history with them. Only then could I understand my developmental deficits and learn to recognize boundary-violating behaviors—in myself and in other people. In doing this work, I recognized the reenactment-trance phenomenon and how I was re-creating in my adult relationships the dilemmas I had experienced in my efforts to differentiate myself from my parents (see Chapter 6).

Building upon these foundations, I've developed a four-pronged approach to creating and sustaining the personal boundaries one needs for successful relationships. The first dimension of this approach focuses on identifying danger signals and assessing them accurately as one interacts with potential and actual partners. The second prong is stopping the blame game. The third prong involves mastering the fine art of what I call tough self-love—setting limits for oneself in order to be firm, loving, and effective as one sets limits with others. The fourth is learning how to stop boundary violations—the subject of Chapter 8.

Identifying Danger Signals

As I discovered and later taught my client Rosie, it is vitally important to know how to recognize signs of potential danger in relationships. Obviously, this is especially critical when you receive warning signals from a person who is an actual or potential intimate partner.

While you may assume you wouldn't be foolish enough to ignore evidence of possible relationship hazards like Rosie and I did, keep in mind that when you lose your heart to a person you see as very special, you are vulnerable to losing your judgment as well. In the romantic bliss of blurred boundaries, it is all too easy to forget to protect yourself and to ignore both inner and outer alarm signals.

Rosie explained away the strange sensation she felt creeping up her spine when she first encountered Slick. The lonely child part of her wanted him to be her true love. Feeling rejected by her ex-husband and hungry for attention, she conned her inner parent and adult instincts. She talked herself into believing that her unpleasant initial reaction to

Slick was an indicator that he and she were destined to share each other's lives.

Though Rosie ignored her first gut-level reaction to Slick, the instant visceral response she felt when she met him was on the mark. Her body told her to beware—told her she was unsafe—told her something was not right with him. She entered the relationship discounting that intuitive signal that she was in danger. Rosie continued to discount her needs, intelligence, and safety throughout the time they were together. Sadly, she learned a very expensive lesson about respecting the accuracy of initial reactions to others.

Most people I've worked with who have been harmed by someone remember experiencing a gut-level "beware" signal when they first met them. They discounted their intuition only to realize after they were robbed or otherwise misused that they should have paid attention to their initial impressions. Becoming conscious of their immediate visceral feedback mechanism helped them cope with repairing the damage they sustained through their unfortunate association with an unscrupulous person. It also reassured them that they could recognize danger when they encountered it in the future.

Rosie also discounted the implications of what Slick told her about being imprisoned for stealing from his ex-wife, harassing her, and disappearing with their child. His dishonesty and his controlling behavior—which should have been obvious from this piece of his history—became painfully apparent once he and Rosie were married.

People who are abusive with their mates usually exhibit a pattern of behaviors that is like flashing red lights—warning signals to be heeded by potential partners. They may be excessively charming and unreasonably optimistic early in a relationship. Once they think they have won their partner's heart, they shift into a controlling style of relating that—if allowed to continue—can be extremely harmful, sometimes even deadly, to their mate.

As one man I worked with put it, "I'm like Groucho Marx. I wouldn't want to belong to a club that would have me as a member." For five years, Gregory had relentlessly pursued his beautiful and professionally successful young wife before she agreed to marry him. But when Fran became "his," he began an equally relentless campaign to destroy her self-confidence and self-esteem. Unconsciously, he reenacted the destructive parenting that had so undermined his own self-worth that he couldn't respect anyone who had the poor taste to love him.

He was excessively jealous and insisted on knowing Fran's every move. He attacked her viciously, accused her of lying, and frequently threatened divorce. Gregory did his best to limit Fran's contact with her family and friends. He didn't want her confiding in anyone who might encourage her to leave him. He insisted that she give up her professional and community activities so she could focus all her available attention on him. When Fran complied, she gave up her financial freedom and felt vulnerable and dependent on Gregory.

About a year into their marriage Gregory's physical and sexual assaults on Fran become more frequent. Along with these obvious boundary violations, he engaged her in mind games aimed at convincing her that she was mistaken in questioning anything about the way he treated her. All these patterns were exacerbated by his abuse of alcohol and other drugs and were particularly difficult to deal with at home because in the outside world he was a well-respected psychiatrist.

There are other signals that—though not necessarily as potentially dangerous as these abusive patterns—are nevertheless important to notice and assess. They are indicators of a strong probability of serious relationship problems in the future.

Lying, for example, is a clear sign of trouble. People who hide the truth, distort it, or tell outright falsehoods cannot be trusted unless and until they make a concerted and sustained effort to change their deceptive behavior and get to the root of the pain that lies beneath the lies. Such profound healing does not happen overnight.

Another indicator of difficulty is a failure to keep commitments. "I'll call you tomorrow." The call doesn't come. "We'll do something next weekend." Friday arrives and there has been no contact to make plans. Or definite plans are made only to be changed or cancelled at the last minute. Worse still, plans are made and not cancelled, and the person who initiated or agreed to them doesn't show up. Obviously, anyone who can't keep a commitment for a phone call or a date is unlikely to be able to make and keep the commitment necessary for a lasting relationship.

An additional and common sign of future trouble that many apparently intelligent people ignore is a history of affairs—or simply the willingness to have an extramarital affair. The excitement of a secret relationship and its forbidden nature too frequently override good judgment. Affair participants—though they may think they have found utopia with their lovers—forget that anyone who betrays one spouse is highly likely to betray another. Sadly they discover that the magic of their liaison changes dramatically when the growth challenges of a committed relationship emerge. Jealousy, insecurity, lack of trust, and fears of betrayal frequently sabotage relationships that began as the most gloriously promising of blissful affairs.

Refusing to ask for help and to learn from others are also warning signals worth heeding. Many people think it is a sign of weakness to seek assistance when relationship problems emerge. They doom themselves and their mates to enduring their misery or severing their connection. People who are good relationship prospects are interested in growing and learning with their partners. They willingly participate in educational and counseling programs designed to enhance their shared lives.

Stopping the Blame Game

Another warning sign—more like a caution light than a flashing red signal—is a persistent pattern of blaming others for problems rather than taking responsibility for one's own part in them. Our culture feeds this habit, fascinated as we often seem to be by trying to ferret out "bad" guys and exonerate "victims." Giving up the blame game is vital to the healing and growth of an intimate relationship.

Blaming either yourself or your partner distorts what happens between you. Your challenge is to start taking responsibility for your part in relationship troubles—without blaming your mate or taking total credit yourself for what is amiss in the partnership.

Prior to realizing the necessity for tough self-love, I focused my attention not on how I was ignoring danger signals and entering relationships that were doomed from the start but on trying to change partners who weren't right for me. Instead of declining to get involved or exiting quickly when it became clear I had made a mistake, I embraced the illusion that somehow he would change if I could just succeed in remodeling him.

I clung to the impossible relationships I created like the needy child I felt myself to be. Yet I complained all the while about what the other person was doing that was hurtful to me. I had twenty-twenty vision about his mistakes while remaining blind to my own.

When our conflicts became serious enough to threaten a rupture, I blamed myself for all that was wrong, promising to change myself and tearfully taking total responsibility for the problem at hand. By doing so I exonerated my partner, rescued him from the need to examine his behavior, and continued to ignore the destructive nature of our interactions. This only put off the inevitable day of reckoning when reality had to be faced—and a relationship that wouldn't work had to end.

By playing both sides of the blame game I denied what went awry in my relationships. I avoided addressing the issues I needed to face while feeding the seductive notion that I was either victim or villain. Unconsciously, I reenacted my childhood victimization and guilt—until I woke up to what I had forgotten about those early years.

Quite naturally it was easy to focus on how wonderful or how terrible the men I dated were. It was much more difficult and threatening to look carefully at my own behavior and notice what was happening inside me.

I failed to realize that I was doing a lot of projecting. Rather than seeing a potential partner clearly, I pictured him as both my idealized Prince Charming come to rescue me *and* as a cruel, hurtful, and abusive villain. I put on rose-colored glasses to make him fit the image in my dreams while also wearing blinders to keep from noticing what I did not yet see—and did not want to recognize—in my own and in my parents' history.

Before I remembered that history, I often wondered how someone as nice as I considered myself to be kept getting involved with angry, abusive men whose explosive tempers I feared. My own anger was as thoroughly repressed as my guilty childhood memories were. The angry men I met mirrored what was in me and in my mother and father that I did not yet recognize.

I was blind to my shadow side and the shadow side of my past. Instead, I was frightened and horrified when I saw intense feelings and behaviors in others that reflected what remained buried in me. I did not yet realize that I could not see anyone else clearly until I began to truly see myself and my history. So long as I projected what I denied in myself onto a potential partner, I gave away my power and responsibility to make a difference in relationships. Only when I stopped playing the blame game did I realize how self-defeating and short-sighted it is to be critical of (and blind to) what we are afraid to see and acknowledge in ourselves and our pasts.

Many of my clients come to therapy because they are concerned about their partner's behavior, like I was in my younger years. In their hurt, fear, and anger over feeling intruded upon, manipulated, avoided, or frozen out, they want their mates to change so life will be better for them. Or they flip to the opposite polarity and take all the guilt and responsibility for their problems on themselves. They are blind to the deeper issues and to the impact of their family history on their present-day relationship dilemmas.

What they fail to notice is that they cannot remodel their spouses or control their choices. Nor can they change things by pretending to be the only one at fault. My first job is to help them see what they *can* do something about! That something is learning to practice tough self-love—a conscious approach to establishing and keeping healthy boundaries as we relate to our partners.

Practicing Tough Self-Love

Practicing tough self-love is the responsibility of our inner parent. A wise inner parent notices danger signals and takes them seriously. It intervenes to ensure that we protect ourselves adequately. Instead of letting us imagine that we can change others by ignoring or complaining about their hurtful behavior, it reminds us that we do a disservice to others by permitting them to hurt us unnecessarily. Nor does a wise inner parent allow us to pretend we are totally responsible for all that is troublesome.

A wise inner parent reminds us that love, rather than being naive and permissive, is clear and firm—both with us and with those who would violate our boundaries. It does not ignore such violations and their current or potential long-term impact. Rather, our wise inner parent is firmly grounded in the principles of tough self-love.

Using tough self-love involves the discipline of developing and maintaining a firm, nurturing, and wise stance with the child self who lives within us. When we practice TSL, we say a respectful "no" to ourselves and to others when saying "no" is necessary. We are also generous with saying "yes" when permission and agreement are appropriate.

We provide a sane structure for our lives, respecting appropriate limits as we plan our time, make financial decisions, and commit ourselves to others. We nurture ourselves in loving ways, making sure we get the food, rest, sleep, play, and time for creative self-expression that we need for optimal health.

Practicing tough self-love, we respect our feelings and allow them to inform us without acting them out impulsively and destructively. We are committed to developing our minds, expanding our wisdom, and continually updating ourselves with the information we need to live well and enjoy life more fully. And we nourish our spirits with inspiring books and teachers, prayer, meditation, personal reflection, or communal worship.

A wise inner parent practicing TSL doesn't play the blame game. As an astute inner guide, it heeds danger signals and does its best to protect us from harm. If we make mistakes in assessing the intentions of others, it insists that we face the difficulties at hand and take corrective action, rather than allowing ourselves to behave as if we are helpless victims or guilty villains, stuck in situations we cannot change.

~ *Tough Self-Love in Action* ~

It takes awareness and effort to begin noticing how we violate our own boundaries—not to mention how we violate our partner's. To create and sustain healthy personal boundaries, we must wake up to the ways we con and cajole ourselves into doing what is not good for us (or our partner). Seeing how we try to manipulate ourselves enables us to recognize when other people—especially our mates and children—try to manipulate us in similar ways.

The needy, jealous, greedy, hungry, demanding, and wounded aspects of our inner child insist on having what they want when they want it. The desire driving our child self may be for a cigarette, a drink, chocolate, a trip to the race track, a shopping spree, putting off something we need to do, or doing something we know we ought not to do. The child inside us pleads, begs, argues, and insists that just this one time it will be okay to indulge ourselves. It attempts to get its way despite whatever earlier decision our parent and adult selves may have made about what is best.

When the inner child tries to get her way, she needs the firm parent and clear-thinking adult parts within us to take charge and tell her "no"—if "no" is the response that is consistent with our goals and intentions. Unfortunately, what too often happens is that our nurturing inner parent and adult are too poorly developed to withstand our inner child's tantrums, demands, and cajoling. They fold under the pressure our child self exerts and allow her to have her way.

The manipulative power so effectively used by the inner child frightens her and heightens her anxiety. This causes her to want more and more—of whatever it is that she imagines might soothe her. So she begs for another piece of cake, more things to buy, just one more cigarette, another date with the man she knows is not right for her, or yet another activity to distract her from her terror.

If she continues to get her way, she becomes even more agitated. Her escalating anxiety is likely to trigger a desperate overreaction from the now also frightened parent and adult parts of her self that previously failed to set adequate limits. They may attack her with vicious, hurtful words to shame her and make her feel guilty for being so "bad." Then, having punished her for getting her way, they step in with impossible-to-enforce resolutions never to allow the "bad" behavior again.

In effect, we go into an internal reenactment trance. In our invisible inner realm we replay hurtful interactions we experienced with our parents. Rather than being firm, clear, and loving with ourselves, we lapse into re-creating their mistakes. We shame, blame, threaten, criticize, and attack our child self. Like our parents when they failed to cope effectively with our childhood tantrums, demands, and manipulations, we try to hurt and intimidate ourselves into "good" behavior.

As a child we longed for consistent, respectful, firm, friendly, and nonjudging parents. Now, as an adult, the child within us still seeks what we missed early in life. What she is really looking for is a firm "no." To give her what she needs we must develop a clear-thinking inner adult and a loving inner parent who understand the healing power of tough self-love.

Our inner child feels safe when she knows she is not allowed to be in charge. She knows she is too young and immature to have so much power. Though she may fuss a bit when we tell her no, she is *relieved* to know that a loving inner parent and an intelligent adult are available to care for her. She feels loved when we stop her from harming us with her impulsive desires.

This doesn't mean she never gets to do what she wants. It simply means that our mature inner parent and adult choose wisely. They allow her plenty of time for fun, play, and nurturing pleasures, while also insisting that she cooperate when it is time to do what is necessary for our health, finances, relationships, and overall well-being.

As with all growth processes, the first step in learning to practice tough self-love is waking up to the pattern we need to address. This means noticing how the child inside us demands what he wants and pushes us to allow him to have it. Our job is to parent him in loving, firm, effective ways. This means we must recognize and appropriately express the unacknowledged feelings that drive him to insist on having something to soothe and pacify his denied emotions.

~ Strengthening Your Ideal Inner Parent ~

An ideal inner parent recognizes when your inner child pushes and demands. He knows to look beneath your agitated behavior for the feelings your child self needs to express. Then he stands available to listen, acknowledge your feelings, and validate them.

Your ideal inner parent might say something like, "Tell me about what you were feeling just before you decided you needed to have this thing you're pushing me to give you." Then listening quietly to discern what your inner child reveals, you may hear or sense something like, "I hated it when Susie forgot she was supposed to meet me for lunch. That really hurt my feelings, and I'm angry. This isn't the first time she's disappointed me. I don't trust her anymore, and I hate feeling this way."

Once your inner child speaks or communicates through an image or a feeling about what is troubling you, your wise inner parent mirrors and validates your feelings. Inside yourself you say something like, "Well, that makes sense to me. Of course you are angry, upset, and disappointed about Susie's standing you up for lunch one more time. I don't trust her either, and I don't like that feeling or having to notice it."

When your inner child feels truly heard, honored, and understood, he may relax and drop his demands. Or he may continue to push for a temporary distraction or false comfort, especially if your feelings tap into painful emotions from the past that you have kept hidden in cold storage.

In the face of a possible meltdown of frozen pain, your inner child may become even more agitated and demanding. Your wise inner parent stands firm with a "no" to comforts or distractions that are contrary to your goals and best interests. At the same time, your inner parent nurtures your child self in appropriate ways to help you thaw and release your pent-up feelings, soothe your anxiety, and get through the experience at hand.

Even as you say "no" to your inner child's immature suggestions, you may decide to take time out—time to be still, to sit quietly, breathe deeply, and reflect on the roots of your pain. You may write in your journal about what is happening inside you. You might take a warm bath, go for a walk, sit outside, pet your dog or cat, or pursue some other activity that helps to ground you and redirect your attention to nourishing and comforting yourself in wholesome ways.

As you become proficient in setting appropriate limits for your inner child and nurturing yourself through your emotional ups and downs, you will find yourself recognizing similar patterns when they emerge in interactions with your partner. Understanding clearly how easily you can manipulate and con yourself, you are alert to similar tactics when the child within your mate also uses them.

Rather than judging your partner for trying to get her way, you simply remain firm about what you believe to be best for both of you. You say "no," releasing any fear about how she may react with anger, disappointment, tears, or more demands. You know she will survive her feelings—even old ones that erupt from her past—and so will you. You are comfortable with being powerful and clear about what is vitally important to you, recognizing that it is your responsibility to care for yourself as you relate to your mate.

I experienced some very painful lessons in developing the adequate inner parent I desperately needed. Gradually, I learned to give myself the love and nurturing I had believed someone else ought to supply. I discovered that no one else treats me better than I treat myself. Other people quite naturally test to discover who I am and where my boundaries are. If I don't have a strong enough sense of my identity and clear limits about what is and is not okay for me in my relationships with others, I am too easy a mark for mistreatment and abuse.

I had to strengthen my spiritual life (the subject of Chapter 10) in order to increase my inner parent's capacity to establish and keep the boundaries I needed in dealing with other people. I also had to learn to set and keep healthy limits for myself. Until I mastered the demands inherent in adequate self-parenting, I wasn't able to meet the challenges of relating successfully with others—especially with a mate.

I came to see that the quality of my relationship with myself is reflected clearly in the quality of my relationship with a partner. If I am at peace with me, I am at peace with him. If I am at war with myself, I am likely to be at war with him. If I am loving, gentle, and nurturing with me, I am filled with the energy I need to be loving, gentle, and nurturing with him too. If I am harsh, critical, and abusive with myself, I am vulnerable to giving him a dose of the pain I shower on myself.

I also began to notice that how I relate to my partner is directly reflected in how he in turn relates to me. How I treat him comes back to me—and sometimes what returns is amplified so I can't miss it. The respect he accords me is a direct reflection of the respect I give myself. If I behave like a doormat, consciously or unconsciously he begins to treat me as if I were one. When I behave as a competent, responsible, potent adult, he gets the message I send and responds to me as a person worthy of consideration and respect. By tuning in to the impact I have on him and learning to really listen to his point of view, I gradually have grown to experience genuine empathy for how he feels living in a relationship with me.

Practicing tough self-love enables me to love my partner without losing myself. It helps me create and sustain the healthy boundaries I need to be all that I am—while living in a committed, growing relationship with the person I love. TSL empowers me to relate to my partner authentically—as the real person I am. It also allows me to honor him by seeing through his defenses into the heart of his authentic self.

EXERCISES

Reflect upon the following questions, perhaps writing or drawing your responses in your journal:

<u>**1.**</u> Think about times when you first encountered someone who harmed you. What bodily signals do you remember from the moment of your meeting? How did you persuade yourself to overlook your "gut" reaction?

<u>**2.**</u> In what part or parts of your body do you tend to feel your "beware" warnings?

<u>**3.**</u> Consider the signals you send to others about whether or not you can be trusted. Are these the messages you want to convey? If not, are you re-creating with potential partners behaviors that left you feeling betrayed by your parents when you were small?

<u>**4.**</u> Are you ignoring danger signals you ought to heed from people who want to be close to you? If so, what are you afraid to face by being honest with yourself about the whole picture of your relationships with them?

<u>**5.**</u> What were some of your favorite strategies for manipulating your parents when you were a child? How do you use similar tactics to con your inner parent into giving the child in you what he wants—even when it is not good for you? Make a list of your inner child's most effective manipulative strategies.

<u>**6.**</u> Visualize a symbol or picture that represents your ideal inner parent. Do not deliberately try to create an image; simply allow one to enter your consciousness. Use the image to help you call on your inner parent when you need to be firm with your inner child.

<u>**7.**</u> Draw pictures of your inner child and your inner parent. Give them loving names or nicknames that appeal to you. Notice their relative sizes. Does your inner parent need to be augmented? If so, draw it larger and give it a more potent visual presence.

<u>**8.**</u> In your journal create a dialogue between your inner child and your wise inner parent. Have your inner child use some of her

best manipulative strategies for trying to get what she wants. Experiment with allowing your inner child to get her way. Notice how you feel after indulging yourself. Then explore what happens when your wise inner parent says "no." If your first efforts to say "no" are not firm enough, try taking a tougher stand until you feel confident and secure in your capacity to be in charge of yourself. Then ask your inner child to talk with you about the feelings that lie beneath your desire for comforting and distraction.

What does the dialogue you have written remind you of from your childhood? Write a typical dialogue you can remember or imagine between yourself as a child and either your mother or your father.

Now create an ideal dialogue between you as a child and your mom or dad about the same issue.

9. Write a letter blaming your partner for all the difficulties you experience in your relationship. Then explore taking responsibility for your part in the problems. What repressed parts of yourself are you reacting to in him? Write about what you can do that will make a difference in how you relate to each other.

10. Find pictures of you and your partner when you were two to five years old. Post them in places where you will see them frequently. Visualize the child in each of you whenever you become aware that it is active in you or in your mate. Have fun with these lovely children playing together. Notice also how they fight, pout, con, plead, and try to intimidate and control what happens between you. Be aware of your wise inner parent and how it can intervene to provide necessary structure and boundaries when the child in either of you needs clear limits.

CHAPTER 8

Stopping Boundary Violations

Afterwards identifying danger signals, stopping the blame game, and practicing tough self-love—all detailed in the preceding chapter—the fourth step in creating and sustaining healthy boundaries is learning how to stop boundary violations.

The key to success in stopping boundary violations is keeping fear in check. It is fear—of your mate, of anger, of power and responsibility, of change, of being alone, of being your authentic self—that keeps you locked into boundary-violating patterns of behavior. To care for yourself and others, especially in the context of your most intimate relationships, you must learn to recognize when fear has you in its grip.

Your fearful self keeps detailed mental records of all the times and ways your boundaries are violated. It calls up these frightening, hurtful memories and uses them to try to protect you when you feel threatened. Operating on the self-defeating principle that worry and negativity can somehow insure you against being vulnerable, your fearful self makes fearful interpretations of other people; fearful predictions about what the future might hold; fearful comments on what you or your mate might do; fearful projections about how you might fail; fearful warnings about how you might be harmed; and fearful comments about what is wrong with you and others. Or it takes the opposite tack and puts you in jeopardy by encouraging you to ignore obvious danger signals that your wise inner parent warns you to heed.

The Internal Saboteur

In earlier chapters I referred to the two sides of this fearful self as the monster inner child and the monster inner parent. They surface when we are frightened and are trying to defend ourselves, fool ourselves, manipulate others, or defeat ourselves. The monster inner child and monster inner parent stand like guards on duty to keep us from looking beyond them into the shadowy depths of ourselves.

Now I want to introduce you to a name that embraces both these threshold guardians—a name that includes both our monster child and monster parent aspects. That name is the Internal Saboteur. It is the whole of the fearful self that guards the threshold to the dark basement of our subconscious mind.[1]

Instead of nurturing you with love and wisdom, the Saboteur specializes in abusing you with negative, discounting comments and interpretations of yourself and others. It confuses your thinking by denying your inner parent's wisdom and loving intuition. It uses your wounded inner child to persuade you to do what is not best for you.

Learning to recognize and name your Internal Saboteur is vital to stopping boundary violations. By noticing and calling your Saboteur by name, you are empowered to tame it. By becoming aware you can witness your Saboteur in action, knowing that what it tells you is not written in stone. When it speaks, what you hear is not truth. Rather, your Saboteur preaches the gospel of self-sabotage, relationship sabotage, and dangerous self-deception.

The Saboteur comes forward within you when your boundaries are violated or you imagine they have been. It also reveals itself when you experience strong feelings that overstimulate your emotional circuits. If you allow the Saboteur to take charge of you, it urges you to follow your "old brain"-dictated fight, flee, and freeze reaction patterns.[2] It encourages boundary-violating behavior.

When it takes control, the Saboteur turns you into an out-of-control child, a paranoid adult whose thinking is distorted, or an abusive, ineffective parent who silently attacks you or takes aim at your mate. Once it has you in its grip, you lose touch with your wise nurturing parent and your loving, safe inner child. You also break connection with the clear-thinking adult part of you. Fear takes charge. Either you harm yourself or you violate others—especially your intimate partner.

Your state of mind and behavior invite your partner's Saboteur onto the scene or, if his Saboteur is already present, escalate his fearful reactivity. Before you know it, your Saboteur and his are entangled in a rapidly unfolding drama that hurts you both. Together you recreate scenes similar to ones that harmed you when you were children.

But there is another possible choice. When your Saboteur urges you to react in a primitive way, your wise inner parent can practice tough self-love. It can say "no" to your Saboteur's efforts to control you. Your wise inner parent can intervene to center you in love so you remain calm, clear, and firm with your partner—even when her Saboteur has her ensnared in full-scale, destructive reactivity. Your self-control and loving—rather than reactive—presence may help your partner relax, too. Your capacity to tame your Saboteur assists your partner in bringing hers under control also.

Ultimately, you discover that your Saboteur is not a "bad" part of you. It is simply the part of you that tries to protect you in the ways you discovered were necessary to help you survive life in your original family. Your Saboteur becomes your ally in healing your life and your relationships when you learn to recognize that its appearance offers a chance for you to grow. When it comes onstage, it signals you that an opportunity is at hand that can help you move beyond the mental and emotional programming you received as a child. Its antics are simply strategies that worked well in your early years to protect you when parents and caretakers violated your personal boundaries.

The Saboteur Masks Our Fears

Saboteur attacks mask what we fear within ourselves. They cease only when we embrace the lost and rejected parts of ourselves that the Saboteur is determined to keep hidden.

Our lost and rejected parts are those aspects of ourself that were pruned away by our parents and our culture when we were children and adolescents. Without them we have huge holes in our identity, like gaping, empty spaces within us. Like magnets, these empty spaces draw what is missing in us from our partners and from other people who are closely connected to us.

As we saw in Chapter 4 with Ellie and Tyler, our mates, children, business associates, and friends often act as mirrors in which we see our missing selves reflected. When others speak, feel, or behave in ways that we believe are wrong or bad, we encounter the feelings, needs, behaviors, beliefs, attributes, and failings that we either deny or disallow in ourselves.

Like children who are afraid of the dark, we are frightened when we encounter reminders of the lost selves we've buried in the dark, shadowy basement of our subconscious mind. Our Saboteur appears at the entrance of this basement territory to make sure we continue to deceive ourselves about what is hidden there. It directs our attention away from our lost selves and encourages us to project responsibility for our fearful feelings, mistakes, and shortcomings onto others. Or it heaps guilt and blame on us—charging us with terrible crimes and trying to convince us that we are bad and responsible for other people's misbehavior. By agitating us, it distracts us from the real issues at hand, helping us sustain the notion that we are either perfect and blameless—or unworthy, undeserving, and lost.

Taming the Saboteur requires understanding its role as guardian of the dark basement where our banished selves languish. We must learn to make our way past the Saboteur into the shadow territory it guards. This demands courage, love for ourselves, and commitment to nonjudging self-acceptance—essential resources that will light our way as we descend into the innermost depths of our being to face what we believe is both dangerous and unacceptable within us. This is graduate-level work in the school of life. The consciousness it demands runs contrary to much of what is modeled for us by our culture.

Reclaiming the Shadow

We are part of a society that denies its shadow side and preaches projecting it onto others. We are taught to see the enemy as "out there"—in other people whose ideas and beliefs are different, whose skin is a different color, whose language and ethnic heritage are different, whose lifestyle is different, who feel what we don't allow ourselves to feel, and who think what we are afraid to examine. Instead of listening to them, we do our best to shut them up. Rather than being curious about what we might learn from them, we see them as agents of evil.

For many years Communism, Russia, and other Iron Curtain countries received our shadow projections. They were the "enemy"—foreign to us and dangerous. Since the dismantling of the Berlin wall, we have been forced to find new foes.

Though certain foreign countries still serve as convenient objects of our projections, we are slowly waking up to also find shadow energy here at home—in our midst. The good news is that gradually we are bringing it closer to home. The bad news is that we still project it on others.

We see the shadow in politicians under siege by their colleagues and the news media hungry for scandal. We find it in teenage gangs who remind us of the awful results of child abuse and neglect as well as the failure to provide children with a meaningful education and discipline. Conservatives point to the shadow in liberals, who respond in kind. One religion sees the devil in another; different denominations within the same religion pit themselves against each other, convinced that theirs is the only valid way.

Every day and everywhere we go, we are called—as a nation and as individuals—to reclaim our shadow. To do so we must find and face within ourselves what the Saboteur helps us hide, deny, and ignore. Only when we are courageous enough to tame our Saboteur and face our shadow selves can we begin to accurately assess the Saboteur when it appears in others. Then we must remember that its mission is to keep their own shadow territory hidden from our view.

Identifying Your Saboteur's Favorite Masks

Taming the Saboteur and seeing it clearly when it manifests in other people requires patience and skill—as well as lots of practice with tough self-love. It also depends on your becoming adept at identifying your own Saboteur's favorite tools for confusing and deceiving you.

I like to think of the Saboteur as a skilled actor with a huge wardrobe of masks that it uses to hide its true identity. When it appears within us or manifests itself outwardly as we interact with others, it chooses from its costume chest any one of many possible disguises. The chart below identifies some of its options. Learning to recognize these masks when your Saboteur uses them—as well as when your partner puts them on—is both amusing and helpful.

~ *Masks Assumed by the Saboteur* ~

The Judge: "You are bad, guilty, wrong."

The Critic: "You ought to be different—more like me."

The Worrier: "Something terrible will happen. You'll abandon me or reject me."

The Pusher: "You really need to do that. These things just *have* to get done—now!"

The Pleaser: "Let me do that for you. Whatever you want. You count; I don't."

The Victim: "Poor me. I'm sick, tired, helpless, confused. What can you expect?"

The Martyr: "How could you, after all I've done for you. You owe me!"

The Abuser: "You'll do what I tell you, or else! I'm the one who counts here."

The Rescuer: "I'll fix things for other people—especially our kids—so I can avoid you."

The Historian: "You did those terrible things way back when. How can I trust you now?"

The Blamer: "If it weren't for you, I would _____. It's all your fault. You make me _____."

The Charmer: "I know how terrible I was. I'll never, ever hurt you again. Let me make it up to you. Just give me one more chance to prove how much I love you!"

The Con Artist: "I'd never do anything like that—trust me! I'm innocent. You know me better than that!"

The Avoider: "I'm not in a good mood. It's too late/too early. I've got a headache. I want to go to sleep. Don't disturb me!"

The Liar: "She's just a friend. I can't believe you would even think such a thing!"

The Seducer: "You are irresistible! I've never met anyone like you. Just this once..."

The Big Spender: "I'm angry, and I'm going shopping." Or, "I've got big bucks; I'll take care of you and show you a really good time. We'll travel. I'll buy you jewels."

The Denier: "I don't know what you're talking about. I'm not feeling anything. I have no growth issues. My family life was perfect when I was a child. I've already worked through all that!"

The Interrogator: "What do you mean? What were you doing? Who were you with? Where are you going? Why are you doing that?"

The Distancer: "I'm not available. Just go away—don't bother me."

The Clinger: "We've got to talk—now! Please don't leave me!"

The Impulsive: "I can't stand this; I've got to get out. I *have* to do this. I want _____, and I want it now!"

The Addict: "I need a drink. I deserve a little relaxation! I want to numb out."

The Controller: "It's my way or the highway. We are one, and I'm the one that counts."

The Adaptor: "We are one, and you're the one who counts. I'll make it easy and okay for you. I'll tolerate whatever you deal out to keep you in my life."

The Victim/Persecutor: "You mistreated me. Now I have the right to abuse you."

The Awfulizer: "This is so awful—I can't believe how awful. Nothing could be worse!"

The Bored Teenager: "I don't know. You're stupid. Everything is stupid. I don't care."

Your Saboteur's disguises are wonderfully clever manipulative tools. It uses them to deceive, confuse, and throw others off guard. A clever Saboteur is particularly skilled at twisting what partners learn in couple's therapy and using it in ways that appear sincere but that actually convey deadly, hurtful messages.

Your Saboteur may put on a mask of superiority to interrupt the Safe Dialogue process, refusing to participate and declaring it too cumbersome, artificial, and difficult. It may mirror what your partner says with sarcastic overtones or act like a parrot, mocking what you or your partner say. Or it may attack your mate or you rather than allowing either of you to reveal yourself honestly to the other.

You can be sure your Saboteur has taken charge when you find yourself hiding behind the mask of a clever child intent on getting his way. Using mean words, exaggerated feelings, threats, gestures, guilt, postures, and veiled meanings, you see yourself trying to manipulate your partner as you once manipulated your parents. You are also under your Saboteur's control when you allow yourself to be manipulated by your partner. His Saboteur may appear in an angry or guilt-inducing parental mask, using strategies that were favorites of your mom or dad.

To stop these things from happening, you and your mate must learn how your Saboteurs mask themselves, manipulate each other, and take you into reenactment trances. Begin expanding your awareness by making a list of your parents' favorite ways of manipulating you when you were a child. Did they use threats, frowns, or other distinctive facial expressions? Did they feign helplessness, create guilt trips, or go into angry tirades? Perhaps they used bouts of tears, pouted, pretended perfection, were blaming, made promises they didn't keep, or were neglectful and/or used abandonment to try to control you. How did you respond? What manipulative tools did you find most effective in trying to protect yourself?

Once you have considered these questions, turn your attention to your present-day relationship. What are the manipulative masks you use with your mate? How does he or she respond when you use them? What are your partner's most effective masks for manipulating you? How do you tend to react to each of them? Are either of you becoming skilled at using elements of Safe Dialogue (or other resources you've learned in therapy), pretending to be genuine while doing your best to undermine and hurt the other?

As you engage in this self-examination, use the Safe Dialogue process with your partner to share what you discover about yourself. Avoid analyzing your mate. That would only violate his or her boundaries and create more hurt. Simply reveal yourself courageously and sincerely, realizing that this is an act of trust and good faith in both of you. Be aware of your Saboteur as you dialogue. It may want to use what you hear about your mate against her in the future. It also may tell you that your mate will use what you reveal against you. This is a great time to practice taming it! Keep reading!

Taming Your Saboteur

You are enjoying a quiet day alone, relaxing and doing things around the home that satisfy and soothe you. Suddenly the phone rings, interrupting your solitude and jarring you a bit. When you answer you hear your partner's voice speaking to you in an excited tone.

"You won't believe what just happened. I went to the lunch meeting of our college class-reunion committee—and you'll never guess who I ran into!"

"Who?!" You respond with equally excited curiosity.

"Ann—my old college sweetheart. I was astounded. She looks just like she did back then, and she and her husband have moved back here. They want us to get together. I invited them to dinner next weekend. I hope that's okay with you."

Your body screams "Beware!" Your vision blurs. Your stomach forms a tight knot, and you feel your face flush. Your "old brain" sounds an alarm: "Danger! Fight! Attack!" Your Saboteur moves onstage inside you and starts to speak. Inside your head you hear, "This is preposterous. Does he think I'm stupid or what! She's the last person I want to see—much less have over for dinner. I'd have to go on a diet—for a month at least. I know I've put on a few pounds. She's probably as skinny and good-looking as she was back then. He's probably wishing he'd stayed with her instead of marrying me."

But you are working diligently to tame your Saboteur, because you and your partner are committed to enhancing your relationship through practicing the principles of conscious loving. So—you take a deep breath and say to yourself, "I know that is my Saboteur speaking."

AWARENESS OF THE SABOTEUR IS THE FIRST STEP IN TAMING IT.

While this sounds simple, it is a giant leap in self-awareness. Moment by moment—as in our imagined example—you are called to recognize the Saboteur when it speaks silently to you and when it emerges in your interactions with others.

To become more aware of how the Saboteur works, practice noticing the Saboteur in others. It is easier to see how it operates when it is "out there" in someone else rather than "in here" in you. *Don't* point it out to them. Simply appreciate *silently* your enhanced awareness. By learning to recognize the Saboteur in others, especially in your mate, you also are opening your eyes to how it manifests in you.

As you observe others, you notice how they change when they are frightened and upset. Tones of voice alter, faces become tense. They may pull back physically as they put up a protective wall. Sometimes you hear words of attack, blame, and criticism. Other times you find yourself being conned and charmed into believing what they want you to think. You see people being pushy, anxious, or harshly judging of themselves and of others. They may try to control what they can't or attempt to placate and rescue others who would be better off solving their own problems.

Pay attention to how you respond to the Saboteur in them. You feel your heart speed up, your stomach tighten, and your lungs constrict as you hold your breath waiting for what will happen next. You notice your "old-brain," self-protective strategies go on red alert. When you feel these physiological changes, access your wise inner parent to soothe and comfort you.

Your wise inner parent reminds you that this is simply a frightened person struggling to cope with terror. Imagine that he is a small child. In your mind's eye, you shrink him into the body of a two-year-old having a tantrum or trying to charm his way out of trouble. Do your best to look for the humor in what is happening.

As you develop this ability to observe the Saboteur in others and to soothe yourself when you see it, you recognize it more readily in yourself. When you notice it emerging, you cultivate your capacity to separate yourself from it—to see it, name it, and not identify with it. This is a giant challenge, because your Saboteur does not want to be recognized. It does its best to distract you from learning to identify it. Even as you read these words, it may try to put you to sleep or tell you that none of this applies to you. It wants to keep its presence and activity in your life out of sight and out of mind. Otherwise it will lose its hold over you.

It is vital that you refrain from judging or criticizing yourself (or others) for having a Saboteur. Having a shadow guardian simply goes with being human. It is not bad. It just "is"—a part of you that is under the spell of fears experienced early in life and reinforced later. Though it pretends to protect you from harm, its behavior actually damages you. Because it operates in fear and illusion, it tries to drive others away from you, forgetting that hurting them also hurts you. It is quick to interpret your experiences in the most negative way possible and then convince you of the truth of its predictions.

Recognizing and naming your Saboteur takes only a few seconds of awareness, for example, in the scenario above, the seconds between when your partner tells you about meeting his old girlfriend, Ann, and when you respond. Before you speak, take a few deep breaths and center yourself in the spirit of love.

BREATHING DEEPLY AND CENTERING YOURSELF IN LOVE IS THE SECOND VITAL STEP IN TAMING YOUR SABOTEUR AND STOPPING BOUNDARY VIOLATIONS.

This becomes a natural response to stressful situations if you consistently practice centering and entering a relaxed state of mind during quiet times of spiritual reflection. You can visualize yourself filled with light and surrounded by a powerful shield of love that protects you from fear and negativity. This shield of love is like a suit of invisible armor. It deflects negative energy and hurtful words that are directed at you.

Then summon your wise inner parent to congratulate and comfort you. Hear it respond quickly, saying "That's great. You are aware! You've recognized the voice of fear. You don't have to let it control you. You can handle this. I'm here to help. Just keep breathing."

Each time—during your daily activities—you feel yourself slipping into the Saboteur's clutches, take a moment to recenter yourself. When you do so, you shift out of the energy of fear and back into the energy of love.

As you continue to breathe deeply, you feel yourself becoming calmer. You are listening to your partner's words but you are also hearing your wise inner parent reminding you in a firm, loving voice, "You can say 'no' to all this agitation. Simply thank your Saboteur for sharing and move on. You don't need to give it any more attention than that. Think of a loving image of you and your partner, and keep that picture strong in your mind while you gather more information. You don't know enough yet to respond appropriately. Remember! You know how to mirror. Just mirror what he is telling you and ask him to tell you more!"

THE THIRD STEP IN TAMING YOUR SABOTEUR IS TAKING A FIRM POSITION WITH THIS FEARFUL PART OF YOU WHEN IT STRIKES.

You can say "no" to it by simply commenting, "Thank you for sharing."[3] Then move on. As you do so, breathe deeply and call to mind your loving image of yourself and your mate. Focus on this image and see it absorbing a mental picture of your Saboteur in action. Then search within yourself for the deeper issues that set off your Saboteur's urge to react in a boundary-violating fashion (see the fourth step, starting on page 167).

You can use this same strategy when your partner's Saboteur manifests itself. You know that its presence tempts your Saboteur to behave destructively, too. Unless you curb the temptation to react, the two of you will engage in a wounding dance that leads nowhere and only serves to hurt you both. Instead, remind yourself that you are a mature adult who can easily curb an impulsive Saboteur. You might repeat a mantra like, "I am calm and centered. Nothing can shake my inner peace." One moment at a time, do your best not to be drawn into battle with your mate.

Meanwhile, ask yourself what your partner needs from you, remembering that beneath his outer behavior a frightened, wounded child is hiding. What might soothe this child? Does he need your presence? Is a hug appropriate? Would he prefer that you give him plenty of space? Remind yourself that you are making a vital contribution to the relationship by staying centered in love and containing your temptation to react.

As best you can, stretch yourself into giving what your heart tells you your partner needs, remembering that the love you express now strengthens the relationship. Know that your generosity will come back to you in many ways as you and your partner work together to grow and heal. And this episode will pass more quickly because you are interrupting sabotaging, boundary-violating behavior patterns. You might decide to invite your partner to participate in the Safe Dialogue process after the two of you take a break and have time to regain your composure.

After the few seconds it takes to recognize your Saboteur in action and center and soothe yourself, you return to the conversation with your mate. Taking a deep breath to support you, mirror what he tells you. As you do so, you are aware of feeling calmer. Yet you also know you are angry—about the old girlfriend and about his issuing a dinner invitation without checking with you first.

In the background of your mind—even as you do your best to listen and hear your mate accurately—your Saboteur is urging you to fight, to respond with anger. It is also busy making jealous interpretations of his actions, telling you this could be the beginning of an affair—that he has been pining for Ann for years and now sees his chance to rekindle an old flame, that you're not as young and beautiful as you were when you met him and swept him off his feet, that you had better stop this before it gets started. "Fight for your marriage," the Saboteur urges. "Now! Before it's too late!"

You hold your ground, continuing to stand firm with your "no" to your Saboteur's suggestion that you escalate this encounter into a full-scale battle.

No sooner have you opted to contain your anger than you hear an-other Saboteur proposition—"Just hang up on him! Cut him off—run away. You are too upset to talk."

Again you refuse to be manipulated. "Thank you for sharing. And no. I will continue to do my best to deal with this in a reasonable, decent way," you respond internally.

"Okay," counters the Saboteur. "Then just be quiet. Let him guess how you feel about this. Give him the old three-day pout treatment. He deserves it—the lousy, inconsiderate. . . ."

"Thank you for sharing and NO. I'm in charge here, and I choose not to behave like an angry two-year-old."

Continuing to center yourself, you mirror your partner and respond to him. "You know, it really makes sense to me that you are excited to run into Ann after all these years and that you want to have her and her husband over for dinner. I can understand that, but I also realize that this has set off lots of feelings in me—lots of reactivity. I want to take time to explore what this is all about for me. Then I'd like to have a Safe Dialogue with you about it tonight when I am more clear about why this is hard for me."

Your partner agrees to your request for time to prepare for an evening dialogue. Breathing a sign of relief, you say good-bye and decide to take a walk to give yourself an opportunity to process what just happened.

THE FOURTH STEP IN TAMING YOUR INTERNAL SABOTEUR INVOLVES LOOKING FOR THE DEEPER ISSUES HIDDEN BENEATH ITS AROUSAL.

Our Saboteur takes over, to guard our deep inner territory, when our boundaries are violated (or we think they are), and we are angry about being invaded. In the example we are imagining, your boundaries are vi-olated by your partner inviting guests to dinner without consulting you. You feel invaded and angry. Your Saboteur urges you to fight and does its best to agitate you with the most negative interpretations possible of what your partner tells you.

This is typical Saboteur strategy. It interprets a situation negatively so that we will feel justified in blaming, attacking, cutting off from, or otherwise discounting the other person. It helps us pretend that others are responsible for our problems—or it tells us that we are worthless, hopeless, and doomed to failure and defeat. It does all this to protect us from feelings emotions it believes we ought not to feel.

The Saboteur also does its best to take center stage when we experience strong positive feelings of intimacy, joy, excitement, sexual bliss, and success. Your partner in the imagined example above is excited about running into an old flame. In his excitement his Saboteur takes over and issues a dinner invitation—despite his knowing that you and he don't make definite plans without consulting each other first. He violates your boundaries and unconsciously sets up a situation designed to short-circuit his pleasure and bring him back to "reality" with a resounding thud.

This, too, is typical Saboteur strategy. It moves in to interrupt and cut off our joy. Until we learn to tolerate, face, and accept all our feelings, especially our anger and grief, we may unintentionally turn away from exciting, happy feelings too—and allow the Saboteur to usurp our triumphs. Its intrusions undermine what is most precious and important to us.

Taming the Saboteur demands that we embrace the parts of us that we would like to hide and honor the feelings we reject. In the example, you take time out to explore the deeper issues that motivate your Saboteur attack. To do so, use four questions to determine if your Saboteur is at work:

1. Have my boundaries been violated? If so, how and by whom?

2. Am I repressing grief, anger, sadness, hurt, or disappointment about the present, old wounds from the past, or anxieties about the future?

3. Am I choosing to interpret the actions of others as boundary violations in order to justify allowing my Saboteur to attack them or control me?

4. Have I recently experienced great joy and success—stronger feelings than I usually allow?

If the answer to any of these questions is yes, explore what you discover, paying particular attention to your feelings and the underlying issues you may find. Give them full acceptance and expression. Writing in your journal as well as dialoguing with your partner or a trusted mentor are great ways to use Saboteur attacks as optimal opportunities for learning and growing.

THE FIFTH STEP IS ADDRESSING THE DEEPER ISSUES.

After you hang up the phone, your partner decides to reflect on his behavior, now that he realizes you are upset. By using the four questions, he becomes aware of how his excitement at running into Ann triggered impulsive, sabotaging behavior that violated your boundaries by committing to social plans without consulting you. He decides that he will begin the evening dialogue by taking responsibility for his mistake.

He also reflects on what he knows about you and what you might be needing from him in this situation. It occurs to him that your parents were divorced when you were eleven and your father married a woman with whom he was having an affair. With a start, he realizes that your stepmother happened to be an old friend your dad reencountered at a professional convention three years before your parents' divorce. Suddenly it is clear to him that you need reassuring that he has no interest in rekindling a romance with Ann. If anything, seeing her has heightened his appreciation of you. In fact, on his way back to his office, he found himself thinking how wise he had been not to marry her—though it was interesting and exciting to see her again, and he was curious about her husband. He decides to tell you how much he values you and how no one—certainly not Ann—could tempt him to betray you and the commitment the two of you share.

Meanwhile, on your walk, you acknowledge that you are angry about his boundary-violating dinner invitation but realize that this is a relatively minor issue given the intensity of your fear. When you ask yourself question number two, about old grief, you don't get an immediate internal response, though you feel distinctly uneasy. Realizing that this anxious feeling is a signal that there is some deeper issue you need to explore, you find a park bench where you can sit quietly.

Closing your eyes and requesting guidance from your higher source, you tune in to your uneasiness and tell the child within that you are listening if she has anything to tell you. Almost immediately the image of your father and mother telling you they are getting a divorce pops into your mind. With a sharp intake of breath, you see the parallel. Of course you are frightened by hearing that your partner has reencountered an old flame. This touches your deepest wound, the one caused by the break-up of your parents.

After shedding a few quiet tears, you return home—feeling some relief but also knowing you have more grieving to do. When you arrive, you make a cup of tea, put on relaxing music, and settle into your favorite meditating place with your journal. You write a letter to your father, expressing this delayed grief about your parents' divorce. Though you've addressed the issue many times before, this phone call from your mate brought it into sharp and immediate focus. Never before have you felt directly threatened by circumstances at all similar to the ones that precipitated your father's affair, and, ultimately, the divorce. You find that you have a lot to say and things to express that have eluded you for years. In your letter, you speak of your anger, your sadness, your fears and regrets. You rage and shed tears and feel enormous relief. By the time you finish, you know you are ready for your evening dialogue. You'll tell your partner what you've discovered and ask him to read your journal letter aloud so he can understand and validate your feelings.

In our example, both you and your partner look for and address the deeper issues beneath the tension that emerged in the telephone conversation. You use the four questions to look for boundary violations, your true feelings, old grief, fearful interpretations, and emotional overstimulation. And you take action. You do important journal work in preparation for the planned evening dialogue. Your mate reflects on his part in what is happening between you. He also looks for ways to understand what is upsetting you.

He decides to open the dialogue by taking responsibility for violating your boundaries. Because he also recognizes how this situation touches an old wound in you, he plans to acknowledge that parallel and reassure you about his intentions. In doing so he intends to make clear that he is who he is and not who your father was.

THE SIXTH STEP IS USING SAFE DIALOGUE TO TELL YOUR PARTNER WHAT YOU DISCOVERED ABOUT YOURSELF BY FACING THE DEEPER ISSUES YOUR SABOTEUR TRIED TO HIDE.

That evening you and your partner agree to begin your dialogue after dinner. Together you put on a pot of tea to enjoy as you talk. Then you select music and set out the dialogue candles and matches. Once you complete your centering preparation rituals, you feel relaxed, safe, and ready to open your hearts and minds to what you each have to say.

As your dialogue unfolds, you are relieved and delighted by your partner's sensitivity to your feelings and needs. Mirroring his words impresses them on your heart. You really get that not only does he take responsibility for violating your boundaries by committing to social plans without consulting you, but also he cares enough about you to think through why you might be threatened by the appearance of his old girlfriend. You are moved to tears when he assures you that he has no interest in rekindling an old flame and, in fact, feels grateful that he was able to realize—through encountering her—just how much he values you.

Seeing you cry, he moves next to you on the sofa and holds you while you tell him about your personal discoveries. He mirrors what you say. He too is relieved to know that you recognize the pain from your past that has emerged in the present context of your relationship. When you ask him to, he reads aloud the letter you wrote your father. This is particularly helpful to you. Hearing the words you addressed to your dad now coming from your partner underscores the distinction between these two important men in your life. You see and fully experience that your partner is not your dad and that he has no intention of behaving as your father did.

After reading the letter aloud, your partner is quiet for a few minutes while you relax in his arms. When he speaks, what he says has a profound impact on you.

"You know, I think it would be important for you to write a letter to your mother, too," he says. "She also had a part in the pain of your parents' divorce. I was just thinking about how you were honest about your feelings and knew we needed to talk about them. I'm also aware that you could have just freaked out on the phone and gotten really angry with me, or you could have cut yourself off and tried to act as if nothing was wrong. But you didn't do that, and I really respect the way you handled this. Perhaps if your mother had done what you did—or at least insisted that she and your dad face what was happening in their marriage—things might have turned out differently. I'm sure glad you are you and not your mom."

Your partner's comment makes you realize something important. You've focused so much anger on your dad over the years. Now you realize you are ready to look at your mother's part in the demise of your parents' marriage. You feel angry that she didn't assert herself more effectively. At the same time you have compassion for her, knowing that in her day women had fewer choices than your own generation does. You also feel empowered, recognizing that you have lots of control over what happens in your own marriage. You will not allow yourself to be a passive victim. It strengthens your resolve to hear your husband say he respects you for the honesty and integrity of your response.

After a bit more talking, you and your partner decide to celebrate your relationship victory by sharing a bubble bath. You thank each other for what each of you contributed to your successful handling of what could have been an explosive conflict but instead became a memorable and transformative experience. Silently, each of you also thanks your Saboteur, embracing it as an invaluable teacher.

EMBRACING YOUR SABOTEUR IS THE FINAL STEP IN TAMING IT.

Embracing it as a teacher transforms its role in your life. Your agenda is not to get rid of your Saboteur. It—like all the other parts of you—

cannot be erased. But it must be acknowledged, accepted, and made a useful partner, instead of remaining an unconscious orchestrator of self-deception, self-destruction, and self-sabotage.

Your Saboteur alerts you to important issues you need to address but are afraid to face. It sounds an inner alarm—an alarm you can allow to wake you up to opportunities for personal growth and healing. By recognizing the Saboteur's signals, you can take charge of those growth opportunities, using them to enhance your life and your relationship. You tame your Saboteur when you name it, set limits for it, and then deal with the issues it challenges you to face.

RECAP ~ *Seven Steps to Taming Your Saboteur*

1. With nonjudgmental awareness, notice and name your Saboteur when it becomes active.

2. Center yourself in love and access your wise inner parent by congratulating yourself for recognizing your Saboteur's presence.

3. Thank your Saboteur for for the alert, but say a firm "no" to its comments and suggestions.

4. Look for the deeper issues your Saboteur tries to hide.

5. Take time out to actively address these issues.

6. Use the Safe Dialogue process to share with your partner what you discover about yourself.

7. Embrace your Saboteur as a teacher, thanking it for alerting you to opportunities for learning and growth.

Uncovering Core Fears

Uncovering the deep fears and insecurities the Saboteur hides is easy if you know where to look. Over the years I have found that asking myself the questions listed below is a surefire way to get to the core fears my Saboteur seeks to mask.

Am I afraid of God/Goddess/All That Is?

Am I afraid of being abandoned?

Am I afraid of rejection?

Am I afraid of anger?

Am I afraid of grieving?

Am I afraid of feeling successful?

Am I afraid of feeling close to my partner?

Am I afraid of acknowledging my mistakes and imperfections?

Am I afraid of feeling vulnerable?

Am I afraid of being powerful and responsible?

Am I afraid of committing and keeping my word?

Am I afraid of reliving pain from the past?

If I answered "yes" to any of these questions, how did I develop these fears?

Framing Life in Love Rather Than Fear

Our connection to the divine and to a wise inner parent provides powerful counterparts to the voice of our Saboteur. Our challenge is to deepen our spiritual life and create a strong, nurturing inner voice. As we do so, we learn to listen for inner guidance and to trust the wise counsel we receive.

The Saboteur views life from a perspective of fear and negativity. A wise inner parent is skilled at viewing life experiences from a loving perspective. Instead of allowing us to react impulsively to other people and violate their boundaries, it helps us become consistent in choosing creative ways to respond.

As my friend Marge Barlow, Ph.D., points out, the only difference between the words "creative" and "reactive" is the placement of one letter—*C*. That clever observation reminds me of the moment-by-moment choice I make: where I put that *C* in my interactions with others. For me, *C* stands for "conscious" and "creative" alternatives to being "reactive" and blind to what I do. I find the following checklist helpful in making discerning choices.

Checklist of Loving vs. Fearful Choices

AM I BEING...	OR...
Awake, conscious, aware?	Asleep, unconscious, unaware?
Responsive?	Reactive?
Creative?	Destructive?
Responsible?	Blaming/projecting?
Grateful?	Critical?
Honest?	Dishonestly nice or mean?
Respectful and empowering?	Invasive of personal boundaries?
Attentive, open, available, listening?	Tuned-out, absent, silent?
Validating?	Discounting?
Letting go, forgiving, accepting?	Controlling, clinging, judging?

Remember, however, that sometimes a fearful reaction to a stranger or even to a loved one is valid. As Rosie (in Chapter 7) discovered, her initial, visceral reaction to Slick of bodily fear was right on. In retrospect she knew she would have been wise to refuse his advances.

The challenge is to recognize when fear is a legitimate signal to beware and when it is the voice of the Saboteur. Legitimate fear comes from love and our wise parent who protects us from immediate or potential danger. Saboteur-generated fears are not based on reality. They are lies designed to keep our lost, rejected selves hidden. Sometimes our Saboteur launches a fearful, conning attack on us. Sometimes it attacks others to keep us from facing our part in what takes place in our relationships with them.

Stopping Boundary Violations Is About Consciousness, Not Control

Stopping boundary violations is about consciousness and choice, not punishment, right and wrong, or control. As an enlightened relationship partner, you realize that you must tame your own fearful Saboteur. But you are not under the illusion that you can control or change your mate's fearful behavior.

You know that she makes her choices just as you do. You cannot coerce, intimidate, plead, or passively wait for your partner to fit your picture of how she ought to be. She is who she is, and your challenge is to accept her as she is—even if that means choosing to leave the relationship because you are unwilling to live in the way she chooses.

Though you cannot change her, you can express yourself honestly, reveal yourself openly, listen carefully, seek to understand her and to be understood, and firmly maintain your own integrity, allowing her to do the same. You can attend to your own growth challenges conscientiously, resisting the temptation to project your blind spots onto her.

Knowing you are capable of controlling your Saboteur gives you the confidence you need to deal with your partner's. Instead of consciously or unconsciously provoking him by nervously overreacting to what he does, your capacity to stay centered and in charge of yourself will help dampen sparks of angry intruding, withdrawing, or freezing behaviors from him that otherwise could easily become raging flames.

The goal here is not to blame the one who appears to be the "victim" of his mate's violation of his boundaries. Rather it is to notice that partners who get into abusive tangles both share responsibility for how their interactions flare out of control. Both can change their role in what transpires between them by learning to tame their Saboteurs.

When you see your partner's Saboteur coming onstage to interact with you, acknowledge how you feel without commenting on what you notice in him. Say something like, "As I listen to you my heart is racing and my shoulders are getting tight. I'm frightened. And I'm really angry and hurt by your words. I also am sad, because I was looking forward to being with you and enjoying a quiet dinner tonight. And I really want you to mirror my feelings before I say anything else."

If your partner is willing and able to shift into conscious relating by mirroring your words, validating your experience, and expressing empathy for you, the two of you may be able to jointly reroute what might otherwise have become an unpleasant encounter. After being mirrored, you might respond by saying, "I trust we will be able to enjoy being together tonight. It really helps to know you are willing to hear and validate my experience. That keeps me from wanting to escalate this into more hurt and pain. I am willing to listen and mirror for you too if you need to talk."

If your mate does not choose to honor your request for mirroring and instead continues to speak in a disrespectful, boundary-violating manner, you might simply hold up your hand to signal "Stop!" and tell him firmly that you are unavailable for judgment, criticism, or blame.

If physical boundary violations should occur or appear likely, they demand definitive action, not passive acquiescence or aggressive counterattack. Clarity, firmness, and keeping fear in check are essential. Otherwise the stakes may escalate like a raging fire and rapidly burn out of control. Say with absolute conviction something like, "I will not tolerate being abused. Stop now and do not attempt to harm me physically!" Then with as much calm and dignity as possible, leave the scene and give your partner time to regain control. Learn to resist any temptation to attack your partner physically or to consciously or unconsciously provoke your partner into attacking you. If physical boundary violations are a problem—or a threat—in your relationship, seriously consider enrolling in a Compassion Workshop or in anger-management classes, as discussed in Chapter 5. In such cases, separation may be necessary until you can both respond to your intense feelings in mature, responsible, safe ways.

If your mate's behavior becomes intolerably destructive, take responsibility for letting go and leaving your relationship rather than allowing yourself to go down with the ship. Short of such an imperative, do what only you can do to heal yourself and be an agent of acceptance and healing for your partner. Practice the Boundary-Healing Process presented in Chapter 9. And remember: help is always available, if you remember to ask for divine assistance—by whatever name you call it and by whatever means you access it. Remain open to the teachers who appear in your life at the times when you need them. Open your heart to receive, and you will find the strength, wisdom, and guidance you need to grow through all your relationship challenges.

Remind yourself frequently that when criticism and blame stop, growth starts. The Saboteur is like a fearsome—and fearful—ogre who stands guard at the gateway to your inner being. As you tame this wounded monster, you gain entry into that rich domain which is your essence. In your deep inner space you find your lost and neglected parts; your old wounds and buried grief emerge for healing and release; your feelings await your embrace; and your immense creativity stands ready to be unleashed. Diving into this rich territory with compassion for yourself and curiosity about what makes you tick is vital to loving your partner without losing your self.

EXERCISES

1. Practice identifying the Saboteur in the various masks it wears as you interact with other people. If you like television soap operas, have fun identifying Saboteur masks as they appear in your favorite screen characters.

2. Make your intention to become aware of your Saboteur and the favorite masks it chooses. When you notice it becoming active within you, call on your spiritual resources and congratulate yourself on your expanded consciousness. By patting yourself on the back you access your wise inner parent. Realize that your Saboteur may want to judge you for having a Saboteur! If so, simply thank it for sharing and give yourself another acknowledgment for recognizing its persistence and cleverness in trying to keep you in its grip.

3. Whenever you notice your Saboteur in action, take time out to look for the feelings and deeper issues it is trying to hide. Address those issues, acknowledge your feelings, and continue to affirm yourself for your wisdom and growth.

4. In your journal write about your most intense fears about your partner and your relationship. Where are those same frightening potentials in you? What did you learn about these scary possibilities when you were a child? Did you fear similar behaviors from your parents? What feelings were you not allowed to express when you were a child? What parts of you were you forbidden to express?

Consider how you would cope should any of the things you fear actually happen. Ask your wise inner parent to remind you of your strengths and resources for handling life, as you also practice not allowing your Saboteur to create catastrophes in your mind.

5. How are you prone to allowing your partner's Saboteur to manipulate you? Write about some of his or her Saboteur's most effective and commonly used strategies for getting you to do what it wants—whether or not you think it is a good idea. Did your parents use similar strategies with you when you were a child? Did you manipulate them in ways similar to the ways you allow your partner's Saboteur to manipulate you? Do you allow your Saboteur to also manipulate you in these ways?

6. Using heavy construction paper and all sorts of creative art supplies, make a mask that symbolizes your mental image of your Saboteur.

7. Give your Saboteur a name that amuses and pleases you—a name that helps you remember that it is not as powerful as it seems.

8. Using your art supplies, make a second mask that represents your mental image of your wise inner parent.

9. Give your wise inner parent a name that feels powerful, loving, and good to you. You might choose to use the name of a person you admire whose strength and presence would be enough to silence your Saboteur.

10. Pick an activity you have always feared. Take lessons and learn to do what you think you can't. Teach yourself to grow beyond outmoded barriers.

11. In your mind review an upsetting interaction with your mate. What was your "old brain"–dictated reaction? How did your Saboteur urge you to follow it? What was your partner's reaction to the choices you made? What more creative responses can your wise inner parent see? How would your wise inner parent interpret this situation in a loving way? How could you turn it into a growth experience instead of a wounding fight? Generate at least six possible loving options—whether or not you like all of them. Develop the habit of looking for at least six possible choices in any situation in which you find yourself feeling frightened and/or trapped.

12. Using the Safe Dialogue process, talk with your partner about nonverbal signals that you both can use to indicate that you are aware of boundary violations occurring between you. For example, you might hold up one hand to signal "Stop." Or you could put a hand over your mouth to indicate that you are aware you just made a boundary-violating statement. Using nonverbal signals can be much less threatening than words when you sense that you may be headed into a potentially hurtful encounter.

13. Assign a different-colored pen to each of the parts of yourself that you reject and tend to project onto your partner. Write a note to them, one at a time, inviting each of these disowned

selves to write a letter of response to you, sharing with you what you need to know about yourself and your history. Assure each one that you will honor what you are told and believe what you discover.

14. In your mind's eye, envision embracing each of your disowned selves with love and compassion for what this part of you needs and feels.

CHAPTER 9

The Boundary-Healing Process

Learning to respect and keep healthy boundaries takes time, consistent effort, and patience—with yourself and with your partner. Neither of you can expect the other to be perfect or to change habitual patterns of relating overnight.

Living together is bound to result in occasionally crossing each other's boundary lines and triggering old boundary wounds that await healing. The times when you unconsciously cross each other's boundaries or the boundary of commitment that defines your relationship are calls to growth for both of you. Instead of wringing your hands in despair or rejecting each other as impossibly difficult, examine the roots of your hurtful behavior with compassion in your hearts.

On these occasions, you and your partner need a safe way to digest what transpires between you. The Boundary-Healing Process presented in this chapter provides a structure to help you do this. It assists you in keeping healthy boundaries, healing your hurts, feeling empathy, and deepening your commitment as you work through difficult times. It can be used again and again to assist the two of you in meeting the growth challenges inherent in such difficulties.

The payoffs for engaging in this process are well worth the effort required. While the steps may seem simple, they take you deep within yourself to parts of you that cry out for healing. The Saboteurs in you and in your partner may react in fear by telling you that this work is too difficult and/or unnecessary. When you notice your Saboteur's voice, remind yourself that it is simply your internal gatekeeper attempting to keep you away from the sources of your pain. Thank this part of you for its efforts to protect you, and say "no" to its suggestion that you back away from healing your buried hurts.

The Boundary-Healing Process is designed to help you interrupt hurtful interactions before they escalate into potentially destructive or even abusive episodes. It is a comprehensive, eight-step structure that summarizes what this book teaches; it can be used in any of the situations we have discussed in previous chapters. It is encapsulated in the following words:

WAIT • BE SILENT • WRITE • SHARE

GO DEEPER • FORGIVE • HEAL • COMMIT

Don't worry about memorizing all the steps involved. If you wish, just remember the first four steps—Wait, Be Silent, Write, and Share—by bringing to mind "WBWS." Pretend these are the call letters of a radio station dedicated to healing relationships. Then, as you and your partner share, refer to the chart at the end of this chapter to prompt you through the next four steps. Be aware of when and how your Saboteurs emerge to block your work.

When you conclude any part of this process, celebrate your victory together. Mark your progress with hugs, special treats, and mutual congratulations. It's important to make healing experiences enjoyable. Laugh at your mistakes, honor your successes, and express confidence in your relationship. Acknowledge the wonderful ways you empower each other through the tough times you inevitably encounter.

Step One — WAIT

WITNESS your feelings and your role in what happens between you and your mate.

ALLOW yourself to feel compassion for both yourself and your partner.

INTERRUPT your interaction with your mate.

TAKE time out.

The first step in the Boundary-Healing Process is: wait before you react to boundary-violating behavior by your mate. Wait also before you continue a boundary-violating behavior yourself.

Your challenge is to be a constant, conscious witness to your feelings and your role in what happens between you and your partner—and to do this without judging either of you. When you witness boundary-violating behavior, wait before you react or continue hurtful words or actions of your own. Then allow yourself to feel compassion for both of you, realizing that the Saboteur in your partner—and perhaps in you too—is active. You are on the verge of reenacting painful patterns of relating that you learned early in life. Let the compassion you feel be like cool water poured over hot, burning skin. Feel it soothing your reactivity and helping you calm down.

Next, interrupt your interaction by saying something like, "I see myself on the verge of reenacting painful scenes from the past. I am calling for a time-out so I can regroup. I don't want either of us to be hurt here. I will be glad to dialogue with you about this when you're ready, and when I've had a chance to cool off." Then take time out to recenter yourself and reflect on what you've become aware of. Do this by going to a quiet place to sit, going outside, taking a walk, or doing something soothing like taking a bath or shower.

Step Two — BE SILENT

BREATHE deeply. Exhale completely, then let your lungs refill naturally and easily.

ENTER your quiet place inside.

SEE with loving eyes.

INVITE yourself to notice your feelings and fears.

LISTEN to what you are telling yourself: your thoughts and interpretations.

EXPERIENCE your power to interpret this situation in a loving, compassionate way.

NOW open yourself to guidance from your spiritual source in reframing what has happened.

THINK in positive, hopeful, creative ways about yourself and your partner.

This step in the Boundary-Healing Process gives you time to center yourself and reflect calmly on what has just happened or was about to happen with your partner. It is important that you allow yourself a leisurely, relaxed break period to become quiet, attuned to your breathing, and connected with your spiritual source. You need at least twenty to thirty minutes to disengage from the tension.

As you relax, be aware of opening your inner eyes so you can view yourself and your partner with compassion. Without judging yourself, notice what you feel and what you fear about the situation. Remind yourself that your feelings are okay. They make sense and are understandable, and you know they don't control you. You can honor your emotions without allowing your Saboteur to bury them and take charge of your behavior.

Then tune in to your thoughts. Pay attention to what you are telling yourself about what has happened. What you choose to think about yourself, your partner, and this situation determines how you feel. If you indulge your Saboteur in fearful, negative thoughts, your feelings will also be frightening and destructive. If you interrupt your Saboteur's fearful thinking by substituting positive thoughts about yourself and your partner, your feelings will be harmonious and creative too.

Remind yourself that you have the power to interpret this situation in a compassionate way. To help you access that power, ask your spiritual source to guide you in reframing what has happened. Listen with an open heart, and allow love to direct your thinking. Bring a loving image of yourself and your partner into your mind. See that image absorbing your anger, fear, and hurt. With conscious intention, think in positive, hopeful, creative ways about yourself, your partner, and your joyous connection. You may wish to use the affirmations listed at the end of Chapter 11 to aid you in this reframing process.

Step Three — WRITE

WHAT was the boundary violation you created or experienced?

REVIEW your responsibility in what happened.

INVITE memories of similar situations from your past to emerge.

THINK about your needs and feelings as a child/adolescent/younger adult.

EXPRESS in writing what you feel, need, and desire right now.

The third step in the Boundary-Healing Process is to write about what you experienced with you partner and what you are discovering during your time-out for personal reflection. Begin your journaling by identifying the boundary violation you created or experienced. You may want to refer to Chapter 5 if you need help doing this.

Review your responsibility in what happened. If you violated your spouse's boundaries, ask yourself what triggered your behavior. If your partner made the first move, notice your reaction. Did you want to fight, flee, or freeze? When and how did you tune in to your "old-brain" reaction and consciously decide to initiate a Boundary-Healing Process?

When you have a clear picture of your part in the exchange, invite memories of similar situations from your past to emerge. Don't try to force yourself to remember. Just be open and allow whatever is relevant to pop spontaneously into your mind. Your unconscious mind knows how your history relates to this present experience. It will tell you—if you are willing to listen and let go of trying to control the process.

Once a memory or memories emerge, record them in your journal. Paint a vivid verbal picture. By making a record of the memory, you honor it and release it. Because it now lives in black and white on the pages of your journal, it no longer has to live and fester inside you.

As you write, think about the needs and feelings you experienced when this occurred during your childhood, adolescence, or earlier adulthood. Express your feelings and needs as part of the account you are creating. Then write about what you feel, need, and desire right now, from your nurturing inner parent as well as from your partner—if he or she is willing and able to give it.

Step Four — SHARE

S̲PEAK with your partner about what you've discovered.

H̲ONOR yourself by taking responsibility for your part in what happened between you.

A̲CKNOWLEDGE your feelings, needs, and desires now.

R̲EQUEST an appointment to go deeper (or stop your sharing now, if you wish).

E̲XPRESS your gratitude to your partner for listening and being available to you.

This part of the Boundary-Healing Process involves reconnecting with your partner. It may take place immediately after your time-out period or at a later time that is convenient for you both. Often it is a good idea to allow additional space and time for recentering and release before you get together to talk about what happened. Returning to your normal round of activities and doing things you enjoy helps you regain your equilibrium as you continue to soothe and nurture yourself back to a normal, well-functioning state.

When you and your partner come together, use the Safe Dialogue structure as you share. Be sure to honor yourself by taking responsibility for your part in what happened between you. Use "I" language, and do your very best to avoid making statements that are blaming and critical of your mate. It is your partner's responsibility to uncover and share his or her part in this experience.

Acknowledge your feelings about what happened, as well as your present needs and desires, so your partner can mirror and validate them. Once your mate has heard all you have to say and has expressed empathy for you, you may end your part in the sharing by inviting her to talk about her reflections. Or you may ask if she is willing to assist you in going deeper into the underlying issues that are relevant for you. If she agrees, continue with the steps that follow.

Your mate may want to share her reflections before you go more deeply into your issues. If so, invite her to reveal herself to you so you can mirror, validate, and express empathy for her. Afterward, you may decide to set a later date for doing steps five through eight—or one or both of you may continue the healing work now.

Step Five — GO DEEPER (Now or Later)

GO into your past, continuing to use the Safe Dialogue process.

OWN your memories about the past that you reenacted in the present.

DESCRIBE your experience as if you were speaking directly to each of your parents.

<u>**EXPERIENCE**</u> your partner mirroring for you as if he or she were each of your parents.

<u>**EXPRESS**</u> your anger, sadness, fears, regrets, and appreciations.

<u>**PUT FORTH**</u> your unmet needs.

<u>**EXPRESS**</u> what you've learned about yourself.

<u>**REALIZE**</u> that your partner is not either of your parents.

Going deeper is a necessary healing experience. It is also a "choice point" in the Boundary-Healing Process. You can do this work now or schedule a specific time to do it later if one or both of you wants more time for personal reflection before going into these family-of-origin issues.

Remember, your Saboteur will encourage you to put off or never do this deeper work. It wants to keep you from exploring your history and your feelings about it. So be aware of the temptation to avoid this part of the process by deciding to delay it. If you have good reasons for waiting for another time—or if you want to take this step with a couple's therapist present—be sure you commit to completing this step.

Going deeper allows you to digest and integrate your feelings about difficult episodes from the past that are at the root of what you and your partner reenacted (or might have reenacted) in the present. While continuing in the Safe Dialogue structure, ask your partner if he would be willing to be a stand-in for your mother, father, or any other important person who was a central player in the relevant episodes from your past. If the answer is yes, thank your mate in advance for assisting you in this way.

Begin by describing what happened when you were a child, an adolescent, or a younger adult. Speak to your partner as if he were one of your parents or another significant person from your history. Your mate listens and, when you pause after a couple of sentences, mirrors for you. When mirroring, he speaks as himself: "So if I'm understanding you correctly, you are telling me that you are very sad and hurt that your mother ignored your feelings when your family moved and you had to leave your best friend behind. Tell me more."

You continue speaking to your partner as if he were your mother until you have said all you have to say. He continues to mirror as himself, then invites you to continue. When you conclude your sharing, he summarizes, validates your experience, and expresses empathy for your feelings, again speaking as himself.

You also may ask your partner to listen to you as if he were other people who were involved in the incident you are remembering. Experience him mirroring for you as himself. Talk to one person at a time, so you directly address everyone who was involved in these incidents.

Be sure you express the full range of your emotions about your earlier experience. Begin with "I" statements about your anger. When you exhaust your angry feelings, describe what you feel sad about, what you fear, and what you regret about what happened. Finally, talk about what you appreciate about these experiences, looking for the lessons they taught you and the ways they've challenged you to grow—both then and now.

Your partner continues to mirror, validate, and empathize with your feelings as you move on to express your unmet needs. Talk about what you desired in the past and still need in the present from your mate, realizing that what you need may not be easy for him to give. If it were, he would already be doing these things. For him to respond to your needs may require his stretching into new behaviors. This will take time and genuine understanding from you. Profound changes do not usually happen overnight.

Conclude this part of the process by telling your partner what you have learned about yourself. Affirm that you know he is distinct from either of your parents. Thank him again for serving as a stand-in for people from your past as you do your personal healing work.

This dialogue experience will help both of you sort out the ways you sometimes mistake each other for one of your parents or other significant people from your past. By speaking to your partner as if he were one of those people, you get in touch with how you sometimes see him as if he *were* that person. When he mirrors for you as himself, both of you are aware that he is not that person but is rather your ally in healing—an individual who is quite distinct from anyone you have known and loved previously.

Step Six — FORGIVE

FREELY

OWN

RESPONSIBILITY for learning your life lessons.

GIVE gratitude.

INTERPRET the entire experience in a loving, compassionate way.

VALIDATE your feelings and the feelings of your partner.

EMBRACE your commitment to new behaviors that promote mutual healing and growth.

Forgiving, the next step in the Boundary-Healing Process, is an ongoing process, not a one-time event.

Forgiveness is a much misunderstood but essential dimension of healing. It does not happen just because you say the words, "I forgive you." Rather, it gradually evolves as you experience, express, and release the full range of your feelings about whatever experiences violated your boundaries and wounded you. It is a process you cannot rush no matter how much you wish to believe that you can simply and automatically forgive instantaneously, on demand.

Some experiences are fairly easily and quickly digested, integrated, and released. Others that involve consistent and continuous patterns of childhood abuse require a much longer time for processing and completely releasing. You may have to work your way through layers of grief, forgiving and releasing your parents many times before you experience lasting peace.

Forgiveness does not mean that you condone hurtful behavior. Rather, it means you have worked through your feelings about behavior that harmed you. You give yourself the gift of release from the pain you experienced. Forgiving others frees you—from the bonds and wounds of the past. It allows you to lay down your emotional burdens, having learned the lessons they provide.

In the Boundary-Healing Process you and your partner take important steps in the forgiveness process. You do this by freely taking responsibility for your behavior with each other. You also express gratitude to your partner and consciously choose to interpret the experience you shared in a loving, compassionate way. You validate each other's feelings and the ways you need to change your behavior. Then you commit to new behaviors that will promote your mutual growth in the context of your relationship.

Step Seven — HEAL

HELP your inner child by intentionally satisfying his or her unmet needs.

EXPRESS in general terms what you also need from your partner to help you heal.

ASK for specific behaviors that will help you heal.

LIST your requests on three index cards.

Having stated your intention to forgive what harmed you in the past, you and your partner now move back to the context of your present-day relationship. Acknowledging your responsibility to satisfy the unmet needs of your wounded inner child, you ask your mate's help in the healing process, stating in general terms what you would like her to do that would help satisfy your previously unmet needs. Then request specific behaviors that will help heal your hurts.

For example, you might make a general request that your partner be more sensitive to your need to be consulted about decisions that affect you both. Then you might make several specific requests. One might be, "I would like you to talk with me before committing to plans with other people that include me or involve time you and I might otherwise spend together." Another could be, "I would like you to talk with me before you make a significant purchase that affects our joint finances—perhaps before you decide to spend more than five hundred dollars." A third request might be, "I want you to talk with me before you consult with your parents about decisions that relate to our children."

Once you have articulated your requests, record them on three cards. One is for you, one is for your partner, and the third is to be posted in a place where both of you will see it frequently.

Remember, these are requests, not commands. Your mate may or may not decide to commit to them. And what he does commit to may be difficult for him to do. The new healing behaviors one partner desires usually represent significant growth challenges for the other.

If he doesn't give you what you ask for consistently, resist the temptation to think that his failure means he doesn't care about you. Instead, remind yourself that failing to honor your request may just mean that it is difficult for him to do. It is a growth step for him that may require time to master.

Do your best to resist the temptation to attack, blame, or criticize him when he disappoints you. That will only delay his growth. Simply tell him how you feel about his behavior by making "I" statements. For example, you might say, "I am disappointed that you made plans with your parents without talking with me first. Checking with me is one of my very important requests. However, I understand that this is not easy, and I know you are doing your best to keep your commitment to me."

Step Eight — COMMIT

COMMIT to giving what you are willing to give to meet your mate's requests.

OWN your responsibility to keep your commitment.

MENTION your new behaviors when you do what your mate requests.

MENTION your partner's new behaviors when he or she honors your requests.

INITIATE a follow-up dialogue with your partner to share the boundary-healing letters you've written to your parents.

TAKE further healing steps by sharing your boundary-healing letters with your parents (optional).

The final step in the Boundary-Healing Process is committing to following through with the growth challenges you have discovered. Each of you commits to what you are willing to do to meet your mate's stated requests. You also own your responsibility to keep your commitments. You may want to make a formal declaration and conduct a special ritual to mark your mutual pledges.

In the weeks to come, you do your best to notice when your partner does the new things promised. You point out when you do a new behavior she requested. You also mention that you notice her exhibiting the new behaviors you wanted from her.

To further strengthen your release of the past, both of you should write a boundary-healing letter to your parents (or anyone else who violated your boundaries during your earlier years). Following the same order of feelings that you used when you dialogued with your partner, write about your anger, sadness, fears, regrets, and appreciations. You may or may not decide to send these letters to the people to whom they are written. They are intended for your healing—not to shame or blame your parents or to try to make them change. If you do choose to share them, you may experience a new level of freedom, understanding, and eventually greater intimacy with your original family members.

Two to three weeks after your Boundary-Healing Process, initiate a follow-up dialogue with your partner. During this session you may swap the letters you have written and read them aloud to each other. This is very healing. Hearing your mate speaking your words mirrors them for you and validates their importance.

RECAP ~ *The Boundary-Healing Process at a Glance*

STEP ONE — WAIT

Witness your feelings and your role in what happens between you and your mate.

Allow yourself to feel compassion for both of you.

Interrupt your interaction with your mate.

Take time out.

STEP TWO — BE SILENT

Breathe deeply. Exhale completely, then let your lungs refill naturally and easily.

Enter your quiet place inside.

See with loving eyes.

Inside yourself, notice your feelings, both good and bad.

Listen to what you are telling yourself: your thoughts and interpretations.

Experience your power to interpret this situation in a loving, compassionate way.

Now open yourself to guidance from your spiritual source in reframing what has happened.

Think in positive, hopeful, creative ways about yourself and your partner.

STEP THREE — WRITE

What was the boundary violation you created or experienced?

Review your responsibility in what happened.

Invite memories of similar situations from your past to emerge.

Think about your needs and feelings when you were a child/adolescent/younger adult.

Express in writing what you feel, need, and desire right now.

STEP FOUR — SHARE

Speak with your partner about what you discover.

Honor yourself by taking responsibility for your part in what happened between you.

Acknowledge your feelings, needs, and desires now.

Request an appointment to go deeper (or stop your sharing now, if you wish).

Express your gratitude to your partner for listening and being available to you.

STEP FIVE — GO DEEPER (NOW OR LATER)

Go into your past, continuing to use the Safe Dialogue process.

Own your memories about the past that you reenacted in the present.

Describe your experience as if you were speaking directly to each of your parents.

Experience your partner mirroring for you as if he or she were each of your parents.

Express your anger, sadness, fears, regrets, and appreciations.

Put forth your unmet needs.

Express what you've learned about yourself.

Realize that your partner is not either of your parents.

STEP SIX — FORGIVE

Freely

Own

Responsibility for learning your life lessons.

Give gratitude.

Interpret this entire experience in a loving, compassionate way.

Validate your feelings and the feelings of your partner.

Embrace your commitment to new behaviors that promote mutual healing and growth.

STEP SEVEN — HEAL

Help your wounded inner child by intentionally satisfying his or her unmet needs.

Express in general terms what you also need from your partner to help you heal.

Ask for specific behaviors that will help you heal.

List your requests on three index cards.

STEP EIGHT — COMMIT

Commit to do what you are willing to do to meet your mate's requests.

Own your responsibility to keep your commitment.

Mention your new behaviors when you do what your mate requests.

Mention your partner's new behaviors when he or she honors your requests.

Initiate a follow-up dialogue with your partner to share the boundary-healing letters you've written to your parents.

Take further healing steps by sharing your boundary-healing letters with your parents (optional).

EXERCISES

1. Practice being a nonjudging witness of what happens between you and your partner. When you feel reactive, initiate the Boundary-Healing Process by calling for a time-out.

2. Think about a repetitive pattern of boundary-violating behavior that occurs between you and your mate. Using the **Be Silent** and **Write** parts of the Boundary-Healing Process, reflect on your part in this pattern and on its origins in your past history.

3. Request an appointment for Safe Dialogue with your partner to share what you discover. Go deeper, if you choose, into healing the pain that lies beneath your behavior.

4. Consciously notice the interpretations you make of what happens in your relationship. When you recognize fearful, negative interpretations that create painful feelings, practice making loving, hopeful, positive interpretations of the same experience. You may wish to use the affirmations listed at the end of Chapter 11 to aid you in this reframing process. Notice the change in your feelings in response to changing the interpretation you choose.

5. Notice when you and your partner do things you like. Comment on what you appreciate, and express gratitude frequently for the ways your mate contributes to your happiness.

6. Create mini-celebrations to enjoy together—a special meal, a favorite dessert, a walk together, playing a game you both enjoy. Be aware of punctuating your life with an abundance of small pleasures.

CHAPTER TEN

Embracing the Whole of You

In our early adulthood we are busy mastering the basics of life: becoming financially independent, finding a life partner, having and raising children, developing our careers, exploring the world through study and travel, creating a home, enjoying sports, music, and entertainment, healing our boundaries, and growing through the painful and joyous times we encounter. With the approach of our later years, we are called to deepen even further our perspective on life.

As we mature, we are less able to live well by focusing exclusively on the surface of things. Through the experiences of aging, we must turn our attention inward to the core of ourselves in order to face all that we fear about both living and dying. When people close to us suffer painful losses, life-threatening illnesses, and sudden death, we come to realize how vulnerable we are. When we are ill or we share a serious health threat with our partner, we face our own mortality with even greater force.

If we avoid the necessity and opportunities for personal growth during our younger years, we will not be able to cope with the difficult issues involved in late-life crises. If we do our homework throughout our earlier years, we have the strength we need to handle these later challenges with grace and peace of mind.

Building healthy boundaries in the context of our close personal relationships prepares us for our final life exams. Doing so takes us gradually through our darkest places to face all that we fear in the shadowy places within us. It teaches us to embrace the whole of ourselves—light and shadow, joy and sadness, health and sickness, successes and disappointments, intimacy and solitude, life and death.

As I conclude this book, I invite you to meet a person you will recognize—someone who is currently involved in life's course-work and thus prepared for whatever lies ahead. Next, I will offer a closing metaphor that summarizes what I have shared with you about appreciating the whole of the wonderful people we are.

Let Me Introduce You

Her identity is complete. Her boundaries are clear, because they encompass all of who she is. She has found her missing parts—there are no gaping holes in her Self. She has healed the fractures in her psyche. She lives embracing both her light and her shadow.

He is in charge of himself and is the conscious master of the choices he makes. His vision is clear—he sees himself as he is. He knows his strengths and challenges—his weaknesses and failings. He knows his shadow and takes responsibility for its behavior when it causes him to hurt himself or harm others.

She is not perfect and does not pretend to be, but she is at peace with herself. Her inner peace is reflected in the quality of her relationships with others. She is accepting of them while also aware of their shadow sides.

He is responsible for the mistakes he makes and learns the lessons inherent in difficult experiences. He knows both his power and his vulnerability and lives courageously—doing what he can do and accepting what is beyond his capacity to change.

She is at home with her feelings and does not shy away from experiencing and expressing them honestly. When she speaks, she does so without blaming her emotions on others. She knows the power of her mind and does her best to be its master. At dark times, when the shadow of fear and the static of anxiety cloud her thinking, she taps into the strength and power of a spiritual source. She honors, enjoys, and appreciates her body, taking the best possible care of her health and actively exercising for fun and fitness, though sometimes she throws caution to the wind and does what is daring, different, and not particularly healthy.

He loves life and sunshine. He accepts clouds and rain. He knows about storms and tragedy. He also knows how there are new beginnings, even after stinging disappointments, losses, and failures. When he hits bottom, he raises himself up toward new possibilities. His spirit is indomitable. His soul is wise. He lives with his feet on the ground—not on a pedestal. His heart is full and open. His eyes look with love and aren't afraid to recognize the presence of evil. He is complex, simple, and complete.

This person is you—with all the selves within you held in the gentle embrace of the bold, beautiful boundaries that define you as distinct from, yet simultaneously connected with, everyone else. You know how to love your partner—and all others you encounter—without losing your self.

Appreciating Your Shadow Side

Such inner peace, self-confidence, and relationship success evolve as you learn to appreciate your shadow side. Knowing your shadow, accepting it, and being discerning about it give you strength and substance and makes you more whole and human—and more loving and accepting of other people as well.

Your shadow gives you depth, perspective, and interest. Knowing that you have a shadow side, you can't act as though you are perfect. Nor do you imagine that a shadow side is only "out there"—in other countries, other cultures, other races, the opposite sex, or in other people, your mate, your children. By claiming your shadow, you can relish its mystery, richness, and potential—for both good and evil, pain and pleasure, self-centeredness and empathy, vision and blindness, rigidity and flexibility, positive and negative, construction and destruction, human failing and miracles of divinity.

Throughout this book we have looked at various aspects of your shadow side. We have talked about your lost and disowned selves as well as about the child, the adolescent, the adult, and the parent parts of you. In Chapter 8 we met the Internal Saboteur who stands guard over your shadow territory. Now I invite you to join me in taking a more comprehensive view of the whole of your shadow side—the dimension of all of us that is hidden behind the curtain of our conscious awareness.

Going Backstage

Our shadow is neither good nor bad. It simply is. It is backstage (or basement) territory—the place where the parts of us that are not on center stage wait for cues signaling them to come out and play an active role in life's drama.

In this backstage space, a vast cast of characters lies hidden from view. Each represents a different facet of the complex person we all are. Some of these characters are frequent players onstage in the drama you create. You—as director of your life play—call on them regularly to take leading roles within you and in your interactions with others.

For example, I am aware of many different parts of me that play various important roles in my life. There is Martha the Therapist who comes onstage when I enter my office and sit down. She is quite a distinct part of me and is different from Martha the Friend, Martha the Mother and Grandmother, Martha Who Loves to Play, and Martha the Writer. These parts of me are backstage when I work with clients. They come forward when changing situations summon them to appear.

You too have various parts that play starring roles in your everyday life. I suggest that you give them names and think about their different strengths, resources, and approaches to the tasks they handle.

Some parts of you appear less frequently. Though they may be excellent actors and possess valuable attributes that could be extremely useful, you don't call them forward when you need them. This is because they got bad reviews from your parents, teachers, and other caretakers when they gave debut performances early in your life. You learned to keep them hidden backstage. They don't come out often enough to develop their talents properly.

These rejected players may include parts of you that feel certain emotions that you were shamed for showing. Whole chunks of your child and adolescent selves with their fun-loving, carefree energy may be shrouded in darkness, hidden behind heavy curtains that conceal them from view. Great talents and personal resources could lurk in the wings, blocked from your awareness and growing rusty from lack of use. Vital aspects of your sexuality may be stowed away in forgotten closets, kept locked in your darkest shadows.

Rejecting these players is costly. In doing so you limit your repertoire of choices by refusing to cast them in the important roles that suit their talents. You also rob yourself of many of the resources you need for creating a successful play.

There is one actor who, most likely, often shows up front and center. His role is to help you keep your rejected cast members behind the curtains. He suddenly appears in your drama when you're feeling vulnerable, threatened, or successful. He seems to be the villain in your production—though he can turn out to be your ally if you learn to work with rather than against him. He's that slippery, complex, sometimes charming character billed as your Internal Saboteur.

The walls in his dusty dressing room are lined with the masks and costumes he likes to wear. (We saw the variety and clever nature of those masks in Chapter 8.) They disguise his identity when he makes his frequent onstage appearances. On those occasions he dons a favorite mask and emerges from the shadows. His mission is to make sure you give rejection slips to forgotten members of your backstage cast who are clamoring for important parts onstage. Your Saboteur bursts into the spotlight in their stead and gives deviously distorted expression to the genuine feelings he helps you hide.

Your Saboteur is clever at conning you into believing his lies and sanctioning his misbehavior. When he succeeds in pulling the wool over your eyes, he manages to undermine your best intentions. If you are alert enough to see through his disguises and recognize him, you call for an intermission, thank him for his efforts, and send him back to his dressing room. He stays put there only if you risk calling forward those of your rejected cast members who need to take active roles onstage.

~ Interactive Dramas ~

You are the director of the life play you create and produce. Refining your directorial skills is vital to playing your drama well and sustaining enjoyable relationships—especially with your life mate. Her stage and yours face each other in the great arena of intimate relating. The actors in your play have frequent dialogues and exchanges with the actors in hers.

Ideally, your players remain on your stage and hers stay on hers as they interact. This keeps the boundaries that define you clear and distinct. At times, when your drama directors are paying inadequate attention, players from your cast may step out of bounds and try to take over her play. Or her actors may intrude on your production.

When this happens, the one whose drama is invaded may abruptly close the curtain and shut down his performance. Short of this, he may simply freeze his players in place and wait for the intruder to retreat to her stage. Or he may secretly feel angry and resentful while appearing to acquiesce to the other's invasion.

If one of you seems to be doing little or nothing on your stage, your lack of activity may tempt your partner to take on responsibilities you appear to be neglecting. If he tends to overfunction and wants to be in control, he may invade your stage and try to take over your drama.

Or you and your mate may do battle trying to control each other's productions. Each of you wants to direct the other's play rather than tending to your own. The power struggles you create are sometimes amusing, but too often they become hurtful and even vicious.

It is also possible in today's busy world that one of you may have so much going on in your own drama that your partner feels ignored and shut out. She may take her play elsewhere, seeking a new companion with whom she can interact more successfully. Or she may become absorbed in generating lots of activity herself, so that eventually you create parallel plays with minimal moments of interaction between you.

~ Playmates ~

In earlier chapters we examined many different patterns of relating that are typical of intimate partners. One way to understand these patterns is by visualizing how certain players from your cast of characters—when they appear on your stage—tend to call forward their favorite counterparts from your partner's backstage. Many of the interactive dramas these favorite playmates create are delightfully fun and pleasant. Others can be dull and boring. Still others may be destructive and ugly—the material from which tragedies emerge if they are not quickly interrupted.

You can interrupt destructive pairings by learning to recognize and name the parts in each of you that tend to tangle. When one of those characters comes onstage in either of you, the other can choose not to allow her counterpart to emerge. Or—if it appears spontaneously—she can send it backstage and bring forward a player who behaves more effectively. Perhaps a story about my own experience will help illustrate what I mean.

My husband and I are very compatible bridge partners. We have playmates within us that love the game and do quite well together. On the night we met we enjoyed a game with the couple who introduced us. Both of us had had years of playing experience and were about equally skilled. We took to being partners as if it were the most natural thing in the world.

Enjoying tennis together, however, proved to be a much more difficult challenge. I'd played as a teenager, but never had lessons. My friends and I simply learned by watching other players. We had lots of fun, but never developed a great deal of skill. When I went to college, I rarely played again—until, not long after we were married, my husband joined a tennis club and gave me a racquet for Christmas.

He loves tennis and had played competitively and successfully for twenty-five years. When we started, he was excited about helping me brush up on my skills. We had a great time with me as student and him as accomplished mentor.

Eventually, I became brave enough to take lessons from a coach. My husband and I wanted to play mixed doubles with our skill levels more closely matched. With the help of my teacher I learned quickly, gaining greater confidence with every lesson. I started playing in a women's doubles league, did fairly well, and had a great time. My husband and I played some mixed doubles and everyone commented on how much my game was improving. All was well until we decided to play in a mixed doubles league.

No sooner had the league competition begun than I became aware of a different part of me coming onstage to play the game. This was not my newly confident tennis-playing self who did so well during her lessons and while playing with other women. This was a scared little girl who wanted desperately to please the competitive daddy I suddenly imagined my husband to be.

If I missed a shot, I was sure he was angry and disappointed—no matter what he said or did. I put so much pressure on myself—while telling myself it was coming from him—that I became less able to do anything I had learned in my lessons.

As I lost more points, I saw a different part of him come onstage, too. His overly competitive self emerged, trying to compensate for my poor playing. Though he said little, I felt what I was sure were his anger and frustration. This fueled my fear and ensured that my game deteriorated even more.

I knew this was a terrific growth challenge for me. It was also an opportunity to bring healing to our marriage. I decided to write in my journal about what was happening and to ask for divine guidance to become a better tennis partner.

As I wrote I realized that Guilty Martha was a good name for my dysfunctional tennis-playing self. She is a very hurt and abused part of me who believes she causes other people's problems. She is convinced that she should be able to function perfectly—no matter what the circumstances. I also decided that Angry Daddy (who would punish me later) was the name I would give to the part of my husband that sometimes comes onstage to play tennis with her.

I didn't tell him about my name for this part of him. To do so would violate his boundaries, because it is more about me than him. But I did tell him what I knew about myself and Guilty Martha. "She simply can't play tennis," I said. "But there is a confident, fun-loving part of me that can. Her name is Masterful Martha and she has several important roles. There is Martha Who Wins, Martha Who Serves Well, Martha Who Can Volley, Martha Who Returns Well, and Martha Who Loves the Game. She likes to play with that radiant, empowering part of you that I call my Twinkling-Blue-Eyed Lover." His response was to assure me that he would do his best to let that charming part of him stay on the courts when he played tennis with me.

Our game changed after that. Though we still have our ups and downs, we avoid getting caught in the self-defeating dance performed by Guilty Martha and her Angry Daddy. If I feel Guilty Martha setting foot onstage after I miss a point or we lose a game, I tell her firmly and with compassion to stay backstage. When either of us misses a shot or we fall behind, and I sense—or think I see—Angry Daddy emerging in my husband, I do my best to stay centered and keep Masterful Martha playing the game. One point at a time I focus on keeping my competent tennis-playing self on the court. As I change my game, my partner changes too. We have fun together again—and sure enough, the score reflects our shift.

~ *Projecting* ~

It is ever so tempting to point out to your partner what you see him doing that you think causes problems for both of you. For a while I was convinced that it was my husband's frustration that caused me to play tennis poorly. But I knew that blaming him and trying to persuade him to change wouldn't work. I had to discover and address my part in the difficulty we had playing doubles together.

Of course there are instances where your stage director may have a sharper perspective on your partner's life play than he does. A shadow part of my husband did come onstage when I got down on myself and allowed Guilty Martha to take over my game. But pointing that out to him—while it may seem potentially useful to me—is likely to feel invasive to him. Though I might be accurate, indulging myself in what I imagine is constructive criticism of him will prove counterproductive. The pattern I see may be what he least wants to notice. And focusing on him is a convenient way for me to avoid noticing my own part in our interactive drama.

What I think I see in him is often what I am blind to in myself. When this happens, I see my shadow players as if they were acting on his stage. Instead of seeing what is happening in *my* drama, I imagine that my play is taking place on *his* stage. In our tennis-playing example, I denied the angry, competitive part of me that dislikes losing, and I saw it in him instead.

Granted, he can be very competitive, too, but what I don't like in his drama usually reflects what I habitually deny in my own. Or when he behaves in difficult ways that strain my patience, he may remind me of immature parts of myself that I do my conscious best to hide.

There are almost endless possibilities for projecting onto an intimate partner what you are responsible for yourself. Sometimes mates become so absorbed in telling the other what is wrong with their behavior that it is almost impossible to understand what is happening between them. Each wants to wear the good guy's white hat while assigning the villain's black hat to his partner. As long as they deny their own shadow players' parts in their interactions, nothing improves between them. Pleading, blaming, and trying to persuade each other to be different are simply ways of prolonging the conflict. When each person wakes up to his part in the action, they can change the outcome. Only then can they create a partnership that works better for them both.

Each partner must find the courage to investigate his or her backstage (or basement, if you prefer that analogy) space. They can begin this investigation by looking within for the feelings, behaviors, and qualities they most dislike in their partner. If one person claims the other is excessively angry, that is her clue to look for the angry part hidden deep within herself.

Coordinating your life play with your partner's is an intricate process—an ever changing and challenging dance among your cast members and hers. The key to sustaining an elegantly choreographed production lies in expanding the vision, consciousness, and savvy of your lifeplay directors. When you are unhappy with what is unfolding between you, keep your director's focus on *your* stage, *your* actors, and what you can do to shift *your* role in the drama. Then watch how your changes affect your partner. Do your best to understand her and to imagine how your play looks from her perspective. Think about what she needs from you and how you can be generous in responding to her. And when you feel stuck, overwhelmed, unable to see clearly, frustrated, and confused— take a few moments to breathe, center yourself, and tap into the strength and courage developed by your spiritual practice.

Remember how tempting it is to let your Saboteur run loose when you feel threatened, vulnerable, or successful. And be aware of how easily your Saboteur can call forth the Saboteur in your partner. Throughout this book you've learned how to interrupt the dance of your Saboteurs, soothe yourselves, and then allow your hidden shadow parts to reveal themselves within the context of Safe Dialogue. Practicing these skills until they become second nature is vital to embracing your shadow side, becoming whole as individuals, and keeping healthy boundaries in your relationship.

Your Higher Self

Embracing the light and dark of your whole being requires expanded consciousness: the ability to hold a complete vision of yourself. I call this extraordinary dimension of consciousness my Higher Self. It is the spark of the divine at my center—the fire of love in my heart that connects me with my God Source.

My Higher Self sees me from a perspective much broader than ordinary awareness. It sees me whole and complete. Much like the astronauts who took the remarkable photograph of the earth from outer space, my Higher Self has a comprehensive view of all of who I am.

My Higher Self keeps both my light and shadow dimensions in sight. While this may seem a simple thing to do, think about the lesser challenge of remembering the natural world in daylight even while gazing in wonder at a star-filled night sky. My Higher Self holds all of me in its watch—even the parts of me that are hidden from view. It knows "what is" in every moment as well as "what is not."

My Higher Self is like the executive director of my life drama. Because it sees the bigger picture of who I am, it is an invaluable guide. It is always available, but it doesn't interfere with the decisions my life director makes. If I ask for help it will answer me. Even when I don't ask, it sends me messages that I may or may not heed.

Dreams, visions, sudden flashes of insight, and simple knowings are among the subtle ways my Higher Self communicates. In night dreams it spins virtual dramas for me—stories that tell me about my life, my challenges, my dilemmas, and my onstage and offstage resources. In dream time, I meet my lost and disowned backstage actors who appear as the cast of characters playing on the stage of my sleeping mind. Their night performances are gentle nudges intended to help me acknowledge them when I am awake.

An old college friend may show up one night in a dream. I haven't seen or thought of him in years. Yet upon exploring the meaning of my dream, I realize he represents one of my lost actors—the fun-loving, carefree side of me that I sometimes send into backstage isolation when my professional life becomes too busy.

Or a cadre of police officers emerges on another occasion. Their appearance symbolizes my effort to bring order to a troubling situation that can feel overwhelming. Another dream is a nightmare that stuns me with its ferocity. I awaken sweating and pumped with adrenalin. Eventually I recognize that the monster pursuing me is my disowned powerful self—released in disguise as a terrifying figure on the attack. By scaring me in my dream, it shows me how afraid I am of this powerful part of me when I leave her languishing and ignored in the shadows of my waking life.

Insights come from my Higher Self, too, often at surprising times and with startling clarity. I may be puzzled trying to understand a pattern I've noticed in the relationship drama I play with my daughter. Then, while driving to an appointment, I have a sudden flash of understanding. I am back in my childhood home watching my mother and me play out a scene so similar to one I sometimes reenact with my daughter that I'm stunned by the parallel. Or I'm looking for a catchy slogan for a brochure I am developing. It comes to me—seemingly out of the blue—while I'm enjoying my morning shower.

Absolute knowings also come from my Higher Self—often just as spontaneously. I could be concerned about a situation involving one of my friends. Suddenly, while I'm absorbed in weeding my garden, I'm filled with a peaceful knowing that all is well and will be well with what concerns me.

As the wise director of my life drama, I actively cultivate my relationship with my Higher Self. I enjoy regular quiet times during which I pray, meditate, or write in my journal. These activities seed my dreaming and open my heart to receiving and trusting the guidance that comes to me from the realm of Spirit.

When I write in my journal I sometimes ask questions of my Higher Self—then I listen and record the words that spring into my awareness from the even greater God Source far beyond my ordinary mind. I discover amazing things in this way and find myself writing with a depth of wisdom and understanding that far surpasses what my conscious mind knows.

In these and many other intriguing ways my Higher Self shows me more and more of my self. It helps me recognize my talents just as it reveals my backstage shadow territory. It speaks in subtle ways that allow me to gently awaken to its meaning. Sometimes it sends me thundering, persistent messages—when it can't get my attention any other way. I may have repetitive dreams I can't get off my mind until I unravel their meaning.

I also encounter situations that force me to grow. Perhaps a business associate reminds me of my mother at her most difficult moments. Or a professional colleague attacks me unfairly, forcing me to stand up for myself in ways that challenge me to grow into greater wholeness. A storm, an illness, or a random senseless tragedy shakes me to my core. Coping with my grief forces me to surrender to Spirit or be swept away by despair.

Gradually—as I continue to cultivate my relationship with my Higher Self—my life director matures, my consciousness expands, and my wisdom grows. I feel connected with my God Source—no matter what happens in my outer life drama. I know that I am never alone—no matter who is present or absent from me in physical form. I don't take the shortcomings of others personally. I draw my energy from the realm of Spirit rather than from other people. I know that the same higher Source is also within them. This helps me resist the temptation to try to rescue them by doing for them what they are called to do for themselves.

Knowing my Higher Self, I see the same spark of the divine in everyone I meet. I am especially attuned to the Higher Self in my partner and honor the holiness that is at the core of his being. I feel my deep connection with him, and with others, knowing we are all part of one all-encompassing Source—whether it be called God, the universe, All That Is, Spirit, or another name. *"Namaste"* is an ancient greeting that translates to mean "the God in me bows to the God in you." I remember this lovely word and see myself bowing in awe to the divine spirit that lies at the heart of my partner—and everyone else I know. Even when their most challenging parts are onstage, I recall the larger truth of their being. Knowing that truth, I don't allow their fearful parts to manipulate me into betraying myself or my relationship with them.

Embracing Your Shadow Side Clears Your Vision

When—with the support of your Higher Self—you are able to see and embrace your shadow territory, you see other people and their shadow sides more accurately, too. Your vision clears. You are not easily deceived—by your own monster parts or by similar parts in others.

As we have seen, the key to handling backstage monster parts is recognizing them, acknowledging them when they appear, and being unafraid to say "no" to them. Knowing the ways you try to manipulate others alerts you when someone else uses the same tactics. Acknowledging how you hide your emotions makes you more sensitive when others hide theirs. Like Rosie in Chapter 7, recognizing the rose-colored glasses you use to hide from difficulties helps you identify the ways others fool themselves about problems they deny.

Because you are unafraid to see what is imperfect in you, you are unafraid of other people's imperfections. You can say "no" and accept others' anger with you. You know that their anger—like yours—is simply a normal human emotion. You can ask for what you want and handle not getting it. You don't interpret someone else's "no" as a personal rejection. You can say what you think without fear of being criticized by those whose ideas differ from yours. Because you know your own critic, you know you don't have to give undue power to that part in others.

Instead of blindly idealizing or vilifying people—and then believing your naive projections—you see the light and shadow sides in them. Your eyes are open to both "what is" and "what is not." You accept yourself and your mate for your humanness—rather than for how perfect you imagine each of you ought to be. You love your partner without fooling or losing yourself, or discounting the whole of him.

Embracing Your Shadow Side Creates Inner Peace

Knowing your whole self and seeing more of the whole of others empowers the director of your life play. It enables this executive part of you to listen to the concerns, feelings, and points of view of all the varied members of your inner cast of characters. It also helps you better understand the inner conflicts other people face.

Instead of consuming your life energy in endless battles among your inner selves, you listen with an open heart to those parts of you that want to speak about a particular issue. Your play director is then able to understand them, validate their points of view, and take them into account. Ultimately, the decisions you make reflect the wisdom that comes with considering all of them—without allowing any one of your inner selves to control what you choose. It is as though your wise Higher Self is the captain of your ship. You experience the inner harmony that comes with genuine self-understanding and self-acceptance.

Your inner peace is reflected in more peaceful relationships with others—especially your partner, your children, and your parents. Because you understand and accept your whole self, you are much better able to understand and accept the whole of them, too.[1]

You listen more carefully and respectfully when they speak. Rather than trying to change, fix, or rescue them, you do your best to understand them. You see them as clearly as you can, love them as they are, and respect their right and privilege to choose the course they set for their lives—whether or not it makes sense to you.

There is no need to engage in endless power struggles for dominance and control. You know you do not direct anyone else's life play. But you are in charge of your own. Respecting your self, you also respect others and teach them to respect you.

You do not allow yourself to be controlled, sabotaged, or silenced by their choices. You express yourself honestly and reveal yourself to them, releasing your fears of what their reactions might be.

You know that you possess no one but your self. You and your partner choose independently to travel together on your life path. Both of you are committed to your shared journey. Yet you know that eventually you will part—unless you die together.

Courageously you honor and enjoy the time you have. You realize that each day could be your last, while also trusting that you have years of life left to relish. You embrace your shadow times as well as your times of brilliant, sunny bliss. You know that all your experiences carry gifts of growth wrapped within them. You look for those gifts and do your best to unwrap them—even in your darkest moments.

Embracing the light and shadow of yourself, your mate, and your relationship, you live a rich life. You value your differences and see them as enhancing your range of choices. You respect each other without expecting perfection. You relax into the fascinating play of contrasts that give substance to your partnership.

Best of all, you let go of trying to control each other. Within the healthy context of acceptance that you share, you are truly free to be the person you are—as an individual, a relationship partner, and a fellow soul walking the path of life. Rather than loving your partner and losing your self, you love the whole of your partner as he truly is and enhance your joy in being the whole of you.

CHAPTER ELEVEN

Letting Go

L etting go is an essential life skill—one we practice every moment of our lives. From conception to death and no doubt beyond, we inhale, and we exhale; we connect, and we release. We bond, and we let go.

We must let go of our mother's womb to make the leap of birth into life. Ultimately we must let go of our bodies to make the leap of faith beyond death into the life of Spirit. During all the years in between, we practice holding and releasing—bonding and letting go, getting together and separating. We are one . . . we are two . . . we are one again.

Letting go is the downbeat of breath—the exhalation phase of each of our life experiences. Breathing out we empty ourselves into the realm of Spirit. Inhaling we reconnect with our bodies—filling ourselves once again on the upbeat. It is as if we are rocked gently back and forth on waves of breath between the physical realm of the body and the invisible realm of Spirit.

Whatever supports the steady rhythm of breath supports life. Whatever interferes with our natural rhythm of connecting and releasing harms us and may ultimately destroy us.

Fear Interrupts Healthy Connecting and Releasing

As we have seen, fear interrupts our natural rhythm of breathing. When we are afraid we tighten our bodies. We hold on to our breath. We cling

217

to what we imagine will comfort us and give us physical security.

Clinging to our partners, we are convinced that we must keep them close in order to feel safe, healthy, and secure. Or we decide that we must keep our distance, because we are afraid to be too close.

Trying to overcontrol ourselves, we fail to express our thoughts, our needs, our feelings, and our dreams. Trying to overcontrol other people, we fail to respect their autonomy and their individual rights. Trying to overcontrol life we hoard money, possessions, and the past, pretending that we can defend against the passage of time, change, and loss by hanging onto whatever we can manage to grasp. Doing so, we gradually squeeze the life out of our relationships.

Thus we fail to "breathe" life fully. We feel depressed. Our energy is consumed by the unnatural effort required in avoiding connection and release. We manage to push people away in our determination to keep them close. Or we run from them, afraid we might need them too much. Closing ourselves to the full experience of what is present—then refusing to let go when it is finished—keeps us from being adequately nurtured by the natural rhythms of life.

The price we pay for clinging and avoiding is losing the joy of simply being in the flow of life. The reward we experience with letting go is the joy of riding the eternal waves of unimpeded connecting and release.

Letting Go Demands Courage and Faith

When we let go we allow ourselves to be vulnerable, to accept what we cannot control, to go with the flow. We open ourselves up—trusting that what we release will come back to us and that we will be safe. It is a bit like jumping off a cliff, riding a roller coaster, or skydiving. Letting go is thrilling. It feels risky, and it demands faith that we'll land safely.

Letting go requires courage and faith. I remember the effort it took for me to kiss my older daughter good-bye and watch her walk down the ramp to board the plane that would take her to Dartmouth for her freshman year. Of course I had already sent her off to Europe for the summer, and both of us had survived. I knew this was just another essential step in her growing into a separate self. It was also a signal to me that a phase of my life was ending—though thankfully I still had five years left with my younger daughter at home.

I was beginning the process of letting go of my child-rearing years. Part of me wanted to rebel—to run after her—to get her to come back and let me do it all over again. Most of me knew better. And I had faith. I knew this amazing young woman would be okay—would do well in the world—was capable, competent, and trustworthy. There was nothing to do but accept what was and give thanks for the great opportunities she had created for herself.

Letting go during life's big transitions is one kind of necessary releasing. We must accept the passage of time and our movement into new phases of life and relationships. Births, deaths, starting school, moving, graduation, marriage, divorce, job changes, natural disasters, illness, and tragedies force us to adapt to profound changes and integrate our feelings about them. If we fail to do so, we doom ourselves to living in the past, pretending that we can control life by denying our emotions and acting as if "what is" is not.

Another, more subtle form of letting go is just as vital and perhaps even more difficult. It is what I call "letting go and letting be." This kind of letting go involves letting people be while also being honest with them and true to you. It is a way of respecting personal boundaries by honoring each individual's right and responsibility to choose for herself what fits for her and what does not.

One of my major lessons in letting go and letting be also came with my older daughter. During a workshop in the desert many years ago, I meditated on my relationship with her. She was sixteen at the time and frequently angry with me. As I sat in the desert and reflected, I visualized opening my heart to her. Soon I felt deep peace and a knowing that she would have to find her way just as I was doing my best to find mine. I saw that I couldn't "make" her perfect and teach her all she needed to know before she left home. I realized that I could accept her as she was—

trusting that she is a work in progress and that she is the one making the choices only she can make. If I don't like what she does I can tell her, but I cannot make her decisions for her and force her to do things my way.

When I returned home, I noticed that I stopped trying to correct her every move. I said to myself, "She'll have to learn about that herself someday." It wasn't that I gave up on her. It was that I felt a new confidence in her and trusted that she would choose wisely. Deep in my heart I knew she would find her way without my trying to control her process or protect her from making what might be useful mistakes.

Later that year she decided to live with her father and stepmother. That was one of the most difficult letting-go experiences I've ever had to face. But out of it came a profound healing in my relationship with her. After a semester away and a summer in a residential education program, she moved home again. In the meantime I had divorced my second husband and done a lot of growing up myself.

Letting others be sounds simple. Yet for me it has been one of the major lessons of my life. My parents did their best to control my choices. I have to be diligent in noticing when I am tempted to fall into the style of relating I learned from them. It is all too easy for me to unconsciously reenact their controlling patterns by playing therapist with my partner and my family.

Soon after I met my husband I told him that I wanted a relationship in which I practiced what I was learning through my work in Imago Relationship Therapy. He interpreted what I said as my wanting him to change—a red flag that felt dangerously invasive to him and triggered his staunchest personal defenses.

As is typical with being in love, I filed the issue away and did my best to ignore that bit of dissonance between us. I assumed that eventually he would become as fascinated as I was with how to nurture our relationship using all the exciting tools I'd discovered in couple's work.

One of those tools is the importance of feeling genuine empathy for your partner. Thankfully, my desire to feel empathy for him helped me realize that being married to a therapist is not an easy task. Helping couples in my office—all day, every day—is seductive business. It can be hard to take off my therapist's hat when I come home. Yet I have to remember that when it comes to my marriage, I'm not the expert—I'm one of the participants.

At first, I flatly refused to believe that I didn't know exactly what was best for us. I was determined to drag my husband into the processes that I knew would transform our difficulties and deepen our joy and commitment. I wanted him to embrace all the ideas I've written about in this book. And I wanted him to do it now! After all, I can't stand not to be actively practicing what I preach.

I was blind to a key piece essential to the nurturing of a marriage. What each of us had to experience before we could move forward was deep acceptance and understanding from the other. I wanted him to accept how important doing this work was to me. He needed me to understand that he was a very sensitive person who didn't respond well to feeling pushed.

We locked horns over a point that was vital to both of us. My challenge was to accept him as he was and to accept that his way of being in the world was just as valid for him as mine was for me. After all, it had worked for him for over half a century before we met.

This was hard for me, because I, too, craved unconditional acceptance—something I felt I lacked from my parents. They wanted to fit me into their mold for me, just as I wanted to fit my husband into my mold for the two of us. He didn't like that any more than I did when I was a child.

From his point of view, being accepted is a bottom-line issue. As a child, and even as a young adult, he experienced his mother's agenda for him that had nothing to do with what he wanted. My having an agenda—though in my mind it was certainly for our common good—replayed his difficulties with her. He was as determined not to be controlled by me as he had been not to be controlled by her. His resisting what I wanted felt like his controlling me—just as my wanting him to explore what I thought was important felt like my trying to control him.

We stayed stuck in that power struggle for a quite a while. In the meantime each of us grew in our capacity to accept and appreciate the other—as is. I saw that I had no choice but to let him be—if I wanted to sustain our marriage. He saw that coming to the Imago conferences and participating in the programs and workshops with me did not harm him or force him to change. And he came and supported me. I gained new appreciation for his being willing to enter into my world and open up to it. At the same time I felt more and more respect for him, for his way of doing things, and for his wisdom and intelligence.

By learning that I simply had to let him be I found great relief. In letting him be and in his letting me be, I came to respect him and his boundaries and to appreciate his point of view in a way I never had before. I think he has come to respect me and accept my ideas as he has learned he can trust me to be respectful of him.

By "letting go and letting be" we gave ourselves the time and space we needed to deepen our trust and understanding of each other. Each of us learned to appreciate the richness of our differences and of our different approaches.

One of the pastimes we enjoy sharing after a trying day at work is the computer game Free Cell. Our different styles of playing are quite striking. I like to let my right brain guide me, simply moving cards and seeing if I can make them all fall into place. His strategy is to study the entire board before making his first move. He carefully establishes a game plan and then follows it. As you can probably imagine, he wins consistently. I, on the other hand, win a lot, too, though without a doubt my way is more risky—and more fun for me. Something magical happens when we share a game, putting our heads together and combining our approaches. Joining forces, we win almost every hand. Accepting our different styles of play, we create a more powerful winning combination than either of us could manage alone.

Letting Go of What Might Be

Despite our best efforts, relationships don't always work out as we hope they will. Honoring your personal boundaries and refusing to accommodate unending episodes of abuse may mean that you and your partner must part. Sometimes letting go of each other is necessary for mental, emotional, physical, and spiritual survival. Facing up to that necessity doesn't mean the relationship was a failure. It may have been a necessary growth experience for both of you—and letting each other go may be the greatest gift of all.

One very difficult life lesson for me was accepting "what is" and letting go of what might be if someone else would only decide to fit himself into my idea of the person he could possibly be—if only...! Living in a fantasy of what could be "if only," I put off facing the reality of what actually was. I did this to avoid letting go of relationships I wanted to sustain—no matter how much they hurt me. Eventually I had to release the imaginary possibilities. Then I could tune in to what I actually observed and experienced. These were vital steps in my growing up, giving up being a victim, and getting on with what I needed to do about me.

Personal growth and change don't just magically happen. They evolve gradually within people who are committed to working toward goals that make sense to them. Feeling loved and accepted by an intimate partner is deeply healing and very important—but it is not everything. Each person involved in a relationship has a part in what happens between them. Each person must take responsibility for doing his part to make growth and healing possible—if he wants the relationship to succeed.

If one person isn't willing to make the effort required to sustain his connection with his partner, the other must face up to the situation at hand. Instead of imagining that things will be different if this, if that, if only, if, if, if, she must let go and let "what is" be.

Often I've observed that when one person truly lets go of her efforts to hold things together, no matter what boundary-violating behaviors she experiences from her mate, he doesn't go away—at least not permanently. Though genuinely letting go may take weeks or months, when she finally frees herself from her enchantment with what might be, the other person sometimes reappears—saying he is willing and anxious to make the changes necessary to repair their partnership.

Then her challenge is to realize that words are cheap. They can be charming and seductive—especially when they are exactly what she once longed to hear. Only time, clear boundaries, and sustained new behavior—often with outside help for both partners to deal with their underlying emotional issues—can insure that good intentions translate into genuine growth. Short of such commitment there is no reason to think that hearing and believing words you want to hear will create necessary change. Stepping back into a magical enchantment with a person who can't be trusted betrays you. It is giving up your self in order to stay with an immature partner.

Letting Go and the Gift of Forgiveness

Giving the gift of forgiveness heals you. It allows you to release your hurts and disappointments, having digested your grief about them. When you forgive, you "give for" yourself and those who hurt you. You move on, letting go of what harmed or offended you.

Forgiveness does not mean blindly walking back into a situation that hurt you with a person who harmed you and demonstrates no solid intention to change. Though you forgive that person, you also keep firm boundaries in place to protect yourself from future harm.

Forgiveness is not blind, and it is not stupid. It is not a simple-minded way of condoning bad behavior. Rather, it is an act of wisdom and enlightenment. Forgiveness affirms that you have unwrapped the life lessons hidden at the core of your pain.

People who are wise enough to forgive are also wise enough not to allow those who hurt them additional opportunities to repeat their damaging behavior. They say "no" to letting themselves be continually violated. If a person who hurts them is remorseful, takes responsibility for her mistakes, and demonstrates—over an extended period of time—that she is both willing and able to make necessary changes, they may gradually rebuild trust and repair their relationship. Otherwise they part.

Letting Life Flow

When I was a child, I remember being fascinated with time-lapse films showing the opening of a flower. I wanted to be able to see for myself the subtle movements that transformed a rosebud into full bloom. But no matter how hard I tried I couldn't manage to witness with my limited human vision a flower's miraculous opening.

I'm reminded of that childhood frustration when people I work with tell me they want to see their relationship change immediately. They wonder how long couple's therapy should take. They want things to be better instantly—and if they're not, they are disappointed and tempted to give up on their commitment.

I point out that we live in a culture that is hooked on speed. We like instant everything—from iced tea to mashed potatoes to emotional maturity. We're frustrated by "slow" computers that once amazed us by their speed and versatility. So why not expect quick fixes for relationship challenges? After all, managed-care insurance policies expect six-session cures of problems that are a lifetime in the making.

Helping relationship partners grow and heal is like watching the rose bloom. The naked eye can't see the subtle movements that ultimately create a beautiful, open flower. Yet those movements occur as long as the rose bush is fed, watered, bathed in sunshine, and allowed to be. A developing flower can't be rushed—it knows the pace of its unique blooming rhythm.

Your relationship has its own blooming rhythm. Its growth is an organic process that requires feeding, watering, being bathed in the light of love, and being allowed to be. The love you and your partner share does its magic work in subtle ways. Patient eyes eventually see miraculous results from both partners' consistently nurturing each other. Gradually you become more conscious, intentional, mature, and understanding.

Of course, as with roses, there are necessary times of pruning. There are seasons when you must let go of what is familiar and redirect your lives. A difficult, unexpected pruning leaves you no choice but to let go and grieve what you are forced to release. You have to cry your tears, wail out your hurt, allow your rage, and share your pain. If you and your partner stay connected and support each other as you suffer, your relationship survives and thrives. Soon it blooms even more abundantly. If you cut each other off and refuse to share the pain, you risk destroying your connection. Like a rose bush, the relationship dies if it is pruned and then left without the food, water, and sunshine it needs to recover from the trauma of sudden change.

So be patient. Remember the limitations of your physical eyes. Ask for help in learning to look with the enhanced vision of your spirit. Your relationship wants to grow and thrive. It wants to support you—if you and your partner respect each other's boundaries, if you are committed to nurturing each other, if you truly want to understand yourselves, if the light of love shines in your hearts, if you embrace your Saboteur selves so you don't allow them to control your behavior.

That's lots of ifs. Loving your partner without losing your self is one of life's most demanding challenges. Unfortunately, it is one for which most of us have precious little preparation. My prayer for this book is that it will enhance your education for intimate partnership. May reading it open your heart, your eyes, your mind, and your spirit to all the selves within you. May you embrace the whole of you in a bold, beautiful boundary of love. May you respect your mate's boundaries as well. And may the two of you travel your life paths within the radiant boundary of your commitment to each other. Basking in the light of Spirit, may you nurture your selves, your children, and everyone whose life you touch with the warmth of your rich and always maturing love.

Letting Go and Letting God

Long ago in the midst of the pain of my first divorce, one of my mentors taught me to say to myself, "I let go and let God." I repeated those words many times every day as I struggled to find my way, stand on my own, and care for my two children as a single parent.

As I release this book to you, dear reader, I reaffirm my intention to let go and let God use this work for the good you deserve in your life and in all your relationships. I also offer you the following additional affirmations to say to yourself as often as you choose. Moment by moment, they will help you enjoy the freedom of releasing what is beyond your power to control.

~ *Affirmations* ~

I love you. I bless you. I release you. May our relationship free you to be all you are created to be.

I forgive you, and I forgive me, giving thanks for the lessons I have learned through a difficult encounter.

I love you, and I let you be.

I say "no" when I must.

I love you, and I trust the growth process we share.

Our relationship is like a rosebud gradually coming into full bloom.

I give thanks for the patience I feel as I learn to accept you and me.

My intention is to love and understand you as you are.

I reveal myself to you because I want you to understand me.

I give thanks for healthy boundaries that define, contain, and protect all of me.

I give thanks for your boundaries and affirm my intention to respect them.

I affirm and give thanks for the boundary of commitment that defines the loving relationship we share.

I affirm my responsibility to be true to myself—even if that means I must ultimately say good-bye to you.

I let go and let God.

Glossary of Terms

Boundaries — Boundaries define one human being as distinct from another and encompass his or her personal identity. The body is our visible physical boundary. Invisible, but very real, emotional, mental, and spiritual boundaries extend beyond the body and encompass our energy field.

Boundary deficits — Ineffective personal boundaries evidenced by failing to adequately protect one's self-interest; or rigidly held personal boundaries evidenced by over protecting one's self-interest. People with boundary deficits have difficulty making contact with others and sustaining satisfying relationships.

Enmeshment — Boundary confusion in relationships in which people act as if there are no distinctions that define them as individuals. They violate each other's boundaries in a variety of ways, alternately behaving as victims, abusers, and rescuers of each other.

Enmeshment-making process — Gradual loss of personal boundaries and the resulting boundary confusion that evolves between intimate partners as their lives become connected and they begin hiding their true thoughts and feelings in order not to upset each other.

Imago Therapy — A therapeutic model for working with couples developed by Harville Hendrix, Ph.D., and Helen LaKelly Hunt, Ph.D. An imago is an unconsciously held composite image of one's original caretakers. This image acts like a powerful magnet that attracts potential partners to each other who are similar, in both positive and negative ways, to their original caretakers. Our imago creates the chemistry of romantic attraction and insures that with our intimate partners, we experience both the bliss we felt as infants as well as the pain and frustration we felt when our boundaries were violated during childhood. In effect, our imago ensures that our mates will challenge us to heal old hurts and grow into wholeness if our relationship is to be joyful and successful. Imago therapy helps couples understand their relationship dilemmas and discover how to consciously choose growth and healing rather than power struggle and stagnation.

Parent ego state — The part within us that nurtures, protects, defends, scolds, punishes, and encourages us, much as our original caretakers did when we were children.

Romantic boundaries — Boundaries that are based upon the separate life circumstances that define potential partners as independent individuals prior to their becoming committed to each other. Romantic boundaries are virtual boundaries as opposed to genuine ones. They exist during the early, romantic phase of a relationship.

Shadow side — The dimension within us that is outside conscious awareness at any given moment. The shadow side includes both the strengths and weaknesses; both the loving and fearful aspects of our being.

Trances/reenactment trances — Altered states of consciousness in which people behave in automatic patterns that are unconsciously determined. In reenactment trances, relationship partners reenact with each other patterns of behavior that were habitual in their families of origin. Reenactment trances are triggered by present-time events that parallel some element of boundary-violating experiences that occurred in the past.

Notes

~ Chapter 2 ~

1. Safe Dialogue is based upon the Couple's Dialogue Process, designed by Harville Hendrix, Ph.D., developer of Imago Relationship Therapy. Safe Dialogue also incorporates elements of the Creative Colloquy Process developed by Joyce Buckner, Ph.D., a Master Trainer at the Institute for Imago Relationship Therapy. In addition, the Safe Dialogue process reflects my work with Brugh Joy, M.D., Carolyn Conger, Ph.D., Jean Houston, Ph.D., and Marge Barlow, Ph.D.

~ Chapter 3 ~

1. Love, Pat. *Hot Monogamy.* New York: Dutton, 1994, 177.

2. This is a basic tenet of Imago Relationship Therapy. See Hendrix, Harville, *Getting the Love You Want: A Guide for Couples*, New York: Harper Perennial, 1990.

3. Chopra, Deepak. *The Path to Love: Renewing the Power of Spirit in Your Life.* New York: Harmony Books, 1977, 66.

4. Easwaran, Ecknath. *Dialogue with Death.* Petaluma, CA: Nilgiri Press, 1981, 171.

~ Chapter 4 ~

1. See *Prosperity Consciousness*, my booklet about money and attitudes about it. It is available through Options Now, Inc.: (800) 345-8477; website www.lovetips.com.

2. For more on healing childhood sexual trauma, see my book *Beyond Victim: You Can Overcome Childhood Abuse—Even Sexual Abuse*, Melbourne, FL: Rainbow Books, 1988.

3. For more on healthy sexuality, see my booklet *Healthy Sexual Response Ability*. It is available through Options Now, Inc.: (800) 345-8477; website www.lovetips.com.

~ Chapter 5 ~

1. Stosny, Steven. "The Compassion Workshop: Compassion as Self-Empowerment Against Attachment Abuse." *The Journal of Imago Relationship Therapy* 4 (1999): 17–44.

2. This is an exercise developed by Jean Houston and practiced at several workshops I have attended with her.

~ Chapter 8 ~

1. I have written extensively about the Internal Saboteur. See Baldwin, Martha. *Self-Sabotage: How to Stop It and Soar to Success*. New York: Warner Books, 1989. My videotape titled *Stop Sabotaging Success* also deals with the Saboteur. It is available through Options Now, Inc.: (800) 345-8477; website www.lovetips.com.

2. The Saboteur is not your "old brain." It is part of the "new brain" that thinks, interprets, and exacerbates your "old brain's" reactivity. It supports and rationalizes your fight, flee, and freeze reactions to boundary violations and strong feelings. It initiates and directs reenactment trances.

3. Ron Roth, Ph.D., suggests the phrase "Thank you for sharing" as a way of saying "no" to the ego.

~ Chapter 10 ~

1. Of course, the opposite is true also. Internal struggles manifest themselves outwardly in fighting with the people who are closest to you.

Index

A

abandonment, 43–44, 81, 82, 115. *See also* boundary violations
abuse, x, 2, 86–87, 177, 183; danger signals, 140; physical, 83–86; refusing, 222–223; self-sabotage, 154; sexual, 70–71; shadow selves, 157
acceptance, 91, 221
addiction, 82, 101, 103; behaviors, 52, 70; inadequate boundaries, 47; to romance, 44
affairs, 71, 82; danger signals, 142; emotional neglect, 96; freezing/denying behaviors, 102
affirmation, 6, 227–228; Safe Dialogue, 24, 30, 31–32
anger, 22, 74–75, 93, 101; acknowledgment, 57; expressing, 106, 190; journal writing, 77. *See also* Anger/Appreciations Exchange
Anger/Appreciations Exchange, 57, 77; explanation of, 58–60; scheduling, 66; summarized, 62–63
anger-management, 84–85, 177
anxiety, 56, 101. *See also* emotional, digestive system
appreciation, 77, 104
attack, 79, 118, 163; Boundary-Healing Process, 193; exercises, 77; power struggles, 50–52; self-sabotage, 168;
attraction, 12, 13–14; fear and, 47; recapturing, 38–39; romantic, 41–42, 229
avoidance, 43–44, 69–71, 144

B

behavior, beneath, 166; Boundary-Healing Process, 193, 194; identifying, 129; pattern of, 122–123; projection, 210; reinforcing positive, 62; replacing, 129–130; triggering, 114, 187
blame, 79, 118, 163, 178; Boundary-Healing Process, 193; exercises, 77; game, 142–144, 145–146, 152; power struggles, 50–52; self-sabotage, 161, 168
bonding, 42, 217; after initial romance, 44–46; with parents, 84; releasing, 43–44, 51; romantic, 39–40, 53
boundaries, x, xi, 8, 128, 205, 229; affirmations, 227–228; blame game, 142–144; developing, 3, 14–15, 75–76, 116, 138–139; dissolving of, 42–43; forgiveness, 224; healthy, 1–2; identifying danger signals, 139–142; inadequate, 5, 46–47, 55, 71, 86; intact, 10–11, 201–202; maintaining, 9–10, 210, 226; romantic, 40–43; Safe Dialogue, 23; sexual intimacy, 68–69; testing, 149; through self-parenting, 150; time, 65; violation of, 48, 56, 72–73, 77, 79, 138. *See also* emotional, boundaries; personal boundaries; physical boundaries; romantic boundaries; spiritual boundaries
Boundary-Healing Process, 182; exercises, 198–199; steps explained, 184–195; summarized, 183, 195–198
boundary violations, 5, 146, 161–162; behaviors, 223–224; as defenses, 106–107; emotional, 83; forgiveness, 191–192; freezing/denying, 81–82; identifying, 107–110, 168, 170, 186; inner parent, 174; intrusive/rejective, 80–81, 83–91; mental, 83; neglecting/abandoning, 81; nonverbal signals, 180; physical, 83; reaction to, 184; self-sabotage, 154–155, 165, 167; spiritual, 83; stopping, 153,

164–165, 166, 176–178. *See also*
    Boundary-Healing Process
breathing, 54, 164–165, 185, 217
budget, 67. *See also* smoke-screen issues

C

centering, 4, 164–165, 171, 185, 188
cheating. *See* affairs
commitment, 141–142, 161, 182, 194
communication, 52; enmeshment, 50,
    61; honest, 49; inner parent, 148;
    listening, 20; nonverbal, 121;
    reenactment dramas, 113; skills, *ix*,
    23; small talk, 104; time, 66. *See also*
    enmeshment, breaking; Safe Dialogue
Compassion Workshop, 84–85, 177
compulsive behavior, 103
connection, 97, 103, 188, 218
control, 221; anger, 57; boundaries, 47,
    176–178, 215–216; danger signals,
    140; freezing behaviors, 104; letting
    go, 218; parenting, 48, 114–115;
    power struggles, 50, 52, 205–206;
    reenactment trances, 119–120, 121
core issues, 76. *See also* smoke-screen
    issues
courage, 15. *See also* fear
criticism, boundaries, 79, 193; exercises,
    77; fear of, 214; power struggles,
    50–52; self-sabotage, 163, 178

D

danger signals, 145; identifying,
    139–142, 175; inner parent,
    145–146; journal writing, 151. *See
    also* boundaries
date night, 65, 77
denying, 81–82. *See also* boundary
    violations; freezing/denying boundary
    violations
depression, 56, 82, 101, 103–104, 218.
    See also emotional, digestive system
differentiation, 55–56, 113, 139
discounting patterns, 114, 115
dreams, 211–212

E

emotional, abuse, 70–71 (*see also* abuse);
    boundaries, 8; boundary violations,
    83, 86, 138 (*see also* abuse; boundary
    violations); digestive system, 56–57;
    neglect, 95–96 (*see also* neglect)
emotions, accepting, 20–21, 56, 168,
    185, 201–202; attraction, 41; as
    bonding experiences, 45–46;
    Boundary-Healing Process, 184,
    192; boundary violations, 2, 83, 87,
    94–95, 102; controlling, 104;
    enmeshment-making process, 52;
    exercises, 77, 108; experiencing, 130,
    133; expressing, 35, 60–61, 105–106,
    189–190; forgiveness, 131–132;
    hiding, 106, 214; honest, 49, 75;
    inadequate boundaries, 46–47; inner
    child, 148–149; interpreting, 198;
    neglect, 95–96; projection, 210;
    reenactment trances, 115, 121; self-
    sabotage, 179; shadow selves, 204
empathy, Boundary-Healing Process,
    182, 188, 190, Compassion
    Workshop, 84; exercises, 133–134;
    expressing, 177, 220–221; needs, 90;
    reenactment trances, 128; Safe
    Dialogue, 35, 66, 91; shadow selves,
    203; tough self-love, 150
"enchantment shades," 127. *See also*
    reenactment trances
enmeshment, *x–xi*, 9, 128, 229; break-
    ing, 55–56, 57, 60–62; creation of,
    48, 53; making, 48–52, 52–53, 114,
    229; sexual, 70
equality, 4, 9

F

fear, of betrayal, 142; boundaries,
    46–47, 79, 153–154; breathing, 54,
    217–218; choices, 175; core issues,
    173–174; exploring, 106; expressing,
    190; growing beyond, 42–43, 180,
    215; inner child, 146–147; journal
    writing, 179; money, 66–68;

parenting, 114–115; pattern of,
31–32; reenactment trances, 115,
134; relationship, 9, 15, 85–86; self-
sabotage, 154–155, 156–157, 164,
174, 186
feelings. *See* emotions
forgiveness, 131–132, 191–192, 224,
227
freezing, 81–82. *See also* boundary
violations; freezing/denying boundary
violations
freezing/denying boundary violations,
81–82, 99–105; reenactment trances,
115; response, 82; transforming,
105–106

G

gratitude, 134; Boundary-Healing
Process, 187, 192; enmeshment-
breaking process, 61–62; exercises,
199; expressing, 104, 130
growth, 178, 182
guilt trip, 89, 161. *See also* manipulation

H

heart-centering process, 78, 90–91
higher self, 211–214. *See also* shadow
selves
honesty, 4, 53, 109, 117, 219;
emotional, 45–46, 49, 75, 201–202;
expressing, 60–61, 176, 215; fear of,
9; inadequate boundaries, 47;
reenactment trances, 121
Houston, Jean Ph.D., 98. *See also*
"mesmeric passes"
humor, 77, 163

I

"I" messages, 60–61
Imago Relationship Therapy, x, 220,
229–230
infidelity. *See* affairs
inner adult, 147. *See also* inner child;
inner parent

inner child, 146–148; Boundary-Healing
Process, 192–193; fear, 166; journal
writing, 151–152; monster, 154;
nurturing, 148–149. *See also* inner
adult; inner parent
inner parent, 145–148, 164–165, 178,
187, 230; fear, 179; journal writing,
151–152; monster, 154; naming,
180; sabotage, 163, 174;
strengthening, 148–150. *See also*
inner adult; inner child
inner peace, 201–203
insecurity, 142
internal saboteur. *See* self-sabotage
intrusive/rejective boundary violations,
80–81; example of, 83–86;
recognizing, 86–90; response, 82;
transforming, 90–91. *See also*
boundary violations

J

journal writing, 212–213; Boundary-
Healing Process, 186–187; emotions,
105, 106, 133; exercises, 53, 77–78,
107–110, 150–152, 180–181; fear,
179; identifying boundary violations,
170; inner child, 149; "mesmeric
passes," 99; reenactment trance
patterns, 130

L

life phases, 217–219
listening, 32, 90. *See also* communication
lying, 141. *See also* honesty

M

manipulation, 144; emotional, 87, 89;
inner child, 146–147, 149; journal
writing, 151–152; recognizing, 123,
214; reenactment trances, 120, 121;
self-sabotage, 146, 160–161, 179
meditation, 105, 212
mental, abuse, 70–71 (*see also* abuse);
boundary violations, 8, 83, 86 (*see*

also boundary violations); digestive
    system, 56–57; neglect, 96 (*see also*
    neglect)
"mesmeric passes," 98–99 (*see also*
    Houston, Jean Ph.D.)
mirroring, Anger/Appreciations
    Exchange, 58–60; Boundary-Healing
    Process, 177, 188, 189–190, 195;
    enmeshment-breaking process, 61;
    exercises, 27, 133–134; inner parent,
    148, 165; neglected parts, 97, 156;
    Safe Dialogue, 17–21, 32–33, 66,
    91; self-sabotage, 160–161. *See also*
    Safe Dialogue
money. *See* smoke-screen issues

N

neglect, *x*, 81; emotional, 95–96;
    mental, 96; physical, 93; reenact-
    ment trances, 115; shadow selves,
    157; transforming, 96–99. *See also*
    abuse; boundary violations
neglecting/abandoning boundary
    violations, 81–82, 91–96. *See also*
    boundary violations
nonverbal signals, 180

P

paradox of healing, 50–51
parent ego state. *See* inner parent
parenting, *x*, 77, 119; reenactment
    trances; affects, *x*, 11–12, 47–48,
    74–75, 107, 137–139; differentia-
    tion, 113; money, 68; reenactment
    trances, 114–115; self, 66, 150;
    time, 65. *See also* inner parent
PEA. *See* phenylethylamine
personal boundaries, deficits, 40, 43–44,
    53; honoring, 219, 222–223; money,
    68. *See also* boundaries.
phases of life, 217–219
phenylethylamine, 41, 44. *See also*
    attraction

physical boundaries, 8, 83; violation of,
    86, 138, 177. *See also* abuse;
    boundary violations
physical health, 56. *See also* emotional,
    digestive system
power, Boundary-Healing Process, 186;
    struggle, *x*, 48, 50–51, 205–206,
    215, 221–222
projection, 41, 143–144, 209–210;
    believing, 214; emotional, 87, 89;
    fearful, 153; reenactment trance
    patterns, 125–128; shadow selves,
    157–158, 202

R

reactive pattern, 129–130
reasoning abilities, 75
reenactment trances, 5, 107, 113, 114,
    139, 230; becoming aware of, 128–
    132; exercises, 132–134; internal,
    147; parental projection, 125–128;
    pattern of, 117–124; purposes,
    115–117; self-sabotage, 161
rejection, 43–44, 80, 82. *See also*
    boundary violations; intrusive/
    rejective boundary violations
relating, 206, 225–226
resentment, 49–50, 52
respect, 215
rituals, activities, 103; centering, 171;
    daily, 66; holiday, 97; money, 67, 78;
    Safe Dialogue, 23–24, 28; sex, 70
romantic boundaries, 40–44, 46–47, 68,
    230. *See also* boundaries
romantic love, ix, x, 39–40

S

sabotage, 163–164, 215. *See also*
    boundary violations; self-sabotage
saboteur. *See* self-sabotage
Safe Dialogue, *x–xi*, 4–6, 17–18, 22,
    90–93; boundaries, 23, 188, 189,
    194; celebrating, 36; connecting,

30–31, 53; cue sheet, 28, 36–37; empathy, 35; enmeshment, 77; environment, 23–25, 28, 29–30; exercises, 108, 133, 198; expanding, 34; five stages of, 28, 29–37; mirroring, 19–21, 27, 32–33; money, 68; nonverbal signals, 180; practicing, 26–28, revealing shadow selves, 210; ritual, 28; scheduling, 25–26, 29, 66; self-sabotage, 160–161, 166; summarizing, 19–20, 34; validation, 20–21, 27–28, 35

self, accepting, 156–157, 215; awareness of, 42–43, 163; confidence, 201–203; love (*see* tough self-love); parenting, 150; understanding, 215

self-sabotage, 5, 154–155, 203, 210; Boundary-Healing Process, 183, 189; centering, 164–165; controlling, 162, 165–167, 173, 176–177; deeper issues, 169–171; embracing, 172–173, 226; fear, 105, 173–174; identifying, 75, 163–164, 167–169, 178; masks, 156–157, 158–162, 178; reclaiming shadow selves, 157–158; Safe Dialogue, 171

senses, 41, 76

separation, 85, 177, 223

sex. *See* smoke-screen issues

sexual, distortion, 69–71; identifying, 69; relationship, 51, 68–69, 78, 101. *See also* smoke-screen issues

sexual abuse, 70–71, 138. *See also* abuse

shadow selves, 157–158, 164, 230; accepting, 157–158, 201–203, 214–216, 226; dreams, 211–212; exercises, 181; lost, 156–157; projection, 157–158, 209–210; recognizing, 203–210, 213. *See also* higher self; projection

shared experience, 45. *See also* bonding

smoke-screen issues, 57, 63–64, 72–73; core issues, 76; enmeshment-making process, 53; exercises, 77–78; money, 66–68, 104; moving beyond, 73–77; sex, 68–71; time, 64–66

spiritual, 6–7, 14–15, 90, 97, 213–214; connection, 42–43, 47, 185; deepening, 174; freezing/denying boundary violations, 104–105; inner parent, 150; intrusions, 89–90; power of, 202; resources, 178

spiritual abuse, 70–71. *See also* abuse

spiritual boundaries, 8, 83, 88, 95. *See also* boundary violations

spiritual neglect, 96–97. *See also* neglect

summarizing, 19–20, 190. *See also* Safe Dialogue

T

therapy, marriage, *ix–x*

time, 77, 219. *See also* smoke-screen issues

tough self-love, 145–150, 155, 158

trances. *See* reenactment trances

V

validation, 66, 90, 148, 177, 215; Boundary-Healing Process, 188, 190, 192, 195; exercises, 27–28, 133–134; Safe Dialogue, 20–21, 35, 91. *See also* Safe Dialogue

violence. *See* boundary violations